ZOROASTI
A GUIDE FOR TE

Continuum Guides for the Perplexed

Continuum's Guides for the Perplexed are clear, concise and accessible introductions to thinkers, writers and subjects that students and readers can find especially challenging. Concentrating specifically on what it is that makes the subject difficult to grasp, these books explain and explore key themes and ideas, guiding the reader towards a thorough understanding of demanding material.

***Guides for the Perplexed available* from Continuum:**

Calvin: A Guide for the Perplexed, Paul Helm
Christian Bioethics: A Guide for the Perplexed, Agneta Sutton
Christology: A Guide for the Perplexed, Alan Spence
De Lubac: A Guide for the Perplexed, David Grumett
Kierkegaard: A Guide for the Perplexed, Clare Carlisle
Mysticism: A Guide for the Perplexed, Paul Oliver
The Trinity: A Guide for the Perplexed, Paul M. Collins
Wesley: A Guide for the Perplexed, Jason E. Vickers

Forthcoming:

Mircea Eliade: A Guide for the Perplexed, Charles Long
Sufism: A Guide for the Perplexed, Elizabeth Sirriyeh

ZOROASTRIANISM:
A GUIDE FOR THE PERPLEXED

JENNY ROSE

continuum

Continuum International Publishing Group
The Tower Building   80 Maiden Lane
11 York Road   Suite 704
London SE1 7NX   New York NY 10038

www.continuumbooks.com

British Library Cataloguing-in-Publication Data
A catalogue record for this book is available from the British Library.

ISBN: HB: 978-1-4411-8995-0
       PB: 978-1-4411-1379-5

Library of Congress Cataloguing-in-Publication Data
Rose, Jenny, 1956-
Zoroastrianism : a guide for the perplexed / Jenny Rose.
   p. cm.
Includes bibliographical references and index.
ISBN-13: 978-1-4411-8995-0
ISBN-10: 1-4411-8995-5
ISBN-13: 978-1-4411-1379-5 (pbk.)
ISBN-10: 1-4411-1379-7 (pbk.)
1. Zoroastrianism. I. Title.
BL1572.R67 2011
295--dc22
                 2010052750

Typeset by Newgen Imaging Systems Pvt Ltd, Chennai, India
Printed and bound in India

To Bruce

CONTENTS

ACKNOWLEDGMENTS

Special thanks are due to those whom I have pestered with many of the questions addressed in this book. These individuals are, in alphabetical order: Ervad Dr. Jehan Bagli, Ervad Parviz Bajan, Prof. Jamsheed K. Choksy, Houtoxi Contractor, Behram Deboo, Malcolm Deboo, Manijeh Deboo, Ervad Soli P. Dastur, Mobed Mehraban Firouzgary, Anahita Fitter, Howard Goldman, Shireen Havewala, Prof. John R. Hinnells, Ervad Dr. Ramiyar Karanjia, Ryna Karnik, Mandana Moavenat, Dr. Bahman Moradian, Prof. Jesse Palsetia, Rohinton Rivetna, Prof. Prods Oktor Skjaervø, Rusi Sorabji, Mobed Dr. Rostam Vahidi, and Dr. Maneck S. Wadia.

I am indebted to Dr. Michael Stausberg and doctoral student Håkon Tandberg, both of Bergen University, Norway, for their invaluable comments and critiques. They challenged me to think more clearly and to write more concisely. To Bruce Benedict, who was my test "Everyman" reader, I am grateful for asking questions about the questions, and for demanding more straightforward answers.

Jenny Rose,
November, 2010

ABBREVIATIONS

A2S	Artaxerxes II inscription at Susa
Av.	Avestan
AWN	*Arda Wiraz Namag*
Bd.	Greater *Bundahishn*
BPP	Bombay Parsi Punchayat
CAP	*Chidag Andarz-i Poryotkeshan*
Dan.	Biblical book of *Daniel*
DB	Darius I inscription at Bisutun
Dd.	*Dadestan-i Denig*
Dk.	*Denkard*
DN	Darius I inscription on his tomb at Naqsh-e Rostam
DP	Darius I inscription at Persepolis
DS	Darius I inscription at Susa
Dt.	Biblical book of *Deuteronomy*
Elam.	Elamite
Ezek.	Biblical book of *Ezekiel*
FEZANA	Federation of Zoroastrian Associations of North America
Gk.	Greek
Heb.	Hebrew
Her.	*Herbadestan*
HN	*Hadokht Nask*
Isa.	Biblical book of *Isaiah*
MHD	*Madayan-i Hazar Dadestan*
MP	Middle Persian
MX	*Menog-i Xrad*
NAMC	North American Mobeds Council
Ner.	*Nerangestan*

OAv.	Old Avestan
OP	Old Persian
Pers.	New Persian
PGuj.	Parsi Gujarati
PRDd.	*Pahlavi Rivayat accompanying Dadestan-i Denig*
SGW	*Shkand Gumanig Wizar*
Vd.	*Videvdad*
Vr.	*Visperad*
WAPIZ	World Alliance of Parsi (and) Irani Zarthoshtis
WZO	World Zoroastrian Organization
XP	Xerxes' inscription at Persepolis
Y.	*Yasna*
YAv.	Young Avestan
YH	*Yasna Haptanghaiti*
Yt.	*Yasht*
Zds.	*Wizidagiha-i Zadspram*
ZTFE	Zoroastrian Trust Funds of Europe, Inc.

THE QUESTIONS

Do Zoroastrians have special dietary rules?
What is the role of fire in Zoroastrian worship?
What do priests do?
What are the Zoroastrian rites of passage?
What festivals occur in the Zoroastrian calendar?
Are there gender differences with regard to praxis?
How do Zoroastrians put their ethics into practice?

INTRODUCTION

The intention of the *Guides for the Perplexed* series is to immerse readers in the various theories of knowledge that relate to the way humans think and act, and to aid navigation through difficult concepts and complex texts. The Zoroastrian religion is an ideal subject for such study, since many of its concepts are already familiar, but its significance in the development of the history of thought is often only mentioned in passing, or completely overlooked.

Zoroastrianism has developed over a span of at least three thousand years, beginning in prehistory as an oral tradition with roots in a common Indo-Iranian culture and mythology, then becoming established as part of imperial Iranian ideology within an Ancient Near Eastern setting, and emerging in variant forms in western and central Asia in late antiquity. The religion continues as a living faith for an estimated 130–150,000 adherents in the world today. Because of its trans-historical and trans-cultural development there are many valid approaches to the study of Zoroastrianism. Any author writing a book about the religion has to decide which methodology—or range of methodologies—to use in presenting the material. I have opted here to focus on the questions that the perplexed seeker might ask of a Zoroastrian, and to attempt to answer those questions using historical and religious ("sacred") sources, alongside personal anecdotes.

Most Zoroastrians if asked, "In a nutshell, what do Zoroastrians believe?" would begin their answer with the moral maxim: "Good Thoughts, Good Words, Good Deeds." This foundational trifold ethic forms the framework for this book, which is divided into three main sections:

1. Thoughts: the ideological complexities and ethical underpinning of the religion;

2. Words: current discussion concerning "text" as oral, visual, and literary expressions of belief, and the "authorship" that validates the text;
3. Deeds: the practical enactment and external impact of the religion.

This threefold division somewhat echoes the three sections of the original *Guide for the Perplexed*, written in the late twelfth century by Moses Maimonides, the great Jewish philosopher. Maimonides' *Guide* took the form of a letter addressing the perplexing questions about Judaism that his students had raised. The first part of Maimonides' *Guide* delves into some complex matters of theology, particularly those concerning the nature of God and reality. The second part examines the authority of the book of Genesis in terms of its exposition of the creation of the world, its theories of eschatology, and concepts of prophecy and revelation as expressed through the Written and Oral Torah. The third section of Maimonides' *Guide* explores the ways of integrating the human and the divine, and of putting religious wisdom into pragmatic and moral action.

QUESTIONS OF THE PERPLEXED

This modern *Guide* to Zoroastrianism begins with the basic questions of a "perplexed" but interested reader, which lead to a discussion of the concepts and texts of the religion (its "Thoughts" and "Words" respectively), and of its socio-ritual articulation through the ages (its "Deeds"). The approach I have chosen balances a focus on contemporary expressions of Zoroastrianism in its "homelands" of Iran and India, as well as in more recent countries of residence, with its historical development and impact on other cultures and religions.

How to ask the questions

In the Jewish tradition, celebration of the Seder meal at Passover includes a scripted asking of questions by the youngest person present, which is intended to unlock the essence of this ritual re-enactment of the Exodus from Egypt. The Passover *Haggadah* (the narrative of the Exodus event recited at the Seder) then alludes to four sons, each of whom asks questions according to his own intellectual development. The answer that each son receives relates to his ability to discern. The son who does not know how to ask questions is given an answer in the form of a statement. Several Zoroastrian texts are similarly constructed in the form of set questions and answers. Perhaps the clearest example of this is the Middle Persian work "Select Precepts of the First Sages" (*Chidag Andarz-i Poryotkeshan*), which is formatted as a kind of catechism.

Most of the questions addressed in the following pages are not unlike those of a catechism. They are the questions that my students, peers, or—more often than not—fellow passengers on airplanes or acquaintances at parties, have asked concerning the Zoroastrian religion. Some are questions that have been addressed to Zoroastrian friends and colleagues when invited to speak at interfaith meetings, or while taking students on a tour of a local Zoroastrian center. Answers to these questions come from both "insider" and "outsider" sources—that is, through the voices of adherents and of external commentators. I have tried to balance the various perspectives. The passages quoted as verbal or e-mailed responses to my questions are from Zoroastrian acquaintances who are identified by name and profession or location.

There may be many more questions raised than are answered, which is, perhaps, par for the course when dealing with a religion which encourages its adherents to develop "Good Thought," "Wisdom," and "Religious Insight." I hope that I have addressed some of the extra questions that might pop into the reader's mind during the course of the book. If not, there is a supplementary reading list at the end of the book to address further questions and to facilitate a deeper investigation. A brief historical timeline and a glossary are also provided.

The most elementary and yet perhaps the most complex question the student of religion will ask is:

WHAT DOES THE WORD "ZOROASTRIAN" MEAN?

In the introduction to her book *Parsis: The Zoroastrians of India* (Good Books, 2000), screenwriter and photographer Sooni Taraporevala writes of encounters with fellow students in America, who would ask "Zorro who?" when she mentioned her religion.[1]

The term "Zoroastrian" derives from a Greek name for the eponymous figurehead of the religion, *Zoroastres*, who becomes "Zoroaster" in English. His Iranian name is Zarathushtra, and many adherents of the religion today identify themselves as "Zarathushtis"—that is, "those who follow the teachings of Zarathushtra"—rather than using the westernized form. The designation "Zarathushti" is preferred in the internal discourse of official organizations of Zoroastrians, such as the Zoroastrian Trust Funds of Europe, Inc. (ZTFE), and the Federation of Zoroastrian Associations of North America (FEZANA). The modern Persian form "Zartoshti" is used by Iranian Zoroastrians.

One of the most ancient labels that Zoroastrians continue to apply to themselves is *Mazdayasni* meaning "Mazda-worshipping," or a later, variant form *Mazdean*. The term "Mazda worshipper" is found in an early statement of faith, known as the *Fravarane*. The *Fravarane* is recited at a Zoroastrian initiation, and in daily prayer. "Fravarane" means "I [will] choose," or "Let me profess," and the statement begins with an acknowledgment of Ahura Mazda, the "Wise Lord" in the phrase, "I profess that I am a Mazda worshipper." This declaration is immediately followed by the expression "*Zarathushtrish*," which is often translated as "a Zoroastrian," but which is closer in meaning to "a supporter, or follower, of Zarathushtra." The sense is, "I will choose to worship Mazda, as Zarathushtra did." The word "Zarathushtri-" is the precursor to the modern form "Zarathushti." The structure of the *Fravarane* points to Ahura Mazda as the primary focus of faith, and Zarathushtra as the human epitome of its conceptual understanding and practical enactment. Zoroastrians today understand the concept of "following Zarathushtra" or "being like Zarathushtra" —in diverse ways.

The phrase *zarathushtrotema*, meaning "the one *most* like Zarathushtra" appears in a couple of late Avestan (Av.) texts.[2] This seems to have been the title of a religious leader, but its use in Middle Persian (MP) texts from the ninth century CE also suggests adherence to an ethical ideal based on the model of Zarathushtra. One such model might have been the influential high priest, Adurbad-i Mahraspandan, who lived in the mid-fourth century CE. According to Middle Persian texts, Adurbad underwent the ordeal of having molten metal poured onto his chest in order to prove that his understanding of the religion was true. Adurbad is said to have emerged from this ordeal unharmed, and so to have proved the validity of his teaching. He is credited with assembling an anthology of the most important religious texts, and with introducing legislation against non-Zoroastrian teachings such as those of Manichaeism.

For some adherents, Adurbad's strength of faith in terms of his understanding, his writings, and his actions provide a prime example of what it means to be "most like Zarathushtra." It can also signify maintaining a steadfast religious conviction alongside a degree of separation from other religions and from teachings considered to be heterodox. For others, however, the ideal of following the paradigm of Zarathushtra is exercised at a more philosophical level, which operates outside cultural and ethnic boundaries.

WHO IS A ZOROASTRIAN?

The question "Who is a Zoroastrian?" is a springboard for a slew of other questions, including:

Is the religion connected with a particular country or ethnicity?
Are there sects within the religion vying for authenticity?
Can Zoroastrians marry non-Zoroastrians?
Can an "outsider" become a Zoroastrian?

Is the religion connected with a particular country or ethnicity?

The ancient Iranian language of the earliest texts of the religion informs us that it developed within an Iranian setting. This took place sometime in the late second millennium BCE, after the Iranians had split from the Indo-Aryans, and both groups had started to move away from their original homeland, generally thought to be somewhere in the Central Asian Steppes. One group of Iranians migrated towards the plateau now known as "Iran," reaching the west of the country by the mid–ninth century BCE. Once they had become established on the plateau, the religion took root and evolved through the three successive Iranian empires: the Ancient Persian or Achaemenid (c. 550–330 BCE); Parthian (c. 250 BCE–224 CE); and then Sasanian (224–651 CE). The Ancient Persian king Darius I (r. 522–486 BCE) recognized the ethno-cultural connection of the Mazda-worshipping religion to the Iranians, when he described himself as "an Aryan of Aryan descent" and Ahura Mazda as the "god of the Aryans." Greek authors writing during the Achaemenid and then Seleucid period referred to "the Persian religion" as if there was only one.

Throughout this millennium, Mazda-worshipping Iranians took their religion with them to wherever they relocated: to Anatolia, Armenia and the Caucasus in the west, and to Central Asia, northern China and northwestern India in the east. The structure and substance of the religion evolved with each successive regime. A systematized form of "Zoroastrianism"—that is, a coherent, developed theology and an established hierarchical religious institution—does not appear to have come into existence until towards the end of the Sasanian period. The theology and ritual of the religion continued to develop for several centuries after the incursion of Islam in the mid–seventh century CE. The migration of Zoroastrian laity and priests to India in the early Islamic period led to the development of expressions of the religion that were often in response to contemporary Hinduism. In more recent times, Iranian Zoroastrians and their Indian (Parsi) co-religionists have brought Zoroastrianism to Europe and the New World, where it continues to evolve. But the homeland of Iran retains its centrality as the place where the religion was established and flourished.

Are there sects within the religion vying for authenticity?

Towards the end of the nineteenth century, "Zoroastrianism" became a common collective description of the religion, but Indian Zoroastrians and Europeans also continued to refer to it as "Parseeism." The designation "Parsi" first appears in reference to the Zoroastrians of India in sixteenth century European travelogues, but must have been in use before then. (At that stage "India" referred to a larger region than its current post-partition boundaries). From about the same time, a collection of Sanskrit texts known as "The Sixteen *Slokas*" applies the term Parsi to those Zoroastrians who had emigrated from Iran ("Persia") to India.

Indian Zoroastrians, such as Sooni Taraporevala, still use the word "Parsi" in self-reference, even if they live outside India or Pakistan. A neatly summarized definition as to who is a "Parsi," and who is a "Zoroastrian" was formulated by a Parsi judge in a legal opinion (*obiter dicta*) of 1908. This opinion formed part of a High Court

Figure 0.1 Sooni Taraporevala on the set of *Little Zizou* with Soonaiji Agiary, Mumbai, in the background. Photo courtesy of Sooni Taraporevala. © Chirodeep Chaudhuri, 2007.

judgment relating to the authority of the Bombay Parsi Punchayat (BPP), the council of elected representatives. Part of the case concerned the rights of Zoroastrian converts to have access to the religious institutions and funds managed by the BPP. The subsequent observations offered by Justice Dinshaw Davar, the Parsi judge who had heard the case, relate primarily to the definition of the term "Parsi," and recognize "Iranis" as part of the Parsi community of India. In the context of Justice Davar's ruling, Iranis are those Iranian Zoroastrians who had migrated to India at a later date than the Parsis.

In his statement, Justice Davar affirmed the normative understanding in determining that Parsi was an ethnic designation, and therefore only referred to:

— those who were descendants of Zoroastrian emigrants from Iran;
— those born of two Parsi parents professing the religion;
— Iranis settled in India who professed the Zoroastrian religion;
— children born of Parsi fathers by non-Parsi mothers who had been duly and properly initiated into the religion.

This remains the standard definition for those Parsis who describe themselves as "traditionalist" or "orthodox." The ethnocentric component is an important marker of religious authenticity for the Parsi traditionalist. In 2005 an association was founded in Mumbai to "strengthen the voice of tradition and protect and preserve the Unique Parsi Irani Zarthoshti identity." It is called "The World Alliance of Parsi Irani Zarthoshtis" or WAPIZ, and its membership consists of traditionalist Parsis and Iranis. The WAPIZ website maintains that it is the "historically fused identity of being Parsi and/or Irani as of race and Zarthoshti as of religion, which has . . . preserved the ancient practices of the Zarthoshti faith."[3] The definition of Parsi/Irani recognizes Iranian descent that is continuous "both historically and ecclesiastically," and that residency may be "in India or outside India." Traditionalists maintain that a person can *only* be a Parsi by birth, not by adoption or conversion. From this standpoint, although a child may be adopted by Parsis and convert to Zoroastrianism, he or she cannot technically claim the rights or benefits available to a Parsi.

Iranian Zoroastrian immigrants who seek asylum in India under the aegis of the BPP must produce an identity card issued by a local *anjuman* (Zoroastrian council) within Iran; they must possess a *sudreh* and *kusti* (the sacred shirt and cord of the initiate), and be able to recite in Avestan the two cardinal prayers of the *Ahuna Vairya* and the *Ashem Vohu*.[4] It is through demonstrating such practical knowledge of daily aspects of the faith that the applicants are recognized as having been initiated into and professing the religion. They then become eligible to receive the support of the Parsi community.

There has been no equivalent historical or practical definition as to who is a Zoroastrian in Iranian legal ruling. Since becoming a minority religion in Iran after the advent of Islam, Iranian Zoroastrianism has faced a different set of parameters in terms of its own status. Under Muslim majority rule, Zoroastrians received *dhimmi* status (that is, as a "protected minority") as one of the "people of the Book." This subaltern standing was marked by the imposition of restrictions and loss of self-regulation in many social and religious matters.

Internal self-definition as a Zartoshti now operates alongside external identification. One example of this external identification is the persistent use of the Persian designation *gabr* or *gawr* for a

Figure 0.2 Plaque marking one of the entrances to the *Gabra-mahalla* (the Zoroastrian Quarter) in Shiraz. The sign reads "Alley of the Fire of Jam [Jamshid]." Photo by Jenny Rose.

Zoroastrian. This is a title of uncertain origin and meaning. It probably derives from the Aramaic ideogram *GBR'* (*gabra*), meaning "man" or "person," which appears to have been used in Middle Persian Zoroastrian texts to refer to members of the religion in general. *Gabr* is used generically of Zoroastrians in the early eleventh-century Iranian national epic, the *Shah Nameh*. A popular derivation is that it comes from a word that can be interpreted as "one with no faith."[5] A more appealing putative source is the Persian word for "cow" (*gav*), which would be in keeping with the centrality of reference to the cow, ox, and cattle in the earliest Zoroastrian texts, the *Gathas*. French merchants who traveled to Iran during the Safavid period (1502–1736 CE) used the form *gaurs* or *guèbres* in a neutral sense in their descriptions of the Zoroastrians they encountered in the capital, Isfahan, and in the desert cities of Yazd and Kerman. At this time, Zoroastrian quarters in these cities were known as *Gabr-mahalla*.

Although Justice Davar's legal opinion of 1908 defined a Parsi as primarily an ethnic designation, and therefore relating to a group that was not open to outsiders, he also allowed that the Zoroastrian religion itself permitted conversion. The notion that the term "Zoroastrian" refers to religious conviction, rather than lineage and birth, is reflected in a resolution passed by the North American Mobeds (priests') Council (NAMC) at its thirteenth AGM in 2000. This resolution reads in part: "A 'Zoroastrian' is a person who believes and follows the teaching of Zoroaster. It is recognized that 'Zoroastrianism' is a universal religion. It is further recognized that a Zoroastrian is not necessarily a Parsi."[6]

Clearly, the identification of who is or is not a Zoroastrian is controversial. Sometimes adherents use the qualifying prefix "orthodox," "traditionalist," or "reform," before "Zoroastrian," or the suffixes "by birth" or "by choice." Each self-identified group applies the stamp of authenticity to itself. Those who describe themselves as traditionalist may outnumber other groups, but they espouse more than one normative Zoroastrian theology. The theological spectrum is most commonly construed in a manner similar to the various branches of Judaism: that is, with the "orthodox/traditionalist" at one end of the spectrum, and the "progressive/reconstructionist" at the other. Sometimes, these labels are thought to represent the range from conservative to liberal respectively, but a quick look at what each group emphasizes undermines the simplicity of that perspective.

In India, the goal of traditionalist Parsi individuals, and groups such as WAPIZ, is to ensure that the Parsi/Irani Zoroastrian identity—including its religious institutions, both physical and ritual—survives, and that the spiritual link with the past is sustained. The term "Neo-traditionalist" is sometimes now applied by outside academics to those Parsis/Iranis who adopt a theological understanding of Zoroastrianism informed by western scholarship, but who retain—and sometimes have sought to reintroduce—"traditional" rituals.[7]

Can Zoroastrians marry non-Zoroastrians?

The issue of self-identification is of particular immediacy given the fact that the Zoroastrian population is rapidly declining. For at least three decades *Parsiana* journal has been tracking the number of births, deaths, and marriages (both endogamous and interfaith) of Parsis in India, and it is clear that the number of deaths far exceeds the number of births, creating a negative population growth. The population of Zoroastrians in Iran is likewise decreasing due to low birthrates and marriages out of the religion, as well as through emigration to other countries. It is somewhat ironic that as the number of Parsis decline, there has been an upswing in Parsi and Zoroastrian studies particularly among historians of religion, anthropologists, and sociologists. Census figures for the year 2001 indicate that the number of Parsis in India had reduced by 39 percent since 1941, whereas the general population of India had more than tripled in the same period. As Sooni Taraporewala writes: "Fifty-three years after independence, we have nothing to fear but ourselves. We are the only community in fertile India that has a diminishing birthrate."[8]

One of my former students, recently tasked with the writing of bio-ethical guidelines for a teaching hospital in southern California, noted that among the Parsis in India the child-woman ratio—a key gauge of fertility—is about 85 per 1,000, whereas the average for the country is 578 per 1,000.[9] This low birthrate is partly due to the fact that both Parsi men and women tend to pursue higher education, and to get married at the relatively late age of between 30 and 35 years old. Many do not marry at all. As a result, Parsi couples are more proactive than any other religious group in finding and making use of the new fertility treatments and artificial reproductive technology available, including donor eggs. Since 2005, a fertility program has been funded by the BPP, which also offers financial incentives to couples to have a second or third child. Such measures appear to have increased the Parsi birthrate in Mumbai by about 10 percent each year.

Although many accept the early twentieth-century definition of who is or is not a Parsi, including the patrilineal clause, some Parsi priests in the past century have quietly initiated the offspring of Parsi mothers and non-Zoroastrian fathers. As one such young woman, the daughter of a Parsi mother and a Hindu father, told me in confidence: "The Parsi community is small enough that often half-Parsis are accepted, as they are the children of family or close, dear friends." In such cases, the ties of family are stronger than the pull of socio-cultural gender discrimination.

The *FEZANA Journal* of Winter 2004 focused on the presentation of a demographic picture of Zoroastrians around the world. It provided a comparative tabulation of both intra-faith and interfaith marriages in North America and Mumbai between 1991 and 2004. Mumbai is home to the majority of the estimated 60–70,000 Zoroastrians in India.

In both regions, interfaith marriages had increased significantly to just over 46 percent throughout North America and 35 percent in

Mumbai. Interfaith marriages continue to be of particular concern to Parsis. As one of my former students, Ryna (a Parsi), recently wrote:

> Parsis are an ethnic as well as religious group; as a result, there are many for whom the idea of "keep[ing] the blood pure" runs deep. There is a fair amount of pressure on young Parsis to marry only within the fold, and to raise their children according to custom . . . There is a conservative minority, who believe it is better for Parsis to condemn themselves to slowly dying away as an ethnicity rather than allow intermarriage. It seems to me that the sides in this argument divide the community largely (though by no means exclusively) across generational lines. For those who have already had children, the concerns that some of my peers and I have are less pressing. On the other hand, having grown up in the States, the burden of tradition bears down much less heavily on me than on those who grew up closer to the community in India. At the ripe old age of 23, it is high time, according to some in the community, for me to find a husband. I worry that if I were (as many of my elders desire) to choose a Parsi as a life partner, it would increase the chance of birth defects for any children I had.

This last comment derives from the fact that, as an unusually homogeneous group, Parsis display high rates of osteoporosis, hemophilia, Down's syndrome, and other chromosome disorders, alongside cardiovascular disease, all of which have increased considerably in the past half-century.

No regular data collection along the lines of the *Parsiana* or *FEZANA Journal* report has been undertaken in Iran, so it is difficult to know what the percentage of marriages out may be. Iranian census figures from 1986 and 1996 indicate a regular decrease in the number of Zoroastrians, which is partly due to interfaith marriage. Zartoshtis who marry a Muslim are expected to convert to Islam. Officially, Iranian Zoroastrianism does not accept converts. Mobed Mehraban Firouzgary, one of the few Zartoshti priests to be authorized to issue Zoroastrian marriage licenses in Iran, wrote that he is "very strict in making sure that both the parties are Zarathushtis. A Zarathushti wanting to marry a Christian or a Jew, would . . . be refused from my office."[10] As a minority religion in Iran, there is little incentive to encourage the conversion of others, particularly Muslims, since such apostasy would have serious social and legal repercussions.

Figure 0.3 Mobed Mehraban Firouzgary officiating at a Zoroastrian wedding in Tehran, Iran. Photo courtesy of Mobed Firouzgary.

Outside Iran, however, a somewhat different attitude prevails among Iranian Zoroastrians. One man who identifies himself as "of Iranian ethnicity" and of "Zarathushti religious identity," and who lives with his wife and children in the United States, summarized his approach to intermarriage: "In the vein of our forefathers who [were] exiled to India, we discourage our children from marrying outside the faith. But we will endorse their right to choose fully enlightened partners of any ethnicity . . . We welcome initiated spouses standing before the fire . . ."[11]

Can an "outsider" become a Zoroastrian?

Concerns relating to assimilation through interfaith marriage are correlated with those relating to the matter of conversion. This issue is addressed by Zoroastrians in radically different ways. The WAPIZ website contends that there has never been a time in the history of the Zoroastrian religion when conversion has been promoted. In contrast, individuals or groups who designate themselves as "progressive" argue that conversion is crucial, not only for the religion to survive, but because it is in keeping with their understanding of the faith as always having been universally applicable.

The wide gap between these polarized approaches began to form in mid–nineteenth century India, stimulated from the outside by Christian missionary activity in Bombay, and from within by a move to modernize from western-educated Parsis. The *Rahnumae Mazdayasnan Sabha* (the Religious Reform Association) was founded in Bombay in 1851 both to strengthen Parsi identity and to introduce religious reform based on a rationalist, modernist perspective that was often wary of perfunctory ritual.[12] The approach of the Religious Reform Association informed the work of Maneckji Limji Hataria, who, in 1854, became the representative of the Society for the Amelioration of the Conditions of the Zoroastrians in Iran. The Zoroastrian reform movement today relates more to the idea of recovering the original teachings—the "inner truth"—of the religion than to its reworking. In this respect, it has a similar impetus to the recent Renewal Theology movement in Christianity.

Several reformist associations have emerged in Mumbai in the past decade. One such organization, founded in 2004, is the Association for the Revival of Zoroastrianism (ARZ). ARZ members maintain that the declining numbers of the religion are due to the exclusion of children of non-Parsi fathers, and of non-Parsi spouses. Parsi priests affiliated with ARZ have therefore begun to perform initiations for the children and spouses of intermarried couples, and marriages for interfaith couples. ARZ also helps Parsi couples to adopt children, who are then eligible to be initiated into the religion.

In early twentieth-century Iran, Zoroastrianism became co-opted as the "original" religion of the country by Iranian nationalists such as Ibrahim Pour-e Davoud. This view formed part of the nationalist rhetoric for political and social change. Discourse promoting the restoration of the ancient "glory of Iran," prompted many Iranian Zoroastrians to study their own religion and cultural history more closely. They were now able to access modern Persian translations of Zoroastrian texts, particularly the *Gathas*. These translations incorporated the Parsi-reformist interpretation that the Old Avestan "songs" attributed to Zarathushtra were the only primary source of the religion. This perspective, which gives precedence to the *Gathas*, also downplays later texts that are concerned with priestly ritual, purity regulations, and lay religious practices. Many urban-dwelling

Iranian Zoroastrians—that is, the majority of the 25,000–30,000 in the country today—take this approach as normative, while allowing that later Zoroastrian scriptures and rituals may be studied in light of the *Gathas*.

Since the inauguration of the Islamic Republic of Iran in 1979, it appears that many Iranian Muslims seeking a new political and religious identity have found appeal in the religion of ancient Iran. Some have even gone so far as to declare public allegiance to the faith, as in the Iranian Census of 1986, when 90,000 are said to have checked "Zoroastrian" as their religion.

There are also some self-identified "Zoroastrians by choice," who come from an ethnically Iranian background and who have chosen to adopt the religion as their own. They are sometimes referred to as "Neo-Zoroastrians" or "Neo-Zarathushtis" by those who are "Zoroastrian by birth." Although the phrase "by choice" implies the notion of an individual conviction that is not based on cultural background, in fact the majority of "Zoroastrians by choice" are Iranians, Tajiks, or Kurds, who regard the religion as their ancestral birth faith. They mostly live outside Iran and some have formally converted to the religion through initiation by Iranian *mobeds* (priests). Many of these "Zoroastrians by choice" emphasize belief and commitment over birth. One such self-described "Zoroastrian by choice," an Iranian who lives in America, described his feelings that neither Iranian nor Parsi lineage should be a factor in determining faith: "Parsi heritage . . . should not be limited to any [one] religion, so . . . [b]eing Iranian or having to become one should not be a condition for being a Zarathushti . . ."[13]

Dr. Jamsheed K. Choksy, a professor of Central Asian and Religious Studies at Indiana University, summarized the range of attitudes toward the issue of conversion in this manner: "[C]onversion is discouraged by many contemporary Parsis, occasionally accepted by some contemporary Iranians, and periodically encouraged without much success to date by a few Zoroastrian settlers in North America and Europe."[14] This synopsis was printed in 2005. In the interim, several "Zoroastrian by choice" groups have arisen and subsequently declined in South America, primarily Venezuela, Equador, and Brazil.

An example of a more firmly established group of "Zoroastrians by choice" exists in Russia, where the Zoroastrian Community of St. Petersburg was registered as a local religious organization in 1994.

The group's "spiritual instructor" is Pavel Globa, who claims Iranian ancestry through his grandfather, and who is particularly interested in "Avestan astrology." Members meet regularly to study the Avesta in Cyrillic transliteration and Russian translation. According to the community's website, in the first decade of this century several members were initiated by visiting Parsi or Iranian *mobeds*, presumably of the "progressive" section of the religion.[15] A commotion was caused in early 2010, when the Russian group's "spiritual leader" Mikhail Chistyakov came to study the rituals of the religion at Zoroastrian College near Sanjan, Gujarat. Zoroastrian College, which was founded by a Parsi woman named (Dame) Dr. Meher Master Moos, offers a holistic curriculum and has an interfaith and cross-cultural outreach program with particular connection to Tajikistan. Some traditionalist Parsis entered the campus and protested at what they understood to be a ceremony forming part of Mr. Chistyakov's initiation as a *navar* (the first stage of priesthood). In response, Dr. Master-Moos filed a writ in the Bombay High Court against the alleged disrupters and asked the Court to safeguard her work and activities including the "religious education and training in the practices of any Zoroastrian person as a Zoroastrian priest for performance of Zoroastrian rituals and religious ceremonies outside India."[16] The writ states that Zoroastrianism is universal, and therefore allows conversion.

Dr. Michael Stausberg, a historian of religion at Bergen University, coined the term "Para-Zoroastrianisms" to encompass such offshoots of the religion, which have some parallels with a nominal "parent" faith, but which have moved beyond and away from many of the forms and functions of "traditional," "ethnic" Zoroastrian institutions.[17] Although traditionalists consider that various emblems and praxes, such as wearing the *sudreh-kusti*, visiting the fire temple, and observing ancient distinctions of purity and pollution are fundamental elements in determining who is a Zoroastrian, others argue that, since these aspects are difficult to maintain in modern life, particularly in diaspora, they cannot be used as a litmus test of an individual's affiliation to the faith. Dr. Michael Fischer, an American anthropologist who spent some time with the Zoroastrian community in Yazd during the late 1960s and early 1970s, maintains that perhaps only the self-identification "I am a Zoroastrian" remains as the defining clause.[18]

Any exploration of the question "Who is a Zoroastrian?" should include not only the spectrum of beliefs and practices attributed to—or claimed by—Mazda worshippers throughout the ages and across cultures, but also the ideological differences that inform the proclamation "I am a Zoroastrian." Today, the matter of self-identification is more likely to be concerned with pragmatic factors relating to the selection pool for a mate, the religious education of children, and the threat of the demise of the religion, than with theoretical issues relating to theology and religious praxis. An Iranian Zoroastrian acquaintance from Yazd recently copied me on a couple of e-mails that put the theological discussion relating to concepts and doctrines into perspective. Parviz wrote that Mazdayasnans should stop "scratching [their] heads trying to figure out what Zoroaster wanted to say or not say in this chapter or that verse" and instead apply themselves to actively "save the cow." He stated that time spent on drawing attention to "non-issue issues"—including deciphering sacred words—does not bring the world anywhere nearer to its renovation. The sentiment expressed in Parviz's e-mails is that Zoroastrianism is as much (if not more) about how beliefs are put into action as about what one claims to be or to know.

WHAT IS ZOROASTRIANISM?

The range of definitions that arise in answer to the overarching question "Who is a Zoroastrian?" signifies the complexity of any attempt to explain and summarize "Zoroastrianism." This difficulty of encapsulating the religion is as true for its contemporary expression, as for its putative historical evolution. Some scholars maintain that we should not even talk of "Zoroastrianism" in terms of a religion with a systematized collection of beliefs and praxes, until the late Sasanian or early Islamic period—that is, until the sixth to tenth centuries CE. Others claim that the original "Zoroastrianism" from which the *Gathas* emerged cannot now be fully retrieved. If either premise is accepted, then the term "Zoroastrian" should not be applied to most of the history of the religion to date. Instead, perhaps the ancient phrase "Mazda worshipping" (Av. *Mazdayasni*) should be substituted.

As with all cultural histories, that of the Iranians does not follow one continuous line, but splits and wanders across the boundaries of other cultures. Some Iranians stayed in the ancient countries of

Chorasmia, Sogdiana, Margiana, and Bactria (modern Uzbekistan, Turkmenistan, northern Afghanistan, and western Tajikistan), which are to the northeast of the region that became known as Iran. In these Central Asian locations, archaeological finds dating to between the fifth and eighth centuries CE, display a form of "Zoroastrianism" that seems to differ in terms of religious praxis, structure, and iconographic motif from that found in Iran of the same period. But the discovery of depictions of worshippers praying before portable fire holders on Sogdian frescoes, and of an eighth or ninth century CE Sogdian version of the *Ashem Vohu* prayer indicates adherence to core elements of the religion that correspond both to Sasanian Mazdeism and to the more ancient expressions of the Achaemenid period.

Another—and earlier—eastern form of the religion has been revealed in Kushan artifacts dating to the second century CE. The Kushan empire was based in the region of Gandhara (modern eastern Afghanistan and northwestern Pakistan). The coins and inscriptions of the Kushan king Kanishka (r. c. 127–151 CE) use Bactrian, a Middle Iranian language that was written in Greek script, and seem to present this eastern variation of Zoroastrianism as the official religion.[19] And to the northwest of the plateau, the Armenians, who held satrapy status under the Ancient Persians, then the Parthians and the Sasanians, were also Mazda worshippers, until their conversion to Christianity in 301 CE.[20]

How can one short, introductory book hope to cover this complex—and, for many, controversial—scope of definitions of "Zoroastrianisms"? It cannot. Since the forms of Mazda worship to the east and west of Sasanian Iran disappeared due to the conversion of its adherents to other religions, I decided that the focus of this book should be on what is known of the religion in Iran, where it continues to be practiced in the present day, and in India, where many Iranian Zoroastrians took refuge. The beliefs and praxes of descendants of both cultural groups who now live in other countries are also included, as are those of some "Zoroastrians by choice." The questions in this book are asked of the religion as it relates to this particular historical development. This forms the parameter for the working definition of Zoroastrianism used from here on.

One of my academic mentors once told me: "Philology should precede theology," and it is that premise that informs my decision to consider some of the themes of the religion as traceable through its texts, from the most ancient to the most recent. Given the long oral transmission of the earliest texts of the Avesta, this approach carries its own inherent problems. Most of the progress of the religion through history until modern times can only be traced in web-like outlines rather than bold brushstrokes, but some of these outlines are given more substance by external literary descriptions and internal "non-scriptural" textual and iconographic materials. The primary internal religious sources extend chronologically from the Avestan texts of the late second- to mid-first-millennium BCE; through Middle Persian Zoroastrian books redacted or composed between the sixth and tenth centuries CE; to the New Persian priestly correspondences and literature dating from the thirteenth to eighteenth centuries; and finally the Sanskrit, Persian, and Gujarati material of the Parsi communities in northwest India. Some of the earlier sources, particularly the *Gathas* and the liturgical text of the *Yasna*, have been subjected to intense philological scrutiny, and their theology and associated religious praxes dissected, and, to a degree, reconstructed. Other sources have not yet been studied in this way, and many of the texts are apparently no longer extant.

The three parts of this book are intended to introduce the religion as a living entity, which has been evolving over several millennia. They do not have to be read in numerical order, however. A glossary at the end explains unfamiliar terms. Chapter 1 presents the central concepts that are generally taken to be the basis of the religion. This may seem to be a rather essentialist perspective, but there are certain themes that reverberate across both internal and external conceptualizations of the religion. The resonances between those themes and the ideologies of neighboring religions and philosophies will also be explored. Chapter 2 tackles the texts, which crystallize those concepts and develop them into a systematic theology, a coherent mythology, and a hagiography that places Zarathushtra at a crucial moment in the history of human existence. Chapter 3 concretizes Chapters 1 and 2 by exploring the "putting-into-action" of the religion in terms of the everyday, ritual, festival and social lives of its adherents. This tripartite format presents the religion as continuing to have a profound effect on and through whoever claims it as his or her own.

CHAPTER 1

THOUGHTS, OR WHAT ZOROASTRIANS BELIEVE

The question "What do Zoroastrians believe?" is a gateway to exploring the main concepts—the "Thoughts"—of the religion. Just as Moses Maimonides' *Guide for the Perplexed* introduced philosophical concepts relating to questions of religion such as the nature of God, the existence of evil, and humanity's role and purpose in the world, so any study of Zoroastrianism should explore its thinking and teaching in relation to these concepts. This chapter focuses on some of the concepts of Zoroastrianism that can be traced from the Old Avestan texts onward, and their expression through some of the liturgical and mythical narratives of the religion. It addresses the following questions:

What is the Zoroastrian concept of God?
What is the relationship of Ahura Mazda to the world?
What is the significance of fire?
Do Zoroastrians believe in one God or many?
Where does evil come from?
What is the purpose of human existence?
What happens at the End?
Do Zoroastrian concepts relate to those of other religions and philosophies?

The beliefs of Zoroastrians today emerge from a long oral transmission of religious thought and word. Many Zoroastrians still learn and recite their daily prayers by heart, and many priests perform daily liturgies and seasonal or festival litanies from memory. The story of Zarathushtra as the epitome of the one who praises Ahura Mazda is central to this oral tradition.

The texts of the religion were first committed to writing in a specially devised script known in Middle Persian as *den-dabirih*, the "writing for the religion." It is not known exactly where the written text, known as the *Avesta*, was produced, but we assume that priests familiar with the oral recitation either transcribed or dictated the words to scribes based in specific religious centers. This process is thought to have reached completion around the sixth century CE. One Middle Persian book, the *Denkard*, summarizes the contents of the Avesta. According to that analysis, the surviving Avesta is only a fraction of the original collection of texts. The material that remains reflects some modifications in terms of its thematic and linguistic structure as a result of the long period of oral recitation, mental reflection, and societal change.

Debate continues as to when the central elements of the religion first began to crystallize. The most widely accepted date is the late second millennium BCE. Some, however, place the earliest oral Avestan texts in a much later period, around the seventh- or sixth century BCE, when the Iranians had become established in southwestern Iran. This later date presupposes that these texts, including the *Gathas*, were composed using an archaic Iranian language that had not been spoken for several hundred years.

When UNESCO declared 2003 as the "3000th anniversary of Zoroastrian culture," it gave widespread cultural and political recognition to the religion's claim to antiquity. Although this was an arbitrarily selected date, it served to commemorate the birth of the religion sometime around three thousand ago. The anniversary was celebrated by Zoroastrian associations around the world: from Mumbai and New Delhi in India, to Singapore, and to Iran, where UNESCO nominated various pre-Islamic edifices to be listed as World Heritage sites. In the United States, the City of Los Angeles, which has a large Iranian population, including an estimated 2000 Zoroastrians, held a celebratory gala and a daylong conference. In Washington, DC, a seminar on "Zarathushtra's Contribution to Humanity," co-sponsored by the World Zoroastrian Organization (WZO) and UNESCO was held at the Library of Congress. The Zoroastrian Association of Metropolitan Chicago co-hosted the first Zoroastrian film festival. The oldest and principal European Zoroastrian association, which is based in London (ZTFE), commemorated the anniversary by producing a two-volume *Gathas of Zarathushtra* CD. For this, the ZTFE senior priest, Ervad Rustam

Bhedwar, recited what is perceived as the world's first recording of parts of the seventy-two section daily liturgy, the Yasna (Y.). The sections recorded—Yasna 27–34, 43–51, 53–4—include the *Gathas* and two prayers, known as the *Ahuna Vairya* and the *Airyaman Ishya*. These were all composed in a language known as Old Avestan, which is similar in syntax, meter, and vocabulary to the Old Indic of the *Rig Veda*, an early Hindu text. The *Ahuna Vairya* is still recited as one of the daily prayers of Zoroastrians today, in a language that is thought to be over three millennia old.

WHAT IS THE ZOROASTRIAN CONCEPT OF GOD?

The Great God

The *Ahuna Vairya* (also sometimes called the *Yatha ahu vairyo* or *Ahunvar*) is the first prayer recited on the *Gathas of Zarathushtra* CD. The focus of the prayer is Ahura Mazda, the creator God. "Ahura Mazda" is a two-part name that is best translated as "Wise Lord." The word "Mazda" can be translated as "the one who is wise" or "the one who keeps mental track." Many Zoroastrians popularly translate it as "wisdom" as if it were an abstract concept, rather than an agent noun. It is said to be by the mental activity—the "thought"—of Ahura Mazda that the cosmos was first ordered and is upheld. The epithet "Ahura" appears to mean "the one who engenders."

Ahura Mazda is frequently referred to in the *Gathas*, the earliest poetic texts of the religion, although the two epithets of the name are not always adjacent to each other. *Gatha* means "song" or "poem," and these ancient songs articulate many of the seminal concepts of the religion, although not always in a way that is easily understood today. The Gathic poems display a continuity of topic in the structure of the stanzas, but this is not always developed in a linear pattern. The same topic is constantly being approached from different angles. The predominant theme throughout the *Gathas* and the other Old Avestan texts is that of the activity of Ahura Mazda in the two areas that constitute his name—"engendering" and "being wise."

It is not known when the Iranians first began to worship Ahura Mazda. The two concepts that make up the name are also found in the *Rig Veda*, but not in combination. The name *Assara Mazaash* was found in an early first millennium ritual text from the library of the neo-Assyrian king Assurbanipal (r. 669–c. 630 BCE). It appears in a list of gods next to Elamite divinities, and may be a unique reference to two separate neo-Assyrian gods. It could, however, reflect the early presence of western Iranians in the Nineveh region, who were still using the Indo-Iranian "s" when referring to their deity, rather than the "*ahura*" of the Avesta.[1] The name appears in compressed form as "Ahuramazda" on the earliest rock inscription of the Ancient Persians, dating to around 521 BCE. This was carved at the order of Darius I high up on a cliff face at an oasis named Bisutun, on the road from Hamadan to Babylon. Although the Ancient Persians spoke a western Iranian language that was significantly different to that of the Avesta, they retained similar terms and appear to have held a similar worldview.

Darius' trilingual cuneiform inscription at Bisutun contains the first tangible internal evidence that the Ancient Persians worshipped Ahura Mazda as their supreme God. Darius, justifying his accession to the throne as a member of a junior branch of the Achaemenids, claims that it was with the aid of the "greatness of Ahura Mazda" that he became king (DB1: 11–12). In the inscription on Darius' tomb, Ahura Mazda is called "The Great God," who is said to have "bestowed wisdom and activity" on Darius (DNa1, DNb5).

Wisdom

The emphasis on wisdom or "guiding thought" (OP *xrathu*) echoes that of the *Gathas*, where wisdom (Av. *xratu*) is an aspect of Ahura Mazda that guides humans (Y. 53.3). Ahura Mazda is perceived as the source of this wisdom, the *Gathas* as the channel through which much of this wisdom is conveyed, and Zarathushtra is the name ascribed to the inspired poet who first gave voice to that wisdom. The *Gathas* suggest the belief that it is through inspiring the human mind that Ahura Mazda is known. Later Avestan references to Ahura Mazda as being called "the one who knows" and "the all-knowing" reiterate this aspect (Yt. 1.13). These titles subsequently appear among the 101 names of Ahura Mazda recorded in Persian and Gujarati texts. Other names in the list denoting the attributes and activities of this Wise Lord include "Omnipresent," "Formless," and "Full of Light," implying the immanence of God. Titles such as "Lord of all life," "Creator of the world," and "Creator of growth," suggest more transcendent activity. In one Gathic stanza (Y. 28.2),

Ahura Mazda is spoken of as the engenderer of both the "life of thought" (Av. *manah*) and of "corporeal existence" (Av. *astvant*—literally "boney").

Order

The *Gathas* mention the word *asha* over 150 times.[2] It is variously translated as "order," "right," "truth," "righteousness," or "harmony." My own preferred translation is often "integrity," which includes most of these concepts. *Asha* is the focus of one of the cardinal prayers of the Zoroastrians religion, which is recited on a daily basis and in all acts of worship.

The prayer (Y. 27.14) is entitled the *Ashem Vohu* after its first two words. It is transliterated from the Avestan script as:

Ashem vohu
vahishtem asti
ushta asti
ushta ahmai
hyat ashai vahishtai ashem

This can be loosely translated as:

"*Asha* is the best good
It is happiness [or 'it is desired'],
according to our desire, there will be
Asha which belongs to the best *Asha*."

The phrase "best *asha*" (Av. *asha vahishta*) refers to the universal order/right/truth that is established by Ahura Mazda. The prayer indicates that humans should want to uphold this orderly, right way.

The order and integrity of the universe that has been engendered by Ahura Mazda is identified as established in both the realms of thought and of material existence. This order is threatened, however, by the confusion and chaos brought by the lie (Av. *druj*), which deceives as to the nature of reality. This distinction between "order" (*asha*) and "deception" (*druj*)—or that which is "true" and that which is not—reminds us that conceptually the religion belongs to the Indo-Iranian thought world rather than to that of the Ancient Near East. The focus is on the guiding thought that comes through inner vision and understanding.

The fact that "good thought" (Av. *vohu manah*) is a term that also occurs frequently in the *Gathas* indicates its centrality as a guiding principle. The *ashavan*—the person who worships Ahura Mazda by maintaining integrity—aspires to reach the "house of good thought" where both Ahura Mazda and *asha* are located (Y. 30.10).

Light

The *Gathas* compare both Ahura Mazda and *asha* with the sun (Y. 43.16; 32.2). There are several later (Young) Avestan (YAv.) references to the sun as "the eye of Ahura Mazda" (Y. 1.11, 3.13). This early solar imagery for Ahura Mazda is retained in the vocabulary of later non-Zoroastrians, such as in the Khotanese Buddhist word for the sun *urmaysde*, and the Chorasmian *remazd*. In the early twelfth century CE, the Muslim theologian Al-Ghazali remarked that the Zoroastrians "worship Absolute Light, which embraces all lights, and think that It is the Lord of the Universe, and that all good things are attributable to it."[3] Many Zoroastrians today recite their prayers when turned towards the light of the sun. For some, the power of the sacred thought-word (Av. *manthra*) is thought to resonate with the light of the universe. Praise and worship for Ahura Mazda and for *asha*, when performed with good thought, is said to enable joy to be visible in the light (Y. 30.1).

WHAT IS THE RELATIONSHIP OF AHURA MAZDA TO THE WORLD?

The *Gathas* present a clear distinction between the world of the mind (*manah*), or the conceptual existence, and the "living" (*gaetha*), or corporeal, world. The origin of the "thought world" is spoken of in terms of a biological action generated from Ahura Mazda's own essence—along the lines of fathering an offspring (Y.44.3; 45.4). Corporeal creation derives from this conceptual prototype and is not therefore *ex nihilo* ("from nothing"). These two conceptual and corporeal existences recur in Middle Persian accounts of creation as *menog* and *getig*. Some prefer to translate these terms as "spiritual" or "ideal," and "physical" or "material" respectively.

Creator

In one of the 17 sections of the *Gathas*, a series of rhetorical questions concerning the origins of the elements of the world present

Ahura Mazda in his role as "engenderer". The questions include:

Who was the first father of *asha*?
Who established the route of the sun and of the stars?
Through whom does the moon now wax and then wane?

Who has held the earth down and [kept] the skies from falling?
Who [established] the waters and the plants?
Who yoked the fleet pair [of horses] to the wind and to the clouds?
(Y. 44.3–4).

The implied answer to these questions is "Ahura Mazda," who not only generates, but also protects and sustains these various elements. The conception of Ahura Mazda is as the engenderer of all (Y. 44.7), the creator of life (Y. 50.11), who gives that which is good (Y. 46.5). The Old Avestan liturgy, the *Yasna Haptanghaiti* (the "Worship of Seven Sections"), describes Ahura Mazda as establishing the various elements of the world in a similar manner. In this ancient liturgical hymn, Ahura Mazda is the focus of worship as creator of both the cow and *asha*; the good waters and plants; the lights and the earth and everything good (YH 37.1).

The description of Ahura Mazda as creator of all that is good is in keeping with the understanding that an inherent order and harmony runs through every element of the conceptual and corporeal worlds. At the conceptual level, order is manifest in good—or best—thought, and understanding. At a physical level, order is visible in the cosmic progression of the world, particularly the daily appearance of the sun, the growth of herds, and the following of the straight path of thought, word, and deed by humans.

One word that occurs in the *Gathas* to describe this progression or growth is *spenta*, which is sometimes translated as "holy," or "virtuous." It derives from a root meaning "to expand," and is therefore more accurately translated as "bounteous," "beneficent," or "life-increasing." Ahura Mazda is instrumental through *spenishta mainyu*—his "most beneficent inspiration" (Y. 33.12; 43.2). The concept of *mainyu* is a neutral term meaning "inspiration," or "spirit." Because it is from the root *man*—"to think," it is sometimes translated as "mentality" or "mental force."

Any thought, word, or action that diminishes the world in any way is considered to be contrary to the life-giving, progressive activity of

Ahura Mazda in both existences. Those motivated by "evil thought" speak "evil words," which are allied to "evil actions," and bring ruin to existence (Y. 32.5, 11). Both the *Gathas* and *Yasna Haptanghaiti* speak of various attributes or abstract qualities of Ahura Mazda at work through the world to promote order and stability, and to stave off such disorder and disintegration. These attributes, alongside the "beneficent inspiration" (*spenta mainyu*) of Ahura Mazda, permeate existence, and include "humble right-mindedness" (*armaiti*), "good thought" (*vohu manah*), "readiness to listen," (*sraosha*) and "religious insight" (*daena*).

In one Gathic passage, the "most beneficent inspiration" of Ahura Mazda is said to "be clothed in the hardest stones" (Y. 30.5). Elsewhere, Ahura Mazda is praised as the "fashioner" of the cow, the waters and plants through the same "beneficent inspiration" (Y. 51.7). This imagery can be interpreted to suggest a physical connection between the abstract qualities of Ahura Mazda identified above, and the material world. Young Avestan texts, composed sometime in the early to mid–first millennium BCE, expand on this intimate connectedness of Ahura Mazda with the material world, particularly in terms of the creation of good lands for the Iranians and other peoples (Vd. 1. 2–19) and the establishment of the various elements of the cosmos. The cosmogonic sequence is listed as: sky, water, earth, plant, cow, and human (Yt. 13.86).

Ahura Mazda's activity in setting everything in place is reiterated at the beginning of the recitation of the Yasna, the priestly liturgy (Y. 1.1). The performance of the Yasna serves to praise and ritually regenerate all the good elements of the cosmos. In India, the Yasna takes place at the start of each day in the main fire temples. As part of priestly ritual praxis, the Yasna is explored in more detail in Chapter 3.

A coherent cosmology is schematized in ninth century CE Middle Persian books, particularly the *Bundahishn* ("Creation"). But a much earlier acknowledgment of the creative aspect of Ahura Mazda is carved into the rock face inscription outside the tomb of Darius I. The epitaph begins:

"The great god is Ahura Mazda,
who established this earth,
who established that heaven,
who established humanity,

who established happiness for humanity
who made Darius king . . . " (DNa 1–8).[4]

The Old Persian list in this inscription follows the same format as in the Avesta, beginning with the earth and sky, and culminating in humanity, of whom Darius was the current prime representative. Water, plants, and animals do not, however, appear in the Old Persian account. The emphasis on happiness for humanity echoes the joy found in praise of Ahura Mazda and *asha* that was noted previously. This concept of happiness appears to signify "an ideal state of peace, tranquility, abundance, pleasure, and well-being that typifies the world as it was originally created . . . "[5] This resonates with the emphasis on good things for humans, including "peace and pasture for cattle" (YH 35.4).

The *Amesha Spentas*

Six of the revitalizing qualities of Ahura Mazda, some of which were mentioned earlier, are grouped together in a hymn of praise to Ahura Mazda (Y. 1.25). They are referred to collectively as the "beneficent immortals" (Av. *amesha spentas*) with Ahura Mazda at their apex. A calendar based on the Avesta is attested in Greek astronomical texts in the Ancient Persian period. In this calendar from Cappadocia, six months of the year were named after these six *amesha spentas*. By the time of the composition of the Middle Persian *Bundahishn*, the *amesha spentas* had become hypostatized as the guardians of the elements of creation working in accord with the will of Ahura Mazda. Each one is attached to one of the seven elements of creation, with *spenta mainyu*, the "beneficent inspiration" as the connecting link between Ahura Mazda and humanity.

The *Bundahishn* states that Ahura Mazda aligned each of the elements of creation with the seven named *amesha spentas*. Its cosmogony parallels that of the *yashts* (Young Avestan hymns) and the Old Persian inscriptions in placing animate beings as the culmination of creation (Bd. 3.7). According to the account in the *Bundahishn*, fire was the last element of creation, which Ahura Mazda infused into the other six elements. The radiance of that fire was from the endless lights of Ahura Mazda (Bd. 3.8).

The elements are listed in order next to the beneficent immortals that protect them (cf. Bd. 3. 12–19):

Amesha Spenta	Quality (translation)	Element of Creation
Xshathra Vairya	"Desired Rule"	Sky
Haurvatat	"Wholeness"	Water
Spenta Armaiti	"Beneficent Right-Mindedness"	Earth
Ameretat	"Immortality"	Plant
Vohu Manah	"Good Thought"	Cattle
Spenta Mainyu	"Beneficent Inspiration"	Humans
Asha Vahishta	"Best Asha"	Fire

Zoroastrian texts from the Avesta onward encouraged humans to respect all of these aspects of creation. The *Gathas* speak of beneficial activity that nourishes the living, both herds and humans. *Yasna Haptanghaiti* indicates that reverence for the elements could help to sustain them, and that Mazda worshippers particularly venerated the fire and the waters (YH 36.1–3, 38.3).

WHAT IS THE SIGNIFICANCE OF FIRE?

As one of the creations of Ahura Mazda, fire warms and brings light to humans, so that they do not feel the cold and dark. The association of Ahura Mazda and universal order with the sun—the greatest cosmic fire—goes part way to answering the frequently-asked question concerning the significance of fire to Zoroastrians.

For many Zoroastrians, fire is both a physical and figurative representation of the order of Ahura Mazda that permeates the world. This notion is articulated in the *Yasna Haptanghaiti*, which speaks of the ritual fire as both "the fire of Mazda Ahura" and "his most beneficent spirit," implying that Ahura Mazda is somehow present within the fire (YH 36.3). The topos of fire as the "son of Ahura Mazda" is found in a Young Avestan passage in the Yasna (Y.62.2).

The mention of the consecration of fire in the *Yasna Haptanghaiti* establishes the central function of fire in early Zoroastrian praxis. The first figurative depiction of fire in an Iranian context is located above the tomb of Darius at Naqsh-e Rostam (see Fig. 1.1, p. 30).

In this rock relief, the king stands on a stepped platform, facing a fire that blazes in a container on another tiered plinth. Both are situated below a figure, who holds a ring of power in his hand and rises out of a winged solar disc. This figure is sometime identified as an expression of the "divine glory" (Av. *xwarenah*) of Ahura Mazda, or of the sun as a representation of *asha*. In one of the Avestan hymns, the *xwarenah* is described as "the strong glory" that is "made by Mazda" (Yt. 19.45).

Figure 1.1. Carving above the tomb of Darius I (r. 522–486 BCE) at Naqsh-e Rostam, Iran. Photo by Jenny Rose.

Fire has been a prominent and constant element of Zoroastrian reverence, ritual, and iconography. In the millennia since the ancient Greek historian Herodotus first wrote that the Ancient Persians considered fire to be "a god" (*Histories* 3.16), to explain why they did not cremate their dead, non-Zoroastrians have often referred to Zoroastrians as "fire-worshippers." The Persian phrase *atashparastan*—"fire worshippers"—appears in Marco Polo's late thirteenth-century record of his encounters with Zoroastrians in Iran, and is still used in Iran by non-Zoroastrians today. It has a derogatory sense, whether intentional or not, and Zoroastrians still find themselves explaining that they do not worship fire, but regard it as a symbol of Ahura Mazda.

Fire in some form—whether the sun itself, a consecrated fire in a fire temple in India, a gas-lit fire in a *dar-i mihr* in California, an oil lamp (*divo*), or even a flickering electric light in the home—is a focus at every Zoroastrian act of prayer. As one of my Zoroastrian friends led a group of students around the *dar-i mihr* (fire temple) in Westminster, southern California, he was asked: "In some religions, such as Christianity and Islam, fire burns the souls in hell—how can this be a symbol of God in Zoroastrianism?" One response to this question is that physical fire is an emblem of the "endless lights"

Figure 1.2. Anahita lights the fire in the *divo* (oil lamp), before reciting prayers from the Avesta. Photo by Jenny Rose.

(Av. *anagra raoca*) that are the visible manifestation of Ahura Mazda, and of which the sun is the most beautiful form (YH 36.6).[6] A later Avestan text states that the individual soul (Av. *urvan*) of the "person who follows order" (Av. *ashavan*) will eventually make its way to those endless lights (HN 2.15). The endless lights are also understood metaphorically as the boundless illumination of the omniscience of Ahura Mazda.

This notion of Ahura Mazda as a combination of both physical light and conceptual order (or "truth") is, curiously, reiterated in a statement by Porphyry, the third century CE Neoplatonist philosopher. Porphyry wrote that Pythagoras had learned from the Magi, that "God himself whom they call Oromazes, resembles light with regard to his body, and truth with regard to his soul" (*Life of Pythagoras* 41).[7]

Herodotus' comment that the Ancient Persians did not cremate their dead so as not to defile fire is supported by injunctions in the Young Avestan *Videvdad*, which censure acts of carelessness or intentional misconduct that pollute the fire, earth, or water through the introduction of "dead matter" (Av. *nasu*).[8] "Dead matter" includes all bodily excreta including breath, saliva, blood, and urine. Herodotus also noted that the Persians were careful not to wash, spit, or urinate into flowing water (*Histories* 1.138). This practical nurturing of certain elements of nature is a recurring focus across the centuries in both Zoroastrian texts and external commentaries on the "Persian" religion. For instance, another Greek-speaking outside observer, Strabo (c. 63 BCE–24 CE) wrote that the Persians did not throw any unclean or dead matter into water (*Geographia*, 15.3.16–18). Although keeping the waters clean is nowadays considered sound ecological practice, the rationale in the *Videvdad* is given as humanity's contribution to dispelling the disorder and destruction brought by those who live in the "lair of the lie" (Vd. 3.7).

DO ZOROASTRIANS BELIEVE IN ONE GOD OR MANY?

The concept of Ahura Mazda as the sole creator of the universe in its state of perfection and goodness continues through the Middle Persian texts. The ambiguous nature of the *amesha spentas* has, however, led some to consider the religion as panentheistic, polytheistic or pantheistic. The introduction of these and other theological definitions such as "dualism" and "monism" has polarized internal Zoroastrian discussion about the essence and activity of Ahura Mazda, particularly that which is now conducted through the internet. Although most Zoroastrians do not choose to spend much time in dissecting arcane matters of theology, any presentation of "Zoroastrian Thought" should introduce at least some of the issues.

A passage in the *Gathas* alludes to "Ahura Mazda and the other *ahuras*" (Y. 30.9, 31.4). This is echoed in references in Darius' inscription to "Ahura Mazda and the other gods who are" (DB 4. 61–3). Such statements raise the question as to whether there were indeed "other gods" who were recognized as having power, with Ahura Mazda as the supreme divinity. Could the "other *ahuras*" of the Gathic poem refer to the *amesha spentas* as being of the same "lordship" as Ahura Mazda? Or were they other "beings worthy of worship" (*yazatas*), who are not mentioned by name in the *Gathas*, but who are praised in the *yashts*, the Young Avestan hymns? One example of a plural reference to "gods" in *Yasna Haptanghaiti* may help in this analysis. YH 38.3 contains the only instance of the term *ahuranish*, the "female lordly ones," which is usually understood to designate the waters being worshipped as "the wives or consorts of the Ahura." The word could, however, refer to the flowing waters as having their source in Ahura Mazda, in the sense of being "lordly" through him.[9] A similar interpretation could be given for the plural references to *ahuras* in the *Gathas*.

The *yazatas*

Just as *Yasna Haptanghaiti* alludes to those who worship the waters through the spoken word and offerings, so individual *yazatas* are directly addressed in a similar way in the *yashts*. These long Young Avestan hymns to Mithra (the male *yazata* of "contract" or "alliance"), to Anahita (the beneficent female *yazata* of the waters), to the *Fravashis* (the "pre-souls" of those who uphold *asha*), and to several other entities, are included in the Zoroastrian prayer book, the *Khordeh Avesta*. Herodotus describes Ancient Persian mountaintop worship of their God (Gk. "Zeus"), who was "the whole circle of the sky," alongside worship of "the sun, moon, earth, fire, water and winds" (*Histories* 1.131). This list suggests that litanies to these natural elements as the creations of Ahura Mazda were widely known as an aspect of Persian worship by the late fifth century BCE. The Cappadocian calendar cited earlier informs us that alongside the six months named after *amesha spentas*, other months were named after *yazatas*, including Mithra and Tishtrya. Tishtrya (MP Tir) is a male *yazata* of the waters and fertility. The *amesha spentas* and *yazatas* seem to have been significant to the Ancient Persian worldview in terms of shaping the liturgical year.

Inscriptions of Artaxerxes II (r. 404–c.359 BCE) at Susa acknowledge both Anahita and Mithra by name after Ahura Mazda. These two *yazatas*—the one female, the other male—are recognized as assisting the king in his construction work and protecting him from evil (A2Sa 2–5). This elevation of Anahita and Mithra—who crosses the sky before the sun (Yt. 10.13)—may relate to their association with water and fire respectively. Around the end of the reign of Artaxerxes II, the Greek historian Dinon is said to have remarked that the Persians' only images of gods were fire and water.[10]

Imagery of Ahura Mazda and some of the *yazatas*, including Mithra, is found on Kushan coins from the second century CE, alongside Indian divine beings, including the Buddha. This indicates that these *yazatas* remained an important part of eastern Iranian religious expression, which is supported by the discovery of iconographic representations of similar entities in the fifth- and sixth-century Sogdian frescoes of Panjikant.

"Progressive" Zoroastrians do not consider these "beings worthy of worship" to be original to the earliest form of Mazda worship.[11] For those who accept only the *Gathas* as authentic religious texts, the idea of individual *yazatas* or personified *amesha spentas* as the focus of reverence is perceived as a challenge to the supremacy of Ahura Mazda. An understanding has developed that the entities that appear in the *Gathas* and that are quantified as *amesha spentas* and *yazatas* are no more than qualities of Ahura Mazda, which can be emulated by humans and lead to spiritual progression as a Zarathushti. From this perspective, those *yazatas* that are first mentioned in the Young Avestan texts are regarded as "bringing the importance of the protection of nature to the attention of all" and as having significant "ethical and spiritual connotations," but constituting no theological threat.[12]

In contrast, the "traditionalist" perspective is that Ahura Mazda remains the supreme God, who has many "angels" (*yazatas*) and "archangels" (*amesha spentas*). The Persian word *fireshte* is often used for these beings. Like "angel," *fireshte* means "one who is sent." The word conveys the sense that these entities, although distinct from Ahura Mazda, are an integral part of the exercise of Order in both existences. This orderly state is reflected in the Zoroastrian calendar, which begins with seven days named after Ahura Mazda and his "task force" of six *amesha spentas*. There is no separate day named for *spenta mainyu*. These first seven days of the month are followed by other days named after different *yazatas*.

The various categorizations of theology, such as polytheism and panentheism, mentioned earlier are generally perceived as challenges to monotheism. It seems to be the case, however, that the Zoroastrian model has been historically capable of encompassing many different dimensions that would ordinarily seem to be incompatible with the concept of monotheism. Nowadays, a more rigid understanding of monotheism has been adopted by many Zoroastrians, perhaps due to the impact of the other monotheistic religions of the Near East. Such standardization of theological terminology tends to leave no room for a broader definition.

WHERE DOES EVIL COME FROM?

The most challenging question regarding the nature of Ahura Mazda relates to the existence of evil. If Ahura Mazda is the creator of all that is good and orderly, then what is the source of evil? How can a good creator God allow the existence of evil? This is a question that perplexes theologians of many religions. The problem is that of *theodicy*: the inconsistency of believing that the universe is created by an omnipotent and perfectly good supreme being, but that it is also full of evil and suffering.

There is no consensus among contemporary Zoroastrians as to where evil comes from. Does it exist solely within human "destructive mentality" as a necessary corollary to free will? Is it the absence of good? Or does evil have a separate metaphysical—and physical—reality?

The Zoroastrian religion addresses the problem of the source of evil partly through the notion of ethical dualism, which operates at the level of human choice, and can transform the world for better or worse. One of the Gathic poems, which has been referred to as "the *Gatha* of the choice" encourages everyone to pay close attention to the recitation, opening their ears to the words, and their minds to enlightened thought, so that they can choose between two potentialities (Y. 30.2–4). The choice is between the "two inspirations" (*mainyu*) who are "twin" in their thought, speech and actions—but the one is good (*vohu*), the other bad (*aka*). Those who are beneficent choose correctly: not so those who bring evil. The choice that is made determines one's future state: those who follow the "lie" (*druj*) will have "the worst existence," but for those who uphold *asha*, there will be "best thought."

Some Zoroastrians feel that perhaps evil exists in order for humans to be free to choose between the crooked and the straight. In a discussion from the Harvard Gatha Study group which had been studying the "*Gatha* of Choice" (Yasna 30), one of its members wrote: "A world in which there is no evil is, by its very nature, a world bereft of moral choice . . . . Can one consider a person to be good who has no opportunity to act otherwise . . . ? The term 'good' only has meaning because it can be contrasted with its opposing twin 'evil.'"[13]

Crooked mentality

The notion of two inspirations co-existing but competing for human attention is stated in a Gathic verse which declares that the two inspirations were at the beginning of existence, the one "beneficent" (Av. *spenta*), the other one "evil" (Av. *angra*). These two "spirits" are separate in thought, wisdom, preference, words and actions (Y. 45.2). Humans have the ability to choose between that which is good or right and that which is evil or corrupt. This suggests a moral theory of the origin of evil, in which evil is thought to arise from some kind of contradiction within human nature. The translation of the word *mainyu* as "mentality," can lead to the understanding that evil only exists within the sphere of human choice. This notion has been expressed in terms of evil arising from "a crooked human mentality," which leans towards destructive behavior, instead of towards alleviating suffering and misery. Many Zoroastrians today understand evil as operating solely at the level of human action and reaction.

This perspective implies that the world that was created by Ahura Mazda in a state of perfection has been subsequently corrupted through the misguided choices of people. Those who adhere to this view accept that natural disasters and human-created miseries, such as poverty and hunger, are caused by humans choosing the path of destruction (*angra*) rather than of progress (*spenta*). The Lie, then, comes into existence only through the minds of fallible humanity, and evil is in essence the product of human ignorance, deceit, and delusion. The notion that evil exists only in the *menog* or "conceptual" world is supported in some Middle Persian Zoroastrian texts. For example, the *Dadestan-i Denig* states that whereas Ahura Mazda is present in the corporeal world through his creations, Angra Mainyu, the "destructive spirit/inspiration," exists only in the conceptual plane (Dd. 36.51).

The stink of evil

Elsewhere, the choice between good and evil is described as being implemented through and affecting not only a person's mind, but his or her very soul (*urvan*). The soul of the person who is "bad in action, word and thought" is said to taste only foul food when sitting to eat in the "house of the lie" (Y. 49.11, HN 3.36). In contrast, the soul of the *ashavan* encounters a "sweet smell" as it journeys towards the place of reckoning, where it receives "spring butter" to eat (HN 2.18). Old Persian inscriptions of Darius, Xerxes, and Artaxerxes II also refer to evil as "foul-smelling," like food that has spoiled. The same concept of putrefaction is used to refer to the "foul spirit" in the Middle Persian eschatological myth (Bd. 34.27). In these end-time accounts, evil is not just a stench, but epitomized as a separate, powerful force.

Although Middle Persian commentary on the Gathic passage about the "twin inspirations" explicitly identifies them as Ahura Mazda and the "foul spirit" (MP *gannog menog*), there is no sense that evil consists of a power equal to Ahura Mazda. As the creator of "all things good" and of "all life" Ahura Mazda is ontologically superior and cannot be the generator of that which is evil or "not-life." The two are mutually exclusive, being incompatible in essence. Such a separation in essence maintains the unqualified goodness of Ahura Mazda, while accounting for the presence of evil in the world. In this sense, evil is construed as a metaphysical reality.

Daevas and dregvants

The *Gathas* also speak of "false gods"—*daevas*—who first introduce the lie, indicating that evil is not limited to humanity (Y. 30.6). The word *daeva* is sometimes translated as "demon." It is not stated who these *daevas* are, but wrath (Av. *aeshma*) is one of their attributes, through which both they and humans inflict suffering. The generation of such negative qualities as *aeshma* causes harm not only to the world of thought, but also to the material world. The cow, as representative and symbol of the animate world, is particularly vulnerable to the onslaught of wrath in the form of physical violence (Y. 29.1).

The bad choices of the *daevas* and of those who "follow the lie" (Av. *dregvant*) are the means through which evil is able to latch on to the world parasitically. In this manner, the stuff of darkness takes on physical reality. The order and harmony in the two existences—"of thought" and "of bones"—is negated by such disruption, which perpetuates the vertical split between that which is *spenta* (incremental) and that which is *angra* (detrimental) (Y. 45.2). This vertical split extends to all abstract qualities. The good qualities of Ahura Mazda and the people of integrity are challenged by negative qualities associated with following the lie. So *vohu manah* is challenged by *aka manah* (Y. 33.4); *armaiti* ("humble right thinking") is countered by *taromaiti* ("arrogance": Y. 60.5); and *sraosha* battles *aeshma* (Y. 57.9–10, 25).

The structural division between the "straight path" or order of Ahura Mazda and the disorder brought by the false gods (*daevas*) and the "destructive inspiration" (*angra mainyu*) becomes concrete in Young Avestan texts, where Angra Mainyu physically assaults the good creation through his miscreations. One such text, the *Videvdad*, describes each of the good Iranian lands created by Ahura Mazda as being afflicted by the destruction of Angra Mainyu. For example, the "Aryan expanse" is assaulted by a harsh winter instigated by Angra Mainyu (Vd. 1.2–3). The *Videvdad* also mentions creeping animals such as snakes, worms, frogs, ants and flies as if they are intrinsically evil (Vd. 14.5–6). These are alluded to in Avestan as *xrafstra* (cf. Y. 28.5, 34.9). Herodotus refers to a similar Persian categorization of animals as "good" or "bad": the bad included ants, snakes, and "flying and creeping things" (*Histories* 1.140).

Elsewhere in the *Videvdad*, the pollution of dead matter is hypostatized as the female Druj Nasu ("the lie demon of dead matter"); and the onset of menstruation is attributed to a female *daeva* named Jahi, whose glance dries up rivers and vegetation, and whose touch withers the ability of a righteous person to combat evil (Vd. 5.28–32; 18.63–4). According to the *Videvdad*, a woman in menses should, therefore, keep a certain distance away from water, fire and humans, so that her touch or glance would not contaminate them (Vd. 16.1–4). The attribution of death, impurity, and disease to such hostile forces denotes an understanding that evil is at work in the physical world, and is not entirely the product of human corruption.

Counteracting the assault of evil

The intelligence, insight, and forethought of Ahura Mazda are understood to keep the world pivoted towards goodness. During the current time of "mixture" when good and evil co-exist in a state of tension, humans can also actively participate in the work of propelling the world towards the good. Traditionalist Zoroastrians consider that individual acts of purification and consecration, as well as those relating to the performance of the Yasna and other ritual ceremonies, help to counteract the destructive impulse of Angra Mainyu, the *daevas*, and those who adhere to the lie.

The conception of a good world open to an assault from evil that operates on multiple levels of reality is articulated in Old Persian texts. In his inscriptions, Darius I describes his role as Ahura Mazda's representative on earth to ensure peace and prosperity for the people, their homes, and their livestock (DB 1.61–71). He asks Ahura Mazda to protect the land from a hostile army, a bad harvest year, and the Lie (DPd 12–20). Evil is here attributed to the differing realms of physical assault, natural disaster, and mental corruption. Such Old Persian inscriptions emphasize the binary opposition between that which is "good" or "beautiful" (OP *naiba*), and that which is evil (OP *dush*).

Figure 1.3. The Gate of All Nations built by Xerxes (r. 486–465 BCE), Persepolis, Iran. Photo by Jenny Rose.

On the Gate of All Nations (Fig. 1.3), through which all visitors to the royal palaces of Persepolis would have had to pass, Xerxes (r. 486–465 BCE) had inscribed: "I built this Gate of all Lands. Much else that is good was built within this Persepolis, which I built and my father built. Whatever good construction is seen, all that we built with the aid of Ahura Mazda" (XPa 11–17).[14] The gateway represents both a physical and figurative threshold expressing the Persian king's function as perpetrator of "the good" throughout all the lands of the realm, not just Persia. The implication is that this good activity, generated with the aid of Ahura Mazda, functions against both external and internal enemies including the forces of evil. Imagery on the stone doorjambs of Persepolis of the Achaemenid king killing a lion or a bull may illustrate this idea.

The two principles

The Greeks seem to have understood that for the Ancient Persians the split between good and evil occurred at a theological as well as ethical level. According to Diogenes Laertius, Aristotle referred to Persian teaching on this matter as one that was ancient and original to them. He said that there were two first principles, a good spirit (*daimon*) named "Zeus and Oromazes" (Ahura Mazda), and a bad spirit named "Hades and Areimanios" (Angra Mainyu). Diogenes notes that this Persian assertion of two primordial principles is also mentioned by Aristotle's contemporaries, including Eudoxus, the astronomer and friend of Plato, and Theopompus of Chios.

The Ancient Persians seem to have been divided as to how to understand this theology of "two first principles." This ambivalence is reflected in statements by Plutarch (c. 46–120 CE) from the late first century CE. In his discussion *On Isis and Osiris*, Plutarch wrote that some Persians believe that there are two "gods" who crafted the world—the one the creator of good things, the other of evil. The word that Plutarch uses for "god" is *demiurgos*, meaning "fashioner" or "shaper" of the material world. He then writes that other Persians, including "Zoroaster the Magus" call the better one "god" (*theos*) and the other "evil spirit" (*daimon*). Plutarch goes on to say that Zoroaster called the god Horomasdes, who "was more like light than anything apprehended by the senses." The *daimon* was called Areimanios by Zoroaster, and shown to be "more like darkness and ignorance."[15]

A few centuries later, a Christian apologetic account from the mid–fifth century CE informs us that the Zoroastrian theologians of the time had produced their own written definition of the source of evil. According to the Armenian historian Elishe Vardapet, Mihr Narseh, the prime minister of the Sasanian king Yazdegerd II (r. 438–457 CE), wrote an edict to the Armenians in 449 CE to persuade them to revert to Mazda worship. The country of Armenia had converted from Zoroastrianism to Christianity a century and a half earlier, in 301 CE. Mihr Narseh's edict was apparently as much a political ploy on the part of Yazdegerd II as a testimony to the minister's own religious zeal.

Elishe provides both Mihr Narseh's edict and a lengthy refutation of what he knew of the Zoroastrian view of the nature of God. Mihr Narseh wrote that creation is divided: everything good in heaven and earth is Ahura Mazda's and everything harmful is the work of Angra Mainyu. Ahura Mazda created humans, "success . . . and glory and honors and health of body, beauty of face, eloquence, and longevity," whereas Angra Mainyu made "diseases, illnesses and death . . . [a]ll misfortunes and disasters that occur and bitter wars."[16] Mihr Narseh specified that anyone who thinks that Ahura Mazda is the origin of death, or of both good and evil, is in error.

It is in the context of this mid-Sasanian era edict reported by Elishe that the myth of Zurvan as hypostatized "Time" is outlined. Another fifth century CE Armenian, Eznik of Kølb, narrates the myth in more details and with some variations. It describes Zurvan as progenitor of both Ahura Mazda and Angra Mainyu. This myth of a common progenitor seems to have been one way that Zoroastrians in the Sasanian period understood the separate origins and natures of good and evil. Although in this schema Zurvan is the source of both, he is not a creator god—that role belongs to Ahura Mazda. The Zurvanite "twinning" of Ahura Mazda and Angra Mainyu as "brothers" from a common origin is rejected as a false teaching in the Middle Persian *Denkard*.

These difficulties of dualities ripple through the Middle Persian Zoroastrian texts in cosmological, theological, and ethical terms. Middle Persian cosmology relates that Ahura Mazda purposefully created the world in order to be able to do battle against evil in a limited time and place (Bd. 1). In ignorantly agreeing to a fixed time for this struggle for power, Angra Mainyu paradoxically becomes implicit in his

own ultimate defeat. Angra Mainyu then destroyed the various elements of creation, darkening the sky, assaulting the water, piercing the
center of the earth, withering the plant, bringing greed, desire, torpor,
pain, disease, and eventually death to the bull and the primal human,
and then mixing smoke into the fire (Bd. 4.10–27). Just as the *yazatas*
who aid Ahura Mazda in the creation of the world have evil counter-
parts, so do the very elements of creation itself: light is contrasted with
darkness, summer with winter, cleanness with dirt (Bd. 5.1).

Although no single Zoroastrian text deals with all the questions of
theodicy, a Middle Persian work by a layman Mardanfarrokh-i
Ohrmazddad tackles the problem that the very existence of evil
implicates Ahura Mazda. In an apologetic treatise that challenged
the teachings of other monotheistic faiths in the region, and promoted the superiority of the Zoroastrian schema, Mardanfarrokh
addressed the question that one of my students just posed in class:
"If Ahura Mazda is omnipotent, then why doesn't he dispel evil
immediately?" In his "Doubt-Dispelling Exposition" (MP *Shkand
Gumanig Wizar*) Mardanfarrokh cleverly redefined omnipotence to
relate to the realm of *that which is possible*. He stated that since Ahura
Mazda is only good, he is all-powerful *only* within the sphere of
good. According to Mardanfarrokh, the substance of evil is
completely separate from the substance of good, and therefore it is
ontologically impossible for Ahura Mazda to exist in the same sphere
as evil and so to change its nature (SGW 8.18).

Not long after Mardanfarrokh, the Sunni Islamic scholar Al-
Ghazali (1058–1111 CE) picked up on this nuanced perspective. He
noted that although Zoroastrians acknowledge that evil exists in the
world, they would not allow it to be attributed to their God: "He
being wholly void of evil, they conceive of a struggle between Him
and the Darkness, and these two are called by them, as I suppose,
Yazdan ['God'] and Ahriman [Angra Mainyu]."[17]

In the intervening centuries since Mardanfarrokh, there have
been few attempts—from within or outside the religion—to produce a critical analysis of the Zoroastrian understanding of the
nature and problem of evil, and its correlation with theological
notions of "dualism," and "omnipotence." A conclusion expressed
in one late twentieth-century academic paper favors the interpretation "that Zoroastrianism combines a cosmogonic dualism and
eschatological monotheism in a manner unique to itself among the

major religions of the world."[18] In other words, the religious narrative portrays a vertical split on all levels that lasts from the beginning of time until the resolution at the end, when the two inspirations will separate once and for all, and the good will prevail (see below, "What happens at the End?"). This theology does not fall neatly into existing familiar categories, but presents a wholly original religious schema. For those Zoroastrians to whom the omnipotence of God is paramount, however, this concept of a "cosmogonic dualism" carries with it the unacceptable idea of two main principles, which can be—and have been—interpreted as two "gods." It is for this reason that many reject the notion of evil as a separate force. Some take this approach to its logical conclusion and attribute death itself to Ahura Mazda, but this is not part of any "official" discourse of the religion.[19]

WHAT IS THE PURPOSE OF HUMAN EXISTENCE?

Despite internal disagreement concerning the origin and nature of evil, the prevailing Zoroastrian view is that both the mental and material spheres of existence are places where good and evil, although essentially different, are mixed together in a constant state of tension. In this state of instability and time of "mixture," humans have the free will to choose to fight on the side of good. Their choice to do so shapes the ultimate defeat of evil. The progress of the world towards a good resolution in which evil is dispelled can take place only if humans choose the good.

Since humans have both a mind and a body, they are urged in the *Gathas* and later texts to develop "good thought," so that they may discern what is "really real" (Av. *haithya*) from that which is false or delusion, and to speak and act accordingly. Humans must work to acquire the wisdom (Av. *xratu*) necessary to distinguish between good and evil, and to remain separate from evil. They have the responsibility to determine, through their thoughts, which is the best choice of words or course of action. This notion of making a conscious choice between the two possible paths—which one scholar has referred to as "embryonic potentials"—represents a significant contribution to the development of human ethics.[20] Within this Zoroastrian ethic, humans are responsible for exercising their freedom of choice and living with the consequences. They must use their own powers of discernment to make the right choice.

The innate desire of humans for wisdom is understood to help them to gravitate to the good, to Ahura Mazda. Actions deriving from good thought, "good understanding" (*huxratu*), and "right thinking" (*armaiti*) are the markers of the one who upholds order and integrity (Y. 34.10, 14). Those who have minds clouded by deceit and confusion are motivated by self-interest, greed, and anger. From the outset, the ideal of bringing order and integrity is applied to both men and women (cf. Y. 53. 5, 6). Both genders are encouraged to cultivate that which is right (YH 35.6) and to "expand the earth" (Vd. 19.26). There is no gender difference in terms of potential for spiritual achievement. Both "man and woman" will be held accountable for their actions in life (Y. 46.10). For all Zoroastrians, the ethical choice between the straight and the crooked is an ever-present reality.

The purpose of human existence is, then, to be an ally of Ahura Mazda. In the Avesta, Zarathushtra is perceived as the first human to actively assist Ahura Mazda in overcoming evil. He is the first to recite the most powerful prayer, the *Ahuna Vairya*, and to combat the *daevas*, making them go underground (Y. 9.14–15). He is the first to put Angra Mainyu to flight (Yt. 17 18–20). Those who are *Zarathushtri*—"in line with Zarathushtra"—are expected to follow this model. The very first words of the *Fravarane*, the statement of faith, are: "I reject the *daevas*." This is followed by the commitment to worship Ahura Mazda "like Zarathushtra did" (Y. 12.1).

The Zoroastrian understanding of Ahura Mazda's engendering activity and continued function within the physical creation places humanity as integral to the cosmic scheme. In the short "prayer of the four directions" (MP *namaz-i chahar nemag*) the worshipper turns towards each cardinal point—East, West, South, and North—acknowledging the order inherent in the universe, and recognizing that humans are part of that orderly structure. The function of humans is to live in the world, not try to rise above it, or to avoid it, but to participate in similar creative activity to that of Ahura Mazda. For this reason, there is no Zoroastrian asceticism along the lines of Buddhist or Christian monasticism, and very few dietary stipulations.

There is no Zoroastrian concept of "original sin," apart from a reference in the *Bundahishn* to a rebellion against Ahura Mazda in thought, word, and deed by the first mortal man and woman, named

Mashya and Mashyanag respectively (Bd. 14.11–21). Mashyanag performs the first human act of false worship when she pours cow's milk in the direction of the north, strengthening the *daevas* who live there (Bd. 14.28–29). Her act is not considered, however, to have enduring repercussions for subsequent humans along the lines of Adam and Eve's "fall" in the Biblical account. Rather, it serves as a lesson in how not to behave.

Human parts

According to the *Bundahishn*, of all the beings in the corporeal world, humans have a special relationship with Ahura Mazda, who "took them as his own" (Bd. 3.12). The *Denkard* declares humans to be the "chief creations of the world" and the person who upholds order and right to be the culmination of human potential.

The *Gathas* refer to various human faculties bestowed by Ahura Mazda, including "[religious] insight" (*daena*), guiding thought (*xratu*), and physical body and life breath (*astvant- ushtana*; Y. 31.11). A couple of Young Avestan texts list the components of the male and female *ashavan* as "life" (*ahu*), "religious insight," "awareness" (*baodah*), "soul" (*urvan*), and "pre-soul" (*fravashi*).[21] Yasna 55.1 also includes the physical parts of the body (*tanu*), skeletal frame (*asti*), and vital force (*gaetha*). These components, physical, mental, and spiritual, are all necessary to engage in the promotion of good thoughts, words, and deeds.

Five main elements of the human being are listed in the *Bundahishn*, but the terms used are somewhat different. The first three parts listed are the body (MP *tan*), the lifeforce (MP *jan*), and a "frame" (MP *ewanag*); these are connected to the physical elements of the earth, the wind, and the sun respectively (Bd. 3.13). The "frame" of the individual relates to a form that differs somehow from the visible physical body, perhaps more like an individual "essence."[22] The other two dimensions of a human are the soul and the pre-soul. The soul (*urvan*), through physical embodiment and mental consciousness, is the aspect of the human that "hears, sees, talks and knows." It is protected from evil by being connected to the incorruptible pre-soul (*fravashi*), which has assisted Ahura Mazda since the beginning of creation (Yt. 13.1–11).

The Avestan word *fravashi* comes from the compound *fra+var*, which is usually understood to mean "to choose for." The *fravashis* choose for the good, in alliance with Ahura Mazda against evil. According to the hymn in their praise, the *Farvardin Yasht*, the *fravashis* chose to become human in order to engage in the cosmic struggle (cf. Yt.13.12, 28–29). The *fravashi* of each living person is said to be more powerful than those of the dead, but not quite as powerful as the beneficent beings who will make the world wonderful again (Yt. 13.17). Some Zoroastrians translate *fravashi* as "guardian angel," "protective spirit," or even "spark of the divinity."[23]

The right measure and the straight path

The emphasis on the human role in establishing order is elaborated in the Middle Persian concept of *payman*, or "right measure." This refers to maintaining a balanced approach in all things. The balance is about trying to counteract the working of evil in the world by thinking good thoughts, speaking good words, and performing good deeds. The intention is, if possible, to tip the scales favorably, so that there is a progress towards an increase in good and decrease in evil.

One text reads:

These things are most important in the religion: union, the right measure [*payman*] and separation.

This is union: one who is associated to the gods [MP *yazdan*] and the good ones in every righteousness in thought speech and deed. That union never perishes.

This is separation: one who is detached in every iniquity and sin from Ahriman, the demons [MP *dewan*] and the evil ones.

This is the right measure: one who is a protector of that union and separation. It will never perish. (Dk. 6. 43)[24]

This idea of tipping the balance towards union with "the good ones" and away from the forces of evil is echoed in Middle Persian descriptions of a bridge that leads to the endless lights of Ahura Mazda. For the soul of the righteous person, that bridge broadens to nine spear widths and is easily crossed in three steps—one for good thoughts, one for good words, one for good deeds. For the evildoer, however, the bridge narrows to a sharpened razor edge, on which the individual cannot balance, but falls tumbling into the depths of hell below (Dd. 20.3–4). (See later, "The Individual Hereafter").

The Achaemenids seem to have identified with an ethical code of promoting the good and opposing evil. The name "Darius" in Old Persian is *Darayavahu*, meaning "he who holds the good." Darius I emphasizes that he received the support of Ahura Mazda, because he stuck to the straight path, neither following the Lie, nor siding with evil (DB 4.61–65). He also claims that he was slow to anger, because he was able to keep his thought (*manah*) in check (DNb 13–15).

Like the Avesta, Old Persian texts display an opposition between that which is "true" (*hashiya*) and "right" (*rasta*) and that which is a "lie" (*drauga*) and "wrong" (*mithah*). From the Old Persian inscriptions, it is evident that the principle of following the straight, true, and orderly path was central to the self-definition of the Achaemenids. The Greeks were familiar with the Ancient Persian notion that to choose the good or the straight was a moral imperative with repercussions in this life, and also perhaps in the afterlife. An often-quoted passage from Herodotus is his remark that Persian boys were taught three things: to ride a horse, to shoot a bow, and to tell the truth (*Histories* 1.137). Herodotus goes on to say that for Persians telling lies is only marginally worse than owing a debt, and so identifies them as making a strong link between verbal honesty and integrity in conduct.

Making the world excellent

The Old Persian inscriptions endorse a strong ethical connection between the beneficial acts of humans and the creative activity of Ahura Mazda. Darius I professes that he has constructed much perfect work, but recognizes that it is the great god Ahura Mazda who established perfection and peace, and who guides him (DSf 55–58; DNb 1–5). Xerxes claims that it was with the aid of Ahura Mazda that he was able to construct something beautiful, and also to replace evil action with good (XPh 41–46). Such efforts to make the material world "excellent" seem to be a conscious emulation of the perfection of Ahura Mazda. The Old Persian word for "excellent"—*frasha*— also refers to the creative work of Ahura Mazda and to the constructive efforts of the king (cf. DNb 1–2; DSa 5, DSo 4).

In the *Gathas*, the word *frasha*, meaning "wonderful" or "perfect," is linked with the word for "existence" or "life"—*ahu*. A petition by worshippers asks that they may assist Mazda in making the world *frasha* (Y. 30.9). This Old Avestan cosmogonic use seems to underlie that of the Achaemenids. The Gathic sense is that existence is progressing towards a state of final perfection with the aid of humans who act as "world healers" (Av. *ahum bish*: Y. 31.19, 44.2). This final perfection will be brought by the *saoshyants*, the "ones who will be strong" and who will combine their knowledge with practical action to dispel evil (Y. 48.12). The word *saoshyant* is grammatically a future participle, which indicates that the concept is already part of an eschatological vocabulary concerning that which will come to be.

Some Young Avestan texts allude to a single *saoshyant* whose arrival will effect the ultimate defeat of evil (Yt. 19.11). The Young Avestan use of *frasha* in the context of life being made "excellent" or "wonderful" relates to this final removal of evil from the world, which can then be restored to its original perfection (Av. *frasho.kereti*). Until that time, all humans who are motivated by good thought have a responsibility to protect themselves and the good creations from the turbulence and trouble epitomized in the Lie and those who promote it.

In another of Xerxes' inscriptions at Persepolis, the king tells those who come after him that they should worship Ahura Mazda according to the order (*arta*) "on high," and should behave according to the law established by Ahura Mazda, so that they might be happy while they are alive and "possessing that order" (*artavan*) when dead (XPh 46–56). In this context, the use of the adjective *artavan* (cognate with the Avestan noun *ashavan*) implies that when humans act in accord with the established cosmic and ethical order of Ahura Mazda, they follow a straight path that continues beyond death. That this activity included ritual order as well seems to be evidenced by the similar phrasing in the penultimate section of the Yasna, which reads:

> As you desire, O Orderly one [Av. *ashavan*],
> here you shall be Orderly
> You shall make (your) soul pass
> Across the Ford of the Accountant
> Up to the best state of existence
> Arriving Orderly (Y. 71.16).[25]

WHAT HAPPENS AT THE END?

Discussions of cosmology and of the possibility of the triumph of good and the defeat of evil eventually lead to discussions of eschatology. To paraphrase T. S. Eliot, ideas about the end are always wrapped up with the story of the beginning. The *Gathas* have cryptic allusions to the end. The adjectives *apara* and *apema*, meaning "later/future" and "last/end" respectively occur in reference to a time of reckoning—a "final turning point" (Av. *urvaesa*), when those people of integrity will be illuminated and achieve "best thought," but the lie-mongers will experience the "worst existence" characterized by "a long lifetime of darkness, bad food and the word 'woe'" (Y. 30.4; 31.20). Zoroastrians today discuss whether this future/end resolution relates to a physical state, in and of the material world, or to a spiritual state of "heavenly bliss" in which the soul resides with Ahura Mazda, or, even becomes one with the "endless lights." For some, the "house of good thought" (Y. 32.15) is understood allegorically, as a mental state of "oneness" with the intention of Ahura Mazda—a state that can be experienced in the here and now. Such deliberation is similar to Christian consideration of the concept of the "Kingdom of Heaven."

This question about "the End" is about the end of life for individuals, and also about the end of time.

The individual hereafter

At an individual level, the question is about life after death, about whether there is any part of a human being that continues in an afterlife. If so, what does that afterlife involve? A physical resurrection? Or a return to a spiritual source?

As mentioned above, the *Gathas* allude to places where the good and the bad will end up "at the end." For those who are good, who sustain order and bring benefit to the world, the reward includes the "house of song", the "house of good thought," and the "best existence" (Y. 51.15, 32.15, 44.2). The bad who follow the lie find themselves as guests in the "house of the lie", the "house of worst thought" and "the worst existence" (Y. 51.14, 32.13, 30.4). Some consider this prototypical heaven and hell to exist only during this life. In this sense, they are allegories of the human condition and consciousness: the "heavenly" house is a metaphor for a life of happiness and fulfillment at both mental and material level; the "hellish" house is a metaphor of psychological and physical alienation. This notion of isolation is dramatically delineated in one Middle Persian book, where hell is described as a dangerous and terrible place, evil-smelling and dark, which, although full of wicked souls, is so silent and dark that each soul feels it is entirely alone (AWN 54). In this particular context, however, hell is a postmortem state for the soul, not an earthly existence.

The *Gathas* mention a crossing place—the *"chinvat peretu"* (Y. 46.11, 51.13), where a reckoning occurs for each person. This point marks the moment that an individual is called to account for her or his life, and crosses over to another stage of existence. The crossing place is a transition, rather than a trial. It is where one faces the consequences of one's decisions: those who have followed the straight path end up in one state of existence; those whose bad choices have led them astray find themselves in another, diametrically opposite state. The two disparate existences are measured by the superlatives "best" and "worst": they are "bright" or "dark"; full of song or lament; they either lead to strength for the individual or to a lengthy period of suffering; to life or not-life.

In the Young Avestan accounts, the soul (*urvan*) of a dead person goes to the place of reckoning and the *fravashi* returns to its place alongside Ahura Mazda. One Young Avestan text describes the journey of the individual soul to the afterlife in answer to Zarathushtra's question about what happens to the soul after death. The narrative is formulated in terms of Ahura Mazda's response. The text, the *Hadokht Nask*, records that at dawn following the third night after death, the soul of the deceased feels the wind blowing towards it, and sees the thoughts, words, and deeds that constitute its religious insight (*daena*) coming towards it (HN 2.7–11). If the soul is of an *ashavan*, the breeze is from the south, and is fragrantly scented. The form of the *daena* is as a beautiful young woman. The soul takes three steps—one for good thought, one for good words, and one for good deeds, and on the fourth step arrives at the endless lights (HN 2.15). A similar scenario appears in the *Videvdad*, where the *daena* accompanies the soul of the *ashavan* over the crossing-place of reckoning into the presence of the throne of good thought, from where they proceed to the thrones of Ahura Mazda and the *amesha spentas* in the house of song.

According to *Hadokht Nask*, the soul of the *dregvant* is met by a stinking northerly wind, and on its fourth step ends in endless darkness, where the food is poisonous (HN 2.36). In the *Videvdad* account, it is the *daena* that drags the soul of the *dregvant* into the "darknesses" (Vd. 19. 30–2).

In various Middle Persian accounts, the bad thoughts, bad words, and bad deeds of the *dregvant* appear as a horrible, deformed female (AWN 17.9; Dd. 24.5–6). These accounts indicate that the sum of one's thoughts, words, and deeds relates directly to one's religious insight. An individual's *daena* is enhanced through the recitation of the *Gathas*, and through making offerings to the good waters, and to the fire of Ahura Mazda (HN 2.13).

These descriptions of the afterlife of the soul seem to be based on contemporary laws of hospitality: the soul is like a guest in a house, and the reception depends upon one's prior life. The parallel today would be, perhaps, the comparison between a cheerful reunion with family and friends in a cozy restaurant, eating good food and being entertained with music, versus an evening at a gloomy D-rated diner where the ambiance, the food and the music are all atrocious, and one feels utterly alone.

The Avestan themes relating to this time of judgment: a bridge or crossing place; a woman representing one's *daena*; a place of darkness and fear; and a place of light and nourishment, all appear in a series of Middle Persian inscriptions by a Zoroastrian priest named Kerdir. In these third century CE accounts, Kerdir records that he "saw" all these elements, when he asked the *yazatas* to reassure him about life after death in terms of heaven and hell. The Middle Persian word usually translated as "heaven" is *vahisht*, which means "best," as in the "best existence" (Av. *vahishta ahu*). The word *dushox*, translated as "hell," probably comes from an earlier Avestan form of "*dush ahu*" meaning "bad existence."

In an inscription at Naqsh-e Rajab near Shiraz, Kerdir states as a fact that there is an afterlife and that the good go to heaven, and the bad to hell. This early Sasanian narrative proclaims the existence of an afterlife for the individual as a central religious tenet. It does not allude to any universal eschatology, and makes no mention of the fate of collective humanity nor that of the material world. This is also true of the later Middle Persian account of the hereafter as experienced by a layman, Arda Wiraz. The name "Arda Wiraz" can be translated as "the Righteous Man" and he could be said to symbolize Everyman (and Everywoman), whose vision of the blissful life in heaven and the fearful torments of hell serve to impel the faithful to keep to the straight path. Both states are vividly described in the account, but with far more emphasis on the denizens of hell and their degradations. The text obviously acted as a *memento mori* for generations. By the mid–seventeenth century, illustrated versions of this book were available in Iran and India, and a couple of extant Gujarati copies contain gruesome pictures of the punishments of those consigned to hell.

Figure 1.4. A scene from the *Arda Wiraz Namag* showing the soul meeting the *daena* at the bridge. Old Gujarati (Devanagri script), mid–seventeenth century. Photo courtesy of Jamsheed K. Choksy.

In Middle Persian accounts, the soul is met at the bridge by a triad of *yazatas*, led by Mithra, who sees all from his position high above the mountains. Mithra is assisted by Rashnu, the *yazata* of justice, who weighs the souls on a balance that takes no account of birth or status (MX 1.115–23). Sraosha is also there, to lead the soul to the bridge, where the *yazata* either accompanies it across or leaves it to be dragged off to hell (MX 1.123, 161–6).

By the ninth century CE, at the time the "Decisions concerning the Religion" (MP *Dadestan-i Denig*) was written, degrees of existence in the afterlife are listed, with the "house of song" as a kind of supra-heaven beyond the "best existence" for those whose good deeds were excessive, and who have chanted the *Gathas* (Dd. 20.3). Similarly, there was a level of hell below the "worst existence," which was entirely dark and evil (Dd. 33.2–4).

The place in between

A question that arises from the image of Rashnu weighing the soul is, "What happens if the person's thoughts, words, and deed are equally balanced between good and bad?" This was obviously a question asked by Zoroastrians a thousand years ago, since an answer is provided in the Middle Persian books. The soul of the deceased person that is neutral, in terms of being neither good nor bad, goes to a neutral place (Bd. 30.32; Dd. 20.3). This place of stasis is referred to as *hamistagan*, and seems to be a kind of borderland where the soul waits.

The Middle Persian descriptions of "heaven" and "hell" are supplemented by accounts of a time in the future, when the soul is reunited with the body, and both are resurrected together. The notion of both a spiritual and a physical reckoning coheres with that of the two existences. Some Zoroastrians who believe that there is only reckoning based on one's "mentality" or "conscience" extend that view to include the somewhat alternative proposition that the soul may be reincarnated several times over before it has become purified of all attachment to evil. Traditionalists challenge that opinion as being incompatible with the teachings of the religion about a final resurrection.

The universal hereafter

Although information about a universal eschatology is missing from both the Sasanian-era account of the priest Kerdir and from the later *Arda Wiraz Namag*, it is a theme that appears in detail in other Middle Persian texts. Some perceive the kernel for this conception in Avestan texts, and others regard them as part of a later development of the religion.

The progression of the world towards a final "turning point" (Y. 43.5) is spoken of in the *Gathas* in terms of charging to victory in a horse race (Y. 50.7). As this race is charted in Middle Persian texts, it is seen to involve movement from a state of "mixture" (MP *gumez-ishn*) of good and evil toward a state of separation and resolution (MP *wizarishn*). This is understood to be a collective, rather than an individual event, and its culmination in the "making wonderful" (Av. *frasho.kereti,* MP *frashegird*) of existence to have universal eschatological implication. The Young Avestan concept of *frasho. kereti* denotes a state of existence in which the rottenness and harm of evil has been removed, and an ideal state of conceptual and corporeal incorruptibility established (Yt. 19.89). In the *Bundahishn*, the activity of *frashegird* begins with the resurrection of the dead and the reuniting of the soul with the body (Bd. 34.7–15). The ultimate resolution of *frashegird* occurs when the dead have been restored, evil has been dispelled, and the world made perfect once more under the rule of Ahura Mazda, who is all good, all-knowing and all-powerful "for ever and ever" (Bd. 34. 22, 30–32).

Resurrection

The notion of a physical resurrection of the body appears to have been as conceptually and philosophically problematic for Zoroastrians of the early Common Era as it was for contemporary Jews and Christians. It is, however, a concept that is found in Young Avestan texts, where it is stated that the dead will be raised again and "shall have life with bones."[26] The rising of the dead is a sign that the destructive activity of evil has not been successful. A couple of the *yashts* refer to an individual named Astvat.ereta, who will revitalize the world through making corporeal existence indestructible (Yt. 13.129; Yt. 19.94). The meaning of Astvat.ereta is "the one through whom *asha* has bones," and the name echoes a passage in the *Gathas* where the reciter petitions "May *asha* become corporeal" (Y. 43.16). These references indicate an early belief that physical resurrection was an integral element of a universal eschatology. This is in keeping with the notion that death—and the corruption and decay which precede and follow death—are the product of evil, and need to be removed.

A statement attributed to the Greek historian, Theopompus, in the fourth century BCE notes that the *magi* (Mazda-worshipping priests) teach that humans "will come to life again and be immortal" (Diogenes Laertius, *Lives of the Philosophers* 1.9) This informs us that such concepts were recognized to be part of the Persian religion of the period. A cryptic allusion in the *Gathas* to some kind of "mark" or "sign" of molten metal that will harm the *dregvant* and strengthen the *ashavan* (Y. 51.9) is expanded in Middle Persian narrative, which describes how the resurrected bodies of all will have to pass through a river of molten metal created from the metals in the mountains and hills. For the *ashavan* it will be like walking through warm milk, but for the *dregvant*, it will be like walking through molten metal (Bd. 38.18).

The body of the individual dies and the bones crumble, but, according to the Middle Persian schema, at the end all those bodies will be resurrected intact to be reunited with the soul. In the *Bundahishn*, Zarathushtra asks how it is possible to resurrect a body that has been carried away by the wind or water. Ahura Mazda responds that it was more difficult to establish the elements of creation than to effect the resurrection, and that he will call forth the bones from the earth, blood from water, hair from plants and the soul from the wind, in the same manner that they were originally created (Bd. 34.5; cf Bd. 3.13).

The world benefactors

According to the *Bundahishn*, the universal resurrection will take place after three world-benefactors (MP *soshyans*) have been born in successive millennia. These three are all said to be conceived of the "seed of Zarathushtra" which is kept safe in Lake Kansaoya, until, in each millennium, a young woman bathes in the waters and becomes pregnant (Bd. 33.36–8). This partly addresses the question one of my students asked as to whether Zoroastrians believe that Zarathushtra will return in a similar sense to the "second coming" of Jesus. In the *Bundahishn* narrative, Zarathushtra represents the turning point which sets the world on its course towards being healed, and his three posthumous "sons" bring this healing to fruition. The third, and final *soshyans*, Astvat.ereta, will aid in the performance of a final priestly offering, with Ahura Mazda and Sraosha as presiding priests. This offering will effect the raising of the dead and lead to the final healing of the world (Bd. 34.22–33).

In the *Gathas*, the term *saoshyant* refers to an individual—perhaps an allusion to Zarathushtra—but is also used in the plural, indicating that there will be several such benefactors throughout history. The term develops in later Avestan and Middle Persian texts and crystallizes in the figure of Astvat.ereta, the ultimate *saoshyant*, who will bring benefit to the entire world through the defeat of evil. The *Persian Rivayats* title this eschatological figure "Behram Varzavand," which translates as "the victorious wonder-worker." The Iranian

Zoroastrians priests who sent communications concerning the religion (*rivayats*) in answer to a range of questions from the Parsis note that at the birth of Behram Varzavand stars will fall from the sky, and other such signs will appear. These deliberations on the eschaton ("last things"), written during the late Timurid and Safavid period in Iran, may indicate a heightened sense of insecurity for the Zoroastrians.

A mystical movement, known as *khshnoomism*, that emerged among Parsis in the early twentieth century expects that Shah Behram Varzavand will be born very soon, if he has not already entered the world. Several internet sites emerging from modern branches of *khshnoomism* refer to this event as the culmination of the ages, for which all Zoroastrians should be prepared. [27]

The final outcome for evil

There are two opinions concerning the outcome for evildoers. These are both expressed in the Middle Persian text, the *Pahlavi Rivayat Accompanying the Dadestan-i Denig*. According to one passage, while the souls of the *ashavan* will be reunited in the afterlife with their family and friends, those who are evil will "not arrive in the end" (PRDd. 36.4). This seems to indicate that they will be doomed— and damned—for all time.[28] In contrast, a few paragraphs later, when the wicked walk through the molten metal they will be purified of all evil and enabled to enjoy the final renovation (PRDd. 48.70). This scenario in which the wicked are purged of all evil is reiterated in other Middle Persian and New Persian Zoroastrian literature.

According to Plutarch, Theopompus was familiar with a teaching of the *magi* that the cosmic struggle would culminate in an end time, when Hades (Angra Mainyu) had been dismissed from the world, and humans would be happy, existing in a state where they required no food, and cast no shadow (Plutarch, *On Isis and Osiris* 47). This last feature echoes the tradition that at the very moment of separation of good and evil, the sun will return to its noontime position at the spring equinox. At this moment, the "time of long duration" that marks the struggle between good and evil reverts to the "limitless time" that preceded creation (cf. Vd. 19.9). In a commentary on an earlier Avestan text concerning the resurrection, the *Denkard* states that the reunited souls and bodies of the dead "will not die," but that the corporeal forms of demons and the "bad spirit" will be broken and buried in the earth (Dk. 9.46.1–5).[29]

The notion that all of humanity will be returned to life forever in a world that has once more been restored to perfection in both conceptual and corporeal existences is supported in the *Bundahishn* account. There, after the ordeal of molten metal, all people will "meet together with great affection for one another" (Bd. 34.20), but the forces of evil will all be burnt by the metal, which will keep flowing into hell and purify it of all pollution, including its stench. The final outcome is that the earth will be as flat as a disc, just as it was at the beginning, before it was pierced by evil. This imagery was apparently familiar to Plutarch, whose account of the Persian cosmic myth ends with the destruction of Angra Mainyu (as "Areimanios") through his own plague and famine, at which "destined time" "the earth will become level and flat, and all men will be happy, and speak one tongue and live one life under one form of government."[30] Such imagery emphasizes the understanding that this is a collective, rather than an individual event.

According to Mardanfarrokh, however, although evil is dispelled from the shell of the world and therefore ceases to operate within that domain, its substance is not destroyed. Because he considered evil to be of a separate ontological, and co-eternal substance, Mardanfarrokh maintained that Angra Mainyu is thrown "impotent" into the "boundless void" so that the good creations can live forever without fear and distress (SGW 8.78–9).

Paradise

The image of a world restored to an original condition of stability and peace is one that is familiar from Jewish, Christian, and Muslim conceptions of the "world to come." In fact, all these traditions describe that perfect, harmonious state as a "paradise," a word that is of ancient Iranian origin. It is curious that an Avestan term for a desolate place encircled by a wall—*pairidaeza*—should be the origin of the word later used by the Greeks to describe the garden paradises of the Ancient Persians. The Avestan *pairidaeza* is the barren place of confinement for a corpse bearer who has not handled the dead correctly and is therefore "contaminated." He is cared for at a distance by other members of the community until he himself dies and his pollution dissipates (Vd. 3.14–21).

The cultivation of such desolate land that is dry, unproductive, and to all intents and purposes "dead," is said to bring satisfaction to the earth. It is a restorative action that becomes a metaphor for the final renovation, when all traces of the corruption of evil have been removed.

By the time of the Greek author Xenophon, who fought as a mercenary against Artaxerxes II, the garden "paradises" of the Persians were renowned. Xenophon describes them as being full of fruit-bearing trees, flowing water, animals and "everything good and beautiful" that could be grown from the earth.[31] The Greek word that Xenophon uses is *paradeisos*. This may have entered the Greek as a borrowing via Akkadian *pardesu*. In the Elamite tablets discovered at Persepolis, the equivalent word *partetash* can refer to cultivated land, such as a plantation or an orchard, or to the storage area for produce such as grain and fruit.

The vast walled parklands of the Ancient Persians seem to have been established with the intention of providing an environment of peace, abundance, and happiness—all the features of a monarch's good rule. These gardens could also be seen as human attempts to replicate the initial material creativity of Ahura Mazda, in which the world was contained and flourished within the solid "shell" of the sky (Yt. 13.2; Bd. 1a6). It is not difficult to understand why the Greek *paradeisos* was chosen by the Greek-speaking Jews of Alexandria in the third century BCE to translate the Hebrew concept of the Garden of Eden. As it appears in the Septuagint, *paradeisos* also translates "fruit orchard" or "vineyard." The Talmudic form *pardes*, meaning "orchard," remains in use today.

By the time of the New Testament Book of Revelations, the concept of paradise with the tree of life in its center had become associated with humanity's restoration to the Garden of Eden, where God's rule is inherent. This connection of "paradise" with the myth of Eden was retained as the Bible was translated into the Latin Vulgate, and was the subject of much discussion and elaboration in the late patristic period.

DO ZOROASTRIAN CONCEPTS RELATE TO THOSE OF OTHER RELIGIONS AND PHILOSOPHIES?

The relatively developed cosmological and eschatological concepts of the Zoroastrians are thought to have stimulated the evolution of similar concepts in neighboring religious traditions. The three successive Iranian empires, and Iranians living under Seleucid rule in the fourth to second century BCE intersected with religious and philosophical traditions on both the eastern and western borders, including those of the Jews, Greeks, Indian Buddhists, Central Asian Buddhists, Christians, and Manicheans. After the end of Sasanian rule in the mid–seventh century CE, Zoroastrianism survived as an increasingly marginalized religion in Iran, but some of its concepts and praxes continued to resonate within Shi'ite Islam.

Formal Jewish contact with the Ancient Persians dates from the time of Cyrus II (r. c. 559–530 BCE). The Jews were in Babylonian captivity from the time of the destruction of the Temple of Solomon in 586 BCE until Cyrus dethroned the king of Babylon, Nabonidus, in 539 BCE. According to Biblical accounts, Cyrus permitted the exiles to return to Judah (Aramaic, "Yehud") if they desired (cf. Ezra 1.1–11).

After the trauma of the Exile, the Jews were positioned to re-examine their own mythico-religious history, and to include Cyrus and subsequent Persian benefactors within that narrative. In the Hebrew Bible, Cyrus is mentioned by name over 20 times. He is perceived as an agent of God, who intervenes in human history and transforms the world. Deutero-Isaiah (Isa. 40–55) describes Cyrus as one "anointed" by God—a *mashiach*. This section of Isaiah is thought to have been composed in Babylon by an anonymous poet-prophet of the Jewish exile. Its expression of a future hope for the restoration of the exiled people of Judah introduces the notion of the *mashiach* as future savior, but does not yet present a fully developed eschatology. In subsequent Jewish thought, the term *mashiach* gradually became applied to a central figure who would be instrumental in restoring the Davidic kingship. It is this Hebrew term for the messiah that was later translated into the Greek as *Christos*— "the Christ."

The Biblical books of Ezra and Nehemiah contain details of the Achaemenid court, in which both narratives are partially set. This is also the case with the books of Esther and Daniel, although these both seem to have been redacted several centuries later. Many Jews had chosen to remain in the region around Babylon after Cyrus' conquest, and a few rose to positions of prominence in the imperial infrastructure. Some became scribes at court, putting their knowledge of Aramaic—the lingua franca of the empire—to use in the chancellery. Some found careers in the Persian imperial army. Fifth century BCE Aramaic papyri inform us about the lives of Jewish soldiers, administrators, and their families living at Elephantine in Egypt, detailing their relations with neighboring Egyptians, as well as their Persian rulers. It was during this post-exilic Second Temple period of interaction with Iranians that new themes emerge in the Hebrew Bible, particularly those relating to cosmology and eschatology.

When the author of the book of Ezekiel, writing in exile in Babylon in the early sixth century BCE, introduces into the Hebrew visual vocabulary a novel image of dry bones being reassembled, it is not certain whether he knew of the Iranian concept of the resurrection. In Ezekiel's description, the dead rise from the dust of the earth where they lay, some like fallen soldiers on the plain, some buried in the ground, to re-establish Israel in the presence of God (Ezek. 37.1–6). This seems to indicate that he thought of the resurrection as a communal spiritual revival, but perhaps it was also a metaphor for national restitution. Ezekiel emphasizes that the resurrection is of the whole of Israel, and that all are redeemed.

The apocalyptic vision of Ezekiel may have derived some of its concepts from the Zoroastrianism of the time.[32] Physical resurrection was certainly a familiar concept by the time of the final redaction of the book of Daniel sometime in the second century BCE. One passage in Daniel tells how those who lie dead in the earth will rise, and some will receive eternal life, some eternal disgrace. The wise will shine as bright as the sky above, and those who lead others into righteousness will shine like the stars for eternity (Dan. 12.2–3). These verses became the focus of later Jewish deliberations on the concept of the resurrection.

The themes of the arrival of a "savior figure," a resurrection, judgment, and new life in a paradisal setting, may all be traced in a section inserted into the book of Isaiah, known as the Little Apocalypse.[33] The Little Apocalypse constitutes Isa. 24–27, and has a terminus ante quem of the early second century BCE. The late appearance of such themes in Jewish eschatology may be attributed to the rise of expectations of the restoration of a Davidic kingdom following the depredations of the Seleucid Greeks, particularly under Antiochus Epiphanes (r. 175–164 BCE). Zoroastrian eschatology may have served as an existing model for the modification of pre-exilic Jewish notions of Sheol, the land of shades (Dt. 32.22; Ezek. 31.15ff).

During this late Second Temple period, the Jewish religion also developed teachings about heaven as a place of rewards, hell as a place of punishment, and a hierarchy of angelic or semi-divine, beings. Jewish apocryphal texts present the figure of Satan, who has developed from the "opponent" or "accuser" of the book of Job (1.6) into the principle of evil, a prince of darkness. Clear evidence for an Iranian influence upon Jewish demonology of the time is found in the book of Tobit, where the chief of Satan's hosts is called Asmodeios (Tobit 3.7–9; 6.14–19; 8.2–3). Asmodeios appears as Ashmedai in Talmudic legend and Rabbinic literature, and is a name deriving from the Iranian *Aeshma Daeva*—the "false god, wrath." A passage in the *Gathas* (Y. 30.6) tells of the false gods (*daevas*) "rushing into wrath" (*aeshma*).

The Ancient Persians also came into close cultural contact with the Greeks, not only while clashing swords on a battlefield, or outwitting them at the "Hot Gates" (Thermopylae). One Greek contemporary of the Achaemenid king Xerxes was the war veteran and playwright Aeschylus (525–456 BCE). Aeschylus' play *The Persians* is the only surviving Greek tragedy based on a contemporary historical incident. It focuses on the Persian naval defeat at Salamis in 480 BCE, but is set entirely in Susa, the southwestern Achaemenid capital, where the king's mother and a chorus of counselors are waiting for news of the outcome of the battle. As the earliest extant European play, *The Persians* is as much an elegy for a fallen civilization, as a general warning against *hubris*—the human attempt to control the divine powers. This hubris on the part of the Persians is epitomized in Xerxes' crossing over the Hellespont from "Asia", his taking of Athens, and his destruction of the temples on top of the Acropolis. In one of Plato's later dialogues, Xerxes' failures are explained by his pampered upbringing in the royal court (*Laws* 3. 695d–96a).

From the mid–fourth century BCE onward, several Greek authors claimed that earlier philosophers such as Pythagoras, Heraclitus, and Plato owed much of their thought to Zoroastrians (whom they referred to as *magi*) if not to Zoroaster himself. Both Plato's friend, Eudoxus, and his student, Aristotle, are said to have placed the Greek development of intellectual thought within a historical line of succession beginning with Zoroaster. According to Pliny, "Eudoxus, who wished it to be thought that the most famous and most beneficial of the philosophical sects was that of the Magi, tells us that this Zoroaster lived 6,000 years before the death of Plato. Aristotle says the same."[34] The conception of Zoroaster as the wisest and most ancient of *magi* is a feature of neoplatonist thought from Porphyry down through the Renaissance.[35]

After the Seleucids came the Roman occupation of the eastern Mediterranean seaboard. Persecution following the Bar Kochba revolt in Palestine under the Roman Emperor Hadrian from 132–135 CE brought many Jewish refugees into the Parthian empire. An *exilarch* or "head of the exile" (Heb. *resh galuta*) representing the Jewish minority at court in the late Parthian period seems to have held an elevated position. The Jewish Roman historian Flavius Josephus (37–100 CE) records relations between Jews and Parthians, including the detail that one Zoroastrian prince and his mother from the Parthian vassal state of Adiabene had converted to Judaism in the first century CE (*Antiquities* 20.17–96). In Talmudic texts Parthian Jews are recognized as being culturally Iranian.[36] By the early third century CE, there were two flourishing Jewish academies in the part of Mesopotamia that was under Parthian rule. In these academies, teachings developed that eventually became formalized in the Babylonian Talmud during the mid-Sasanian period.

In the synagogue at Dura Europos, Syria, which was dedicated early in the Sasanian period, wall paintings of the Biblical story of Esther present the rule and character of the Persian king Ahasuerus (usually identified as Xerxes) in a positive way. Both the king and the Jewish hero Mordecai are painted wearing the Parthian costume of a belted tunic over baggy trousers, with a long-sleeved coat and a Phrygian hat. It was at this stage that Christianity was developing in the western part of the Parthian realm, and an iconographical as well as literary topos relating to the Zoroastrian *magi* seems to have taken root. The sixth-century mosaics in Ravenna, Italy, show the *magi* of Matthew's Gospel account visiting the Christ child (Matt. 2.1–12). These *magi* are wearing similar Parthian-era costumes to those illustrated in the Dura Europos synagogue.

The *magi* are introduced as a religio-political motif in the Greek original of Matthew, written in the late first century CE. The English translation of *magi* in this context usually reads "wise men," or "astrologers." Matthew does not relate how many *magi* came from the East following a star, nor does he name them; the number three comes from the number of gifts that they brought to Jesus—gold, frankincense, and myrrh. In later Syriac Christian commentaries on this passage in Matthew's Gospel, the *magi* are said to be the only sages of the period who perceived and followed the star to the cave in Bethlehem. One legend states that after the death of Jesus the apostle Thomas baptized the *magi*. Early Church fathers note that Thomas had been commissioned to preach the gospel in Parthia. In the *Acts of Thomas*, Thomas is said to have been sent to India, and to have been brought as a carpenter to the court of the Indo-Parthian king Gondophares.

It was during the time of the Indo-Parthians and then the Kushans that the Parthians came into close contact with Buddhists in the region of southern Uzbekistan, Afghanistan, Pakistan, and north-western India. Some of this area had been part of the extensive Mauryan Buddhist kingdom under Ashoka (c. 272/68–231 BCE), whose proselytizing edicts in Aramaic appear to have been directed at local Zoroastrians from the region of Gandhara, known as "Kambojas." During the Han dynasty (206 BCE–222 CE), trade routes were established between Iran and China, which furthered the contact of both Parthian and Sogdian Zoroastrian merchants with Buddhist communities along the so-called Silk Route. Some Parthians converted to Buddhism during the Han period, and were among the earliest translators of Indian Buddhist texts into Chinese. Chinese chronicles mention one An Shigao, a Parthian prince, who was a pioneer Buddhist translator in Luoyang in the mid– to late second century CE.

Sogdian Zoroastrians also converted, and translated many Buddhist texts into Sogdian and Chinese. One of the 30 Sogdian Buddhist texts found at Dunhuang in modern Xinjiang province does not seem to be a direct translation however, but a Sogdian retelling of an incarnation story (*jataka*) of the Buddha. This Sogdian version of this *Vessantara Jataka* mentions "Mithra, the Judge of Creation" along with other spiritual beings that do not appear in the Pali original. Chinese Buddhist hagiographies record that from the second century CE onward, Sogdian Buddhist monks settled in the Xinjiang region and the main cities of inner China, including the capital of Xian. One legendary Sogdian Buddhist monk from southern China was Kang Seng Hui, who had converted after the death of his parents. Kang Seng Hui is said to have been the first to teach Buddhism in the Nanking region. Buddhism does not seem to have taken root in Sogdiana itself, however, where the predominant culture and religion remained close to that of its Sasanian neighbors.

It has been suggested that the Buddhist motifs of the solar disc and the pillar of fire could have been stimulated by contact with

Zoroastrians. The Kushan empire incorporated many Zoroastrian terms into their texts. The predominance of Zoroastrian, rather than Buddhist, themes in second century CE Kushan inscriptions and coinage, suggests that they may have officially followed an eastern Iranian variant form of Zoroastrianism, while adhering to Buddhism in their personal life. Official Kushan texts and coins name and illustrate Ahura Mazda, the *yazatas* Mithra, Atar (fire), Sraosha, Mah (the moon), Verethragna (victory), Vohu Manah (good thought), Vayu (the wind), and Ashi (recompense), as well as Farr (the divine glory or fortune). These far outnumber depictions of Indian and Greek divinities. Bactrian documents of the early Sasanian era are dated with day-names that belong to the Zoroastrian calendar (see Chapter 2, "The Religious Calendar"). Although these aspects of Kushan iconography and nomenclature come from the same tradition as the western Iranian Zoroastrianism of the time, a female divinity named Nana appears to hold an elevated position. There is no *yazata* named "Nana" in Zoroastrian texts, but the goddess has been identified by some scholars as an eastern Iranian form of Spenta Armaiti, the *amesha spenta* connected with the earth. Later Kushan Buddhist iconography on the cave frescos at Bamiyan in Afghanistan incorporates several Zoroastrian symbols such as the boar representing Verethragna, and Mithra riding on his solar chariot.

The Sasanian Empire encompassed many ethnic and religious communities. It served as a backdrop for the development of the Babylonian Talmud (*Bavli*), which took place alongside the rise of Manichaeism and several other Gnostic movements, as well as the spread of "Nestorian" Christianity. Prior to its adoption of Christianity in the early fourth century CE, Zoroastrianism was the official religion in Armenia. Armenian religious vocabulary retains many terms borrowed from Zoroastrianism, particularly the names for malevolent beings. Until the Armenian conversion to Christianity, "the lady" Anahita was a central *yazata* in both Iranian and Armenian dynastic religion.

In the fifth and sixth centuries CE, many anti-Byzantine dissidents sought refuge in Iran, including Christian theologians who had fled from Edessa in 457 CE due to religious conflicts. The so-called Nestorian Christians were again exiled in 489 CE, when an edict of the Emperor Zeno closed their School at Edessa. When the Byzantine Emperor Justinian I ordered the Neoplatonic Academy in Athens to be closed in 529 CE, several important Greek philosophers made their way to the Sasanian court at Ctesiphon. The refugees included the head of the school, Damascius, and his colleague Simplicius, whose commentary on Aristotle's *Physics* is extant. After one or two years, these philosophers moved from the Iranian capital to settle in the region of Harran, which was within the boundaries of the Sasanian empire,. At around the same time, a Christian "Nestorian" philosopher known as Paul the Persian is said to have presented an introduction to the philosophy of Aristotle at the court of Khosrow I Anushirvan (r. 531–79 CE). Paul is credited with commentaries on Aristotle's *On Interpretation* and his theory of logic. Such direct encounters with classical Greek ideas seem to have had a considerable impact on some of the Middle Persian texts.

Alongside an interest in Greek philosophy, the *Denkard* records that Khosrow I was also well informed about the literature and culture of India. His physician Burzoe traveled to India and brought back several books, including the *Panchatantra*, which he translated from its original Sanskrit into Middle Persian. The Persian form of the work is called *Kalila o Dimna*.

In 532 CE, Khosrow I secured a treaty of "Eternal Peace" with the Byzantine Emperor Justinian I, which lasted for eight years. It was under Justinian that the mosaics at Ravenna depicting the *magi* bringing gifts were installed. The first scene is found on the robes of the empress, Theodora, in the Church of San Vitale, the second in a separate mosaic on the restored and renamed Sant'Apollinare Nuovo.

Khosrow Anushirvan's grandson, Khosrow II Parviz (591–628), was married to a Byzantine Christian named Maryam, who was the daughter of the Roman Emperor Maurice. As a prince, Khosrow Parviz had spent some time in Constantinople. His favorite wife, according to the narrative of the *Shah Nameh* and of later Persian poetry, was an Aramaean Christian named Shirin, who brought her physician Gabriel with her to the Sasanian court. Syriac texts report other Christian court physicians, ambassadors, and astrologers gathered at the Sasanian court during the reign of Khosrow II.

After the introduction of Islam to Iran in the late seventh century, and its rise to the dominant religion in the region, many Zoroastrian customs continued. Ancient Iranian festivals dating back to Achaemenid times, particularly Nav Ruz (the springtime new year), are still times of community celebration. Some elements of Zoroastrian belief and practice have close parallels in Islamic thought and practice, including that of prayer at five specific times each day. Zoroastrians appear as *al-majus* in *Sura* 22.17 of the *Qur'an*, and references to the "two angels in Babel" named Harut and Marut (*Sura* 2.96) indicate an awareness of the function of the *amesha spentas* Hordad (*Haurvatat*) and Mordad (*Ameretat*). Various *hadiths* provide eschatological descriptions of "the straight path" (*as-sirat al-mustaqim*) of *Sura* 1.6. At the time of final judgment, this path is followed to the *pul-e Sirat*, a bridge over hell to paradise that is described as being as thin as a hair or as sharp as a sword. This imagery resembles the *chinvad pul*—the Zoroastrian "bridge of accounting" in Middle Persian books. Some scholars maintain that the Shi'ite concept of the Imam Mahdi, who will lead the forces of good in a final battle to defeat the forces of evil has similarities with the Zoroastrian concept of the *saoshyant*.

Before the discovery and translation of Zoroastrian texts by European linguists, travel literature describing Iran and India was the most accessible source of information concerning the Zoroastrian religion for post-Renaissance scholars. By the mid–seventeenth century, this had become a popular and widespread genre. Although full of hyperbole and orientalist bias, travelogues remain a valuable source of historical information regarding both the Persian and Indian Zoroastrian communities from colonial times up to the modern period. Zoroastrians were considered to be an ancient, but surviving, religious community. The accounts of the French merchant Jean-Baptiste Tavernier (1605–1689) were widely available, but both Voltaire and Montesquieu used the multi-volume account of Jean Chardin (1643–1713) as their chief source of information regarding Zoroastrian beliefs and practices. Chardin's portrayal of the Zoroastrians, whom he called "the Persian heathen," was from the perspective of his own religious and cultural bias. His account gives particular significance to the two principles, the one of light, whom he knew by the Persian name, Ohrmazd, and the one of darkness, Ahriman.

For the European philosophers of the Enlightenment, this perceived "dualism" constituted a truer model for religion than the Jewish or Christian tradition of the period, particularly as it seemed to dispense with the problem of evil inherent in those belief systems. The religion of the *Gaurs* or *Parsees* appealed to European philosophers through its presentation of the human condition as innately good, and as having the capacity to discern the difference between good and evil.

A century after Voltaire's death, Friedrich Nietzsche was struck by the identification of Zarathushtra as the first teacher to make an ethical distinction between good and evil, and to implement an authoritative code of morality. In his philosophical poem, *So Spoke Zarathustra*, Nietzsche brought the voice of Zarathushtra into the public arena once more, although in a new language and with a new message.

The next section of this book aims to bring to the forefront the "voices" of the religion, from the earliest utterances to those who speak with authority today, with a particular focus on Zarathushtra's part as the pre-eminent "spokesperson" for the religion.

CHAPTER 2

WORDS, OR WHAT ZOROASTRIANS SAY AND WHO HAS THE VOICE

The questions in this chapter concern the authority of "the Words"— the oral and literary texts—that are integral to the Zoroastrian religion. Such questions include:

What are the sacred texts of the religion?
How did the teachings of the religion spread?
Who is/was Zarathushtra?
Who holds religious authority?
Can women become priests?
What voice do Zoroastrians have as a minority religion?
Who determines the religious calendar?
What is the reason for the western fascination with Zarathushtra?

WHAT ARE THE SACRED TEXTS OF THE RELIGION?

Sacred words

In the literary traditions of both the Zoroastrian and Hindu religions, the earliest texts were not written, but oral. These "sacred words" were understood to have been revealed to the minds of select individuals: in the case of the Zoroastrian religion, to a person named Zarathushtra; and in Hinduism to a group of nameless *rishis*, or "seers." The words that verbalized the spiritual insight of such wise persons were known as *manthras* or *mantras* respectively. These "thought-words" were committed to memory through constant repetition. Such oral recitation has been part of the transmission of the Zoroastrian religion since its inception.

The concept of receptivity not only to the words as they are intoned, but to their very resonance, is a feature of both early Iranian and Indic sacred poetry. A Parsi high priest from Mumbai, Dastur Dr. Firoze M. Kotwal, summarized this notion: "*manthras* by themselves . . . as printed or unuttered words, are dead things. They do not contain the same kind of inherent power that exists when abstracted from the verbal act of reciting them."[1]

Shirin Simmons, a Zoroastrian born and raised in Yazd, Iran, evokes this sense that the resonance of the words has a powerful impact:

> Everyone sat in silence listening to the Zoroastrian priest (*mobed*), who was dressed in a traditional white gown and cap. He recited passages from the holy Avesta, chanting away in a low musical voice, his eyes half-closed . . . [2]

Ryna, a young Parsi from India, described to me her childhood experience of a similar practice of recitation within the home: "I was introduced to our religion in a very different, and, I thought for a long time, an unusual way. When we were very young children, my mother used to chant the prayers as lullabies, patting our heads to the rhythm of the ancient prayers . . . I learned later that this form of learning is not unusual for young Parsis."

Ryna explained her own transition from childhood to adulthood within the religion in terms of her participation in the chain of oral transmission:

> Zoroastrianism was passed orally from one generation to the next for several hundred years before becoming literature, so it makes sense that practitioners rely on memorization rather than reading. The idea of prayers as an oral tradition first became relevant to me when it came time for my *Navjote* [initiation]. While memorizing the required prayers, I never once looked at a *Khordeh Avesta*, our book of prayer. The prayers were written in a language I didn't know, with a completely foreign pronunciation. For hours, my mother coached me on the cadence, tone, and pronunciation of each phrase. I was taught that the vibrations of the prayers imparted to them a certain power—that the way prayers were spoken was as important as the words themselves. Looking back,

prayer seems to be the dominant way my mother, grandmother, and great-grandmother actively exposed me to the Zoroastrian religion.

Oral recitation is believed by some to activate the power inherent in the *manthra* so that it will generate both insight and reaction in those who speak and those who listen. This notion is encapsulated in the Gathic concept of *sraosha*, "the willingness to listen and respond." This power of the *manthra*—which is both informative and formative—is thought to be activated when the *manthra* is pronounced aloud in a correct and careful manner, so that it reverberates between the mental and material existences. The activity connected with *sraosha* is described as *tanu-manthra*—"possessing the *manthra* for a body," suggesting that participating in the recitation of a *manthra* promotes the embodiment of its insights within the worshipper.

A female Zoroastrian acquaintance, Shireen, explained this idea to me in practical terms:

> Zoroastrian prayers reinforce the idea of embracing good, to support the community and be a humble person. They are a constant reminder of how we can aspire to translate our good thoughts, good words and good deeds into action. I usually begin my day reciting them, which sets me in a positive frame of mind. And at the end of the day, if I manage to practice some of these positive ideas as actions, I consider it to be a successful day.

In the *Gathas*, listening, and then speaking with "control of tongue" and "correct utterance of the words" are qualities of the *ashavan* who wants to heal the world (Y. 31. 19). In this understanding of *manthra*-reciting, the focus is on the sound of the words, rather than an intellectual grasp of their meaning. This is not to say that the interpretation of the Avesta by modern scholars is ignored, or that the words are thought to be meaningless. Many printed prayer books now have the Avestan prayers transliterated into Gujarati, Persian, or English, with translations underneath or alongside.

Two Old Avestan prayers bookend the *Gathas* in their setting within the 72-section liturgy known as the Yasna. The *Ahuna Vairya* comes before the *Gathas* (Y. 27.13) and the *Airyaman Ishya* at the end (Y. 54.1). These two ancient prayers are both recited on a daily basis today and are thought to be effective in combating evil at all levels. The *Airyaman Ishya* is considered to be a prayer that brings healing, and is invoked as such in the *Videvdad* (Vd. 20.11). A narrative in the same text also expresses the efficacy of the *Ahuna Vairya* prayer as used by Zarathushtra to fend off Angra Mainyu (Vd. 19. 9–10). According to the *Bundahishn* this 21-word *manthra* was first recited by Ahura Mazda 3000 years after he began his creational activity. At this point, Angra Mainyu had stumbled upwards from the darkness of his ignorance to challenge Ahura Mazda (Bd. 1.15–16). Ahura Mazda in his omniscience persuaded his adversary to agree to a fixed period of 9000 years until the final battle, and then recited the *Ahuna Vairya* to send Angra Mainyu reeling back into unconscious for another 3000 years (Bd. 1.20–30).

The *Ahuna Vairya* prayer is probably pronounced very differently now than it was when Old Avestan was a living language. Although this prayer would have been recited on a regular basis, regional differences of phonology would have occurred, and variations in pronunciation introduced, once the language was no longer the vernacular. Such changes mean that today, Iranian Zoroastrians often find it difficult to understand familiar ancient prayers as recited by their Parsi co-religionists, and vice versa.

The *Gathas* as sacred text

For Zoroastrians around the world, the *Gathas* retain their centrality as the earliest verbal expression of the religion. The authority attributed to the *Gathas* stems from the belief that they reveal the "mind" of Ahura Mazda, in so far as that mind can be apprehended by humans. One scholar notes that the Avestan tradition concerning the *Gathas* is that "God was their author, the divine Sraosha their first performer among gods, and Zarathushtra their first performer among men . . . "[3] A passage in a Middle Persian text reflects a long tradition that it was a meritorious act to memorize the *Gathas*. There, Ahura Mazda tells Zarathushtra that "no-one in the human race will be blessed and worth of the 'house of song' who has not learned by heart the *Gathas* . . . "[4]

Because they form 17 sections (*haitis*) of the 72-section liturgy (the Yasna), the *Gathas* are often mistakenly referred to as 17 in number. It is more accurate, and in keeping with the oldest tradition, to talk about "five *Gathas*," or five "songs", each characterized by its own meter. Literary analysis of the *Gathas* has discovered that they contain many examples of the poetic form of ring composition. This literary technique places a key theme or word at the center of a poem, with other prominent themes occurring both before and after in a symmetrical arrangement, like a radially concentric circle, or the rings of an onion. The theme may be re-visited both within and across the five songs and the 17 sections. Such chiastic patterns have long been recognized in other ancient literature, such as the poetry of Homer and parts of the Hebrew Bible.

The vocabulary and thematic content of the *Gathas* place them within an ancient mindset, but it is not now possible to determine whether the five main songs or the 17 parts were composed for specific occasions. Tradition has it that the final poem, now numbered Yasna 53, was composed for the wedding of Zarathushtra's daughter, Pouruchista. Some see a linear progression of thought and thematic criteria in the *Gathas* that could reflect the progressive unfolding of either a personal revelation, or a ritual performance. Others are more intrigued by the idea of unpeeling the layers of text to uncover a core of meaning relevant to each individual.

As expressions of belief, the *Gathas* differ from those of other "revealed" religions in that, as *manthras*, their informative impact seems to have been relayed through performative repetition. The fact that all the Old Avestan texts including the *Gathas* are mentioned in the Young Avestan *Visperad* (a supplementary liturgy to the Yasna) in the same order as in the Yasna indicates that from quite early on, they must have formed part of a ritual recitation.

Some Zoroastrians maintain, however, that the *Gathas* should be considered apart from any ritual context, and that they stand alone as an independent, primary text. This "*Gatha*-only" approach views these Old Avestan poems and four ancient prayers as containing the only authentic message of Zarathushtra. From this perspective, the other Avestan texts are considered to be later and not religiously authoritative, although they are of historical interest. This modern perception of degrees of sacredness of scripture, that places the *Gathas* as the most authoritative text, has a precursor in a Middle Persian summary of the degrees of spiritual awareness. The *Denkard* refers to three types of people: *gahanig*, *hada-manthrig*, and *dadig* (Dk. 6.70). Those who are *gahanig*, "the people who are of the *Gathas*," have a developed level of spiritual awareness that keeps them on the right path. The other two types manifest less spiritual insight and attainment. *Hadha-manthrig* refers to those who follow the precepts of the religion because of concerns about how others will perceive them, and *dadig* to those who follow the rules of religion out of fear of punishment.

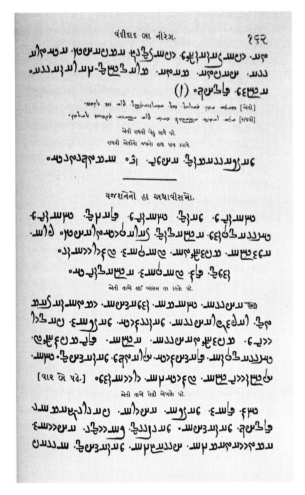

Figure 2.1 A page showing Yasna 28, the first section of the first *Gatha*, in Avestan script, with instructions for ritual actions and the titles of the prayers in Gujarati script. Photo courtesy of Ervad Soli P. Dastur.

The Avesta

The term "Avesta" comes from a Middle Persian word that is thought to mean "praise" or "sacred utterance." It refers to the written corpus of Avestan texts, which also includes Middle Persian translations and commentaries or *zand*. (This is why older European translations are sometimes titled the *Zand-Avesta*). The only known example of the Old Iranian language that is now called "Avestan" comes from this written Avesta, which is the origin for the name of the language. The Avestan language includes both Old Avestan and Young Avestan.

The earliest existing description of the Avesta is found in Book 8 of the *Denkard*, which classifies 21 *nasks* or "bundles" of Avestan texts by name and categorizes them into three groups according to the three types named above. It is not known how reliable this description is, nor whether it refers only to those Avestan texts that had been translated into Middle Persian. In the *Denkard* analysis, seven of the *nasks* are *gahanig*, including the *Gathas*, some commentaries on them, and parts of the Yasna; the seven *hadha-manthrig* texts relate to the formulaic prayers of the ritual; and the final seven *dadig* collection contains law books and some of the *yashts*, the Young Avestan "hymns." This tripartite classification of content designates the texts as the formal expressions of the "thoughts, words, and deeds" of the religion respectively. The *Denkard* notes that the number of *nasks* echoes the 21 words of the *Ahuna Vairya* prayer, indicating a belief that all the texts were equally powerful in combating evil. According to Middle Persian accounts, the 21 *nasks* were given by Ahura Mazda to Zarathushtra, who then brought them to his patron Vishtaspa. The notion that the entire Avesta was a coherent revelation is retained by traditionalist Zoroastrians.

Despite the *Denkard's* breakdown of the content of the *nasks*, it is not clear exactly what material was included, since the majority of the texts identified as belonging to the Avesta are not extant. If the *Denkard's* analysis of the texts is accurate, the existing Avesta that serves as a foundational "scripture" of the religion is only a small part of the original corpus. Some scholars estimate this fraction to be around a quarter or a fifth. Others question whether the *Denkard* should be taken as a reliable summary of the Avestan anthology in its earliest Sasanian form, but agree that much material has been lost. Parts of the Avesta seem to have been preserved, however, in Middle Persian translations made during or shortly after the Sasanian period.

Philologists are now looking at the Middle Persian texts more closely to see if they can work out which parts of the lost Avesta these translations might represent.

Old Avesta

The Old Avestan texts form the oldest part of the extant Avesta, and appear to have been preserved fairly intact. This would cohere with their status as the most sacred texts of the religion, and therefore as a central element of the priestly transmission. The Old Avestan language has been dated to the late second millennium BCE. This is the language of the *Gathas* and the two prayers mentioned earlier—the *Ahuna Vairya* and the *Airyaman ishya*. Two other prayers that also appear to be ancient are the *Ashem Vohu* and the *Yenghe Hatam*. These two prayers are placed immediately after the *Ahuna Vairya* in section 27 of the Yasna.

A late twentieth-century focus on the *Yasna Haptanghaiti*, the "worship in the seven sections" that is preserved at the core of the Yasna, has shown that it is in the same Old Avestan dialect as the *Gathas*. Within the structure of the Yasna, one of the five *Gathas* is placed before the *Yasna Haptanghaiti* (that is, in Yasna sections 28–34), and the other four follow on immediately afterward. The *Yasna Haptanghaiti* itself is placed in the central part of the 72 sections, in Yasna 35–41. The formulaic phrases it contains provide insight into the earliest fixed form of worship practiced by Mazda worshippers, and seem to relate to actual events occurring during a ceremony. It has probably always formed "the liturgical kernel" of Zoroastrian ritual.[5]

Young Avesta

Apart from the Old Avestan texts mentioned above, the Avesta also includes the following Young Avestan compositions, which date to around the mid-first millennium BCE. They seem to reflect an eastern Iranian geographical location, perhaps around the Afghanistan or Sistan region. Surviving Young Avestan texts include:

Yasna: "worship." The other parts of the 72-section liturgy recited during the Yasna ritual. This liturgy includes several different genres of literature.

Yashts: the 21 "hymns" to the various *yazatas*. There are also fragments of other *yashts*. Some of the *yazatas* praised—such as *sraosha* and *ashi*—are mentioned in the *Gathas*.

Videvdad (*Vendidad*): "the laws dispelling the *daevas*." This is a prose text of 22 chapters that includes regulations concerning ritual purification after contact with "dead matter" such as blood, or a corpse. It also includes some mythology about the Iranian lands and their assault by Angra Mainyu (Vd. 1); the rule of Yima (Vd. 2); the struggle between Zarathushtra and Angra Mainyu (Vd. 19); and the various means of healing (Vd. 20–22). The *Videvdad* is thought to be the only one of the 21 *nasks* of the Avesta to have been preserved intact.

Khordeh Avesta: the "small Avesta." A collection of hymns, prayers, and litanies that are recited regularly (see below).

Visperad: prayers to "all the masters." A 24-part liturgy that supplements and intersperses the performance of the Yasna during the six seasonal festivals (*gahanbars*).

Hadokht Nask: "book of the *nasks*." The first part of the surviving text is about the effectiveness of the *Ashem Vohu* prayer; the second part concerns what happens to the soul in the afterlife.

Herbadestan and *Nerangestan*. Two texts consisting of Avestan passages and their commentaries (*zand*), which relate to priestly activity and ritual.

Pursishniha: "questions." A religious catechism of questions and answers.

Aogemadaeca: "we declare." A text about the acceptance of death.

The *Khordeh Avesta* or "small Avesta" includes extracts from the Avesta. This collection of prayers was not compiled as a single text until the nineteenth century. It is often referred to as the "Zoroastrian Book of Common Prayer", as it contains hymns and ritual texts used by the laity in regular prayer. These include:

— Five *Niyayishn*: prayers that are addressed to the sun, Mithra, the moon, waters, and fire. The first four prayers are mostly made up of fragments relating to their respective Yashts, but the praise of fire is an extract from Yasna 62. The *niyayishn* to Mithra and to the waters are regularly recited in abbreviated form during daylight hours. The *Aban Niyayishn* ("Praise of the Waters") may only be spoken while standing by flowing water.

— Five *gahs*: prayers corresponding to the five prayer-periods (*gah*) of the day—morning, noon, afternoon, sunset to midnight, and midnight to dawn. (See below, "The Religious Calendar").

— Four *afrinagans*: "blessings" that are recited in honor of the dead; on the five days at the end of the year; at the seasonal festivals; and at the beginning and end of summer.

Other Young Avestan texts include:

— *Siroza*: formulas in praise of Ahura Mazda, the *amesha spentas* and the *yazatas* to whom the "thirty days" (Pers. *si roza*) of the month are dedicated.
— The 101 names of Ahura Mazda.
— *Nirang*: invocational prayers that provide comfort in times of distress or illness.

There are also a few Avestan fragments, which are titled after Iranologists, such as the *Fragment Westergaard* (*FrW*), named for the Danish scholar Niels Ludvig Westergaard (1815–78). This fragment was mentioned in the previous chapter as an early source for the Zoroastrian concept of the resurrection.

HOW DID THE TEACHINGS OF THE RELIGION SPREAD?

The history of the spread of Mazda worship occurs alongside the history of the Iranians. This history begins in a region known in Avestan mythology as *Airyana vaejah*, meaning "the Aryan expanse." To the extent that a Zoroastrian place of origin can be said to exist, this mythical location of the "Aryans"—that is, the early Iranians—is it. The Aryan expanse is said to have included wide, fertile pastures, which were the irenic grazing lands of the Iranians (Vd. 1.2; Yt. 10.14–15). As some Iranians moved to the south and west from Central Asia, the "Aryan expanse" came to designate the region that they occupied—"Iran."

The three successive Iranian empires were:

Ancient Persian (Achaemenid) c. 550–330 BCE
Parthian c. 250 BCE–224 CE
Sasanian c. 224–651 CE

The Ancient Persians (c. 550–330 BCE)

The Achaemenid king, Darius 1, records that he is not only an Aryan, "of Aryan lineage" but also "a Persian and the son of a Persian"

(DNa 2.13–15). Both "Aryan" and "Persian" are ethnic definitions, but it is uncertain how or whether the two terms should be distinguished in the context of the inscription. What is clear is that the form and meaning of many of the Old Persian expressions in inscriptions from Darius I onwards are in line with the phraseology and general ethos of the Avesta.

Although the Avesta was apparently not committed to writing until long after the oral composition of its various elements, such Old Persian inscriptions from the late sixth century BCE onward indicate that the Achaemenids were familiar with an Avestan worldview. Achaemenid cuneiform carvings on buildings or cliff faces at the key sites of Bisutun, Persepolis, Susa, Naqsh-e Rostam, and the Elvand Gorge provide clues as to their imperial religion, and indicate that it was conceptually close to elements of the *Gathas* and some of the *yashts*, and the focus of worship is Ahura Mazda. Achaemenid kings from Darius I onward invoked Ahura Mazda to legitimate their rule.

References to Persian *magi* in the Persepolis Fortification Tablets, and in Herodotus' *Histories* and Xenophon's *Cyropaedia*, inform us that in Achaemenid times, the male Iranian priesthood functioned in the court on behalf of the king. It is assumed that these priests continued the recitation and transmission of Avestan texts in both a ritual and instructive context, explaining their significance to student priests in Old Persian, or another Iranian language. Some years ago, I visited the Dadar Athornan Madressah, one of the schools for priests in Mumbai, India, and was privileged to see a group of young Parsi trainee priests demonstrate the performance of a Yasna ceremony. The principal of the school explained the Avestan and Middle Persian words and the accompanying actions of the liturgy to the boys who were watching. This method of learning by heart through repetition and performance probably reflects the earliest process of transmission.

In the mid–fifth century BCE, Xanthos of Lydia is said to have reported that the Persian soldiers of his time knew the "sayings of Zoroaster." This, alongside Herodotus' contemporary reference to a "theogony" chanted by the *magi* at the time of a lay offering, suggests that oral recitation of parts of the Avesta existed among both priests and laity in the western part of the empire. There is no indication from these, or later Greek sources including Xenophon, that the "Persian religion" was ever practiced by non-Iranians. During the fourth century BCE, however, it seems that some Zoroastrian eschatological material was widely circulating in western Asia. Both Plutarch and Diogenes Laertius refer to the Greek historian Theopompus of Chios (c. 378–320 BCE) as a source of information on Iranian cosmology and "end-time" teachings.

It is thought by certain scholars that some Young Avestan texts— including some of the *yashts*—may not have been incorporated into the Achaemenid worldview until around the fourth century BCE, during the reign of Artaxerxes II.

The Parthians (c. 250 BCE–224 CE)

The hiatus in Iranian rule after the conquest of the Ancient Persians by Alexander of Macedon is presented in Middle Persian Zoroastrian books as causing a major disruption to the progress of the Mazdean religion. Middle Persian legends tell how Alexander had disposed of a sacred text written in gold on ox hides that were kept at the religious center of Istakhr. The subsequent castigation of the Seleucids and then the Parthians as bringing a dark time of irreligion partly reflects the Sasanian desire to legitimize their own rule. We now know that the Parthians retained the Avestan calendar used by the Achaemenids, and that some kings and commoners had "Zoroastrian" personal names. Rituals relating to fire were also maintained, alongside praxes relating to exposure of the dead and the non-contamination of water.

Strabo, who is one of our main sources of information concerning "Persian" beliefs and practices in the mid-Parthian period, wrote that an oral tradition of the religion continued in Cappadocia. It is possible that oral versions of Avestan texts and commentaries could have existed in local regions such as Persis (around modern Fars province), Bactria (northern Afghanistan, southern Uzbekistan), and Media (modern northwestern Iran). Basil of Caesarea (330–379 CE) and some later Christian Syriac texts refer only to an oral transmission of the Avesta well into the Sasanian period.

There could, however, have been a written version of parts of the Avesta elsewhere. This is suggested in a statement by Pausanias in the mid–second century CE, which records that the *magi* in Lydia read the words that they chanted during their ceremonies from books (*Graeciae Descriptio* 5.27.5–6). According to the *Denkard*, the fragmented Avesta and Zand "both oral and written" was reassembled under Valakhsh, one of the Parthian kings. This is usually taken to refer to Valakhsh I (r. c. 51–78 CE). There is, though, no evidence of the influence of any Parthian collation or redaction in the preserved parts of the Avesta.

The Sasanians (c. 224–651 CE)

From the outset of the Sasanian era, royal proclamations acknowledge the protection and support of Ahura Mazda. Inscriptions on rock and coinage of the first Sasanian king, Ardashir I (r. c. 224–240) profess his religion to be that of Mazda worship. The *Denkard* maintains its tidy description of the preservation of the Avesta with reference to a gathering of material under Ardashir I that was vetted for its religious authority by the chief priest Tosar. This was followed by the collection of extra-religious writings by Shapur I (r. c. 240–270 CE) that were "fitted into" or "annexed" to the Mazdean religion.[6]

It does seem that by the time of the powerful Sasanian priest, Kerdir, who flourished in the mid– to late third century, a compilation of the Avesta was in progress. One of Kerdir's inscriptions mentions the "revelation in the *nask*." Kerdir also refers to a group of people whom he has confronted, who are *zandik*. This term is found in a list of peoples of other religions, included Jews, Buddhists, and various Christians, whom Kerdir says he has also "struck down." It appears to refer to those whose understanding of the religion is based on interpretation (*zand*) of the Avesta, rather than the actual Avesta—in other words, to "revisionists."[7] Kerdir's allusions point to the emergence of a body of Zoroastrian texts and their commentaries, which were the focus of active study and transmission.

According to the *Denkard*, Shapur II (r. 309–379 CE) considered all the oral traditions, and, after the validation of the faith by the high priest Adurbad-i Mahraspandan, an authoritative form of the religion was fixed. Adurbad is said to have been instrumental in compiling the 21-*nask* anthology of the Avesta. The *Denkard* relates that the collected texts of the Avesta, including the Zand, were not written down in their specially devised script until the rule of Khosrow I (r. 531–579 CE). This would cohere with a date of around the sixth century CE for the written Avesta that is favored by many philologists. The oldest existing versions of the Avesta are dated to the thirteenth and fourteenth centuries CE.

One of the motivating factors in the Sasanian push to collate the Avesta and its *zand* seems to have been the rise in number and power of neighboring religious traditions. A Manichaean Coptic text, the

Kephalaia, contains records of discussions held between Mani and other religious sages of the era in the court of Shapur I. In this text, it is pointed out that, because Zarathushtra's disciples did not write down his teachings until after his death, the Zoroastrian scriptures lacked the authority of Manichaean teachings, which Mani himself had written down. A written Avesta would have enabled Sasanian Zoroastrians to combat both heterodox alternate readings within the faith, as well as the powerful appeal of the sacred writings of other text-based religions in the region, particularly Christianity, Buddhism, and Manichaeism. By this stage, the words of the Avesta would, however, have only been understood through their Middle Persian translation and exegesis.

Alongside the anthologizing of "sacred text," came the growth of power of the priesthood and the establishment of various religious institutions including fire temples with endowed fires.

Middle Persian texts

The earliest Middle Persian writings take the form of rock and coin inscriptions. The most extensive rock inscriptions are by the Sasanian kings Shapur I and Narseh (r. 293–302 CE) and the priest Kerdir. These rock writings are not considered to be scriptural, but do provide some insight into Sasanian belief and practice.

Those surviving Middle Persian literary texts that set out to record and codify Zoroastrian beliefs mostly originated in priestly families from Fars province. One such priest, named Adurfarrobay Farroxzadan, is attributed as the first redactor of the various materials in the *Denkard*—the "Acts of the Religion"—during the early Abbasid caliphate (750–1258 CE). Most Middle Persian Zoroastrian books were written down in the ninth or early tenth century CE, but contain materials that had developed through a long period of oral transmission and then textual compilation.

The Middle Persian texts that evolved within a priestly context often claim their authority as deriving "in" or "through" the religion. They are considered to be significant repositories of older authoritative material that reflects the lost Avesta, particularly relating to cosmology, eschatology, and the person of Zarathushtra. Some passages in the *Bundahishn* and *Denkard* seem to be direct translations of parts of the Avesta. The Middle Persian *zand*, or discursive commentary, provides information about how the Avesta was interpreted during and after the Sasanian period. To a degree, this interpretive gloss continues to inform how priests today understand some of the ritual praxes, and how some of the laity negotiates its place in terms of religious regulations and expectations.

Some Middle Persian books

Ayadgar-i Zareran: "Memorial of Zarer." The verse account of the first war of the religion between the Iranians and the Chionians.

Arda Wiraz Namag: the "Book of the Righteous Wiraz." An account of Wiraz's vision of heaven and hell.

Bundahishn: "Creation." This important and lengthy compilation is also called *Zand-agahih* ("Knowledge from the Zand"). There are two recensions from differing manuscript transmissions, the longer one is known as the *Greater Bundahishn* and the shorter as the *Indian Bundahishn*. The *Bundahishn* includes myths of cosmogony and eschatology. It also includes speculations on the phenomena of the natural world, and information about the legendary history of Iran.

Chidag Andarz-i Poryotkeshan: "Select Precepts of the First Sages." This book includes maxims relating to belief and behavior, presented in the form of questions and answers.

Dadestan-i Denig: the "Decisions of the Religion". A text providing answers to questions of religion that Zoroastrians in Fars and Kerman province had asked one of the *dasturs* (priests)

Denkard: "Acts of the Religion." The *Denkard* originally had nine books, but the first two are lost. It is the largest extant Middle Persian text, and the information it presents is, like the *Bundahishn*, often encyclopedic, and reliant upon much older source material. Book 3 is largely an apologetic defense of Zoroastrianism against other religions, with information about doctrine, belief, and behavior; Books 4 and 5 concern theological matters raised during the Sasanian and then Muslim periods respectively; Book 6 is an anthology of precepts (*andarz*); Book 7 is a central source for the life of Zarathushtra and the tenets of the "good religion" (MP *weh den*); Book 8 contains details of the 21 *nasks* of the Avesta; Book 9 provides more details of the Gathic (*gahanig*) material.

Karnamag-i Ardashir-i Papagan: "Account of the Deeds of Ardashir, son of Papag." A romantic narrative about Ardashir I, the first Sasanian king.

Madayan-i Hazar Dadestan: "A Thousand Legal Decisions." A late Sasanian-era text containing case histories and legal decisions, particularly those relating to civil, contractual, and family law.

(Dadestan-i) Menog-i Xrad: (Decisions of) "The Spirit of Wisdom." A book of religious instruction for the laity.

Pahlavi Rivayat Accompanying the Dadestan-i Denig: A Middle Persian communication relating to the "Decisions of the Religion," written for Zoroastrians living under Muslim rule in Iran. It was intended to consolidate the community in difficult times, and to offer practical information as well as ritual and theological support.

Shayest ne Shayest: "Proper and Improper Conduct." A book of religious stipulations relating to purity and outlining reparation for sinful acts.

Shkand Gumanig Wizar: the "Doubt-Destroying Exposition." A series of treatises in support of the Mazdean religion against other faiths of the region. This was composed by the theologian Mardan-farrokh-i Ohrmazddad.

Wizidagiha-i Zadspram: the "Anthology of Zadspram." This book contains details about the life of Zarathushtra that are not found elsewhere. It also displays an awareness of human physiology.

Zand-i Wahman Yasn: the "*Zand* on the *Vohu Manah Yasht*." It is not known for certain whether there was a Young Avestan hymn to *Vohu Manah* on which this text was based. It is a developed apocalyptic work with teachings concerning the fate of the soul at death.

New Persian texts

After the introduction of New Persian as the main literary language in Iran in the late tenth and early eleventh centuries, several important and informative texts emerged. These did not have scriptural authority, in the sense of presenting a schematic system of belief, but they are thought to contain authoritative information concerning the history of the religion, or how to put the religion into action.

Some New Persian writings

Shah Nameh: the "Book of Kings." The early eleventh-century Iranian national epic composed by Ferdowsi narrates the story of the Iranians from the first rulers to the defeat of the last Sasanian king, Yazdegerd III, in 651 CE. (See below).

Zartosht Nameh: the "Book of Zarathushtra." A thirteenth-century verse narrative of the life of Zarathushtra.

Persian Rivayats: A collection of communications about the religion (*rivayats*) from the Iranian Zoroastrian priests in Yazd and Kerman to the Parsis of the Gujarat region of India between the mid-fifteenth and mid-eighteenth centuries. These mostly concern practical and ritual observances, and include topics relating to marriage, divorce, and relationships with non-Zoroastrians.

Qesse-ye Sanjan: the "Story of Sanjan." This narrative of the arrival of the Iranian Zoroastrians on the shores of Gujarat was compiled at the end of the sixteenth century by the Parsi priest Bahram Kay Qobad Sanjana.

The poet Ferdowsi completed the *Shah Nameh* in around 1010 CE. He undertook the work initially under the patronage of the Samanids, the first Muslim Persian dynasty, and finished it under Mahmud of Ghazni. The *Shah Nameh* presents a coherent mythico-history of Iran from the time of the "first rulers" (*Pishdadians*) through the legendary kings (*Kayanians*) to the last historical king, the Sasanian monarch Yazdegerd III. Although not a Zoroastrian text in the sense of presenting a worldview entirely consistent with the Avesta, nor having its religious authority, the *Shah Nameh* is nonetheless considered to be a source of inspiring stories of Iranian (Zoroastrian) heroes that provide lessons for life today. The millennial anniversary of the completion of *Shah Nameh* and the death of Ferdowsi in 2010 was commemorated in the cover story of a *FEZANA Journal* (24/4, Winter/December 2010), and the Zoroastrian Association of Houston Library organized an essay competition for North American Zoroastrians under 25 on the connection between *Shah Nameh* and Zoroastrianism.

The religion arrives in India

In a similar manner to the *Shah Nameh*, the *Qesse-ye Sanjan* has entered Parsi lore as a historical narrative of the growth and glory of the religion. Whereas the former is set in Iran, the *Qesse-ye Sanjan*—"The Story of Sanjan"—is about Zoroastrian emigration to India and the establishment and survival of the religion in the Gujarat area. After the advent of Islam, Iranian Zoroastrians may have chosen to go to the Gujarat coast of India because they had long-standing trade contacts, and perhaps branch offices, there. The *Story of Sanjan* serves as a testimony to Parsi steadfastness: they are portrayed not only as keeping up the tenets and praxes of the religion that they brought with them from Iran, but also managing—on the whole—to maintain a harmonious co-existence with their Hindu neighbors.

According to the narrative of the *Qesse-ye Sanjan*, when the refugees from Iran arrived on the shoreline at Sanjan they were met by the local Indian Raja. They appealed to the ruler's kindness and compassion to provide them with sanctuary, but the Raja became worried that the strangers would cause trouble. At this point in the written story, the Raja addresses the *dastur* (priest) and requests some information about the religion and customs of the newcomers. He is reassured to find out that they have many beliefs and practices similar to those of the Hindus, and that they will be willing to adapt their dress, and adopt the local language in order to fit in.

Alongside this written story, every Parsi child also learns the "Sugar and Milk" version of the arrival of the "good religion" on the shores of India. In this oral narrative, when faced with the boatload of newcomers, the Raja asks for a cup of milk that is full to the brim. He holds it out to the *dastur*, telling him that there is no room for another group of people on the shores of his kingdom. The *dastur* then takes some sugar and adds it to the milk. The sugar is absorbed into the milk, which does not overflow the bowl, implying that the immigrants will only bring sweetness to the land.

This oral account belongs to the sphere of dynamic legend that has lent support and legitimacy to the Parsi community in the Indian subcontinent for generations. As a Parsi from Pakistan remarked about the "Sugar and Milk" story: "[W]hen we learn this from our parents and grandparents, somehow we internalize its implications, and continue to uphold an ancient promise made by our forefathers to integrate and enrich the lives of those around us."[8]

In some respects, the figure of Zarathushtra also belongs to this type of didactic narrative. Rather than being fixed into a specific time in history, his story is seen to have continued relevance and meaning for Zoroastrians through the ages, wherever they happen to be. Earlier this century, a Zoroastrian in Yazd, encountered by an English author researching a book on Persian carpets, declared that the dating of Zarathushtra is not that important: "What's important is that what he taught is still alive today."[9]

WHO IS/WAS ZARATHUSHTRA?

As seen earlier, the *Gathas* or "sacred songs" attributed to Zarathushtra are considered to provide the foundational concepts of the religion, particularly concerning the nature of Ahura Mazda and the nature of reality. The general perception is that Zarathushtra as author gives authority to text. But who was Zarathushtra? Nowadays, Zarathushtra is conceived by Zoroastrians in many different ways: as a fire-tending priest; an inspired and inspirational prophet; a wonder-worker; or a profound philosopher. Perhaps an overarching identification for Zarathushtra is as the spiritual genius of his age who by extension "speaks" to every age.

The Zarathushtra of ancient Iranian memory and myth, who became Zoroaster in the classical Greek and Latin texts—and was known by this name in Europe until Nietzsche brought the Iranian name into the public eye—stands as a powerful, central figure for Zoroastrians today. They retain a clear sense of the image of their eponymous "founder" figure—not as a physical likeness (which did not feature in the religious iconography of the religion until the nineteenth century), but rather in terms of the imprint of Zarathushtra's life and teaching on the religion.

This understanding of Zarathushtra as having authority through his putative authorship of the *manthras*, the sacred thought-words that underlie the beliefs and praxes of the religion, raises several questions:

How central was the person of Zarathushtra to early Mazda worshippers?
Does the life-story of Zarathushtra resemble that of other founders of religion?
To what extent does the voice of Zarathushtra resonate through the centuries?

How central was the person of Zarathushtra to early Mazda worshippers?

Most Zoroastrians accept as a fact that there was an historical individual named Zarathushtra, who propagated the religion and whose name the religion now bears.[10] They contend that the *Gathas* were the work of a single, insightful person, known as Zarathushtra, whose name appears 16 times in the five songs. This perspective echoes the axiomatic acceptance of Zarathushtra as an authority figure in Young Avestan texts that recognize his "voice" speaking through the *Gathas*. In the past few decades, the position of Zarathushtra as "author" has been supported by the linguistic analysis of the composition and structure of the *Gathas*, which has revealed that many structural elements and themes occur both within single sections and across the *Gathas* as a whole. Such poetic technique, particularly the feature of ring composition mentioned earlier, has led many scholars to identify the *Gathas* as the compositions of one individual.

This conclusion has been summarized by one of its academic proponents in this way: "A single, distinct personality speaks to us out of the poems, and in several places the poet names himself as Zoroaster, or rather (in his own language) Zarathushtra . . . In the later parts of the Avesta as well as in other Zoroastrian literature he is frequently spoken of, with never a doubt as to his historical reality. His existence is as well authenticated as that of most people in antiquity."[11]

Other philologists, however, have examined the *Gathas* and come to the understanding that, although Zarathushtra was acknowledged as the first exponent of the religion, its expression in the form of the Avesta was the product of repetition and performance by a priestly group. This deduction comes partly from the fact that the narration of the *Gathas* moves between the first person "I" and the plural "we," and that Zarathushtra is referred to in the third person. In a couple of instances the choral "we" is clearly differentiated from Zarathushtra, which suggests a plurality of speakers.[12] It has, however, been counter-argued that the phrase "to Zarathushtra and to us" in Yasna 28.6 could be a reference to "Zarathushtra and the Mazda worshippers who are listening," and that the use of the third person was a common Indo-Iranian poetic device, which was also used in the *Rig Veda*.[13]

For the most part, these somewhat esoteric hermeneutic concerns have remained within the domain of scholarly discourse. The contention that Zarathushtra might be the inspiration for, but not the immediate author of, the *Gathas* has, however, been unsettling to some members of the faith. But even those academics who propose a gradual elaboration of the initial revelation recognize the central place of Zarathushtra in the religion. As one such scholar, Jean Kellens, wrote: "If he is neither the reciter, nor the author of the

Gathas, Zarathushtra is at least their star. It is clear that in the religious life of the Gathic society he plays a predominant role."[14]

The *Gathas* present an image of Zarathushtra as one who is wise through his powers of mental perception, and who is therefore able to converse with and be guided by Ahura Mazda (Y. 29.8, 43.7). He is both *vidvah* "one who knows," and *manthran* (Y. 29.6, 48.3; 50.5, 6). As *manthran*, Zarathushtra is able to process the religious insights—the "divine plan," as it were—received from Ahura Mazda, and to verbally express those insights to others. Several Gathic and Young Avestan passages present Zarathushtra as being chosen to be the messenger of Ahura Mazda, to spread the religion and galvanize the process of separation from evil (cf. Y. 33.14; 43.8; 12.13). In both existences, he is *spenta*—"beneficent," and *ahum.bish*—a "healer of existence." In this way, Zarathushtra becomes part of the unfolding of a cosmic schema.

Within this schema, Zarathushtra is the *ratu*, the "exemplar" or the "guide," who stands on the fulcrum of time and order, which he pivots to turn the material world and its human inhabitants towards renewal (cf. Y. 46.13, Yt. 5.89, Vr. 2.4). His authority extends to his founding of a coherent religious philosophy, which has its own internal time scale and eschatological resolution. This understanding of Zarathushtra as the prototype for others to follow is preserved across cultural boundaries and historical ages, so that he epitomizes the possibility for each Mazda worshipper to function as a "world healer" (Av. *ahum.bish*). Today, when adherents recite the *Fravarane*, declaring their choice to be a Mazda worshipper "like Zarathushtra", they are pledging to emulate this quality.

The fact that there is no ancient Zoroastrian text exploring the significance of the name "Zarathushtra" may denote that this was not thought to be a meaningful aspect of his person at the time. The Iranian form of the name—*Zarathushtra*—should probably be taken to mean "(owner of) old camels," although this meaning is still debated. The constituent parts of the name have also been popularly translated as "Golden" and "Light/Dawn." This imagery relates to the perceived function of Zarathushtra as illuminating the straight path. It conveys, perhaps, a greater degree of authority than the zoophoric translation.

The interpretation of "Golden Light" with its metaphysical connotation also has a direct association with the Greek *Zoroastres*. Diogenes Laertius stated that earlier Greeks of the time of Plato had interpreted the name of Zoroaster as meaning "star worshipper" (*Lives of the Philosophers* 1.6–9). In a letter of 1883, Friedrich Nietzsche, who had earlier composed a prize-winning essay on Diogenes, wrote that he understood the name of the protagonist in his "little book" (*Also Sprach Zarathustra*) to mean "Gold star," and that this coincidence made him happy![15]

Figure 2.2 A Picture of Asho Zarathushtra in the *Atash Bahram*, Yazd, Iran. Imagery of Zarathushtra was unknown until the mid-nineteenth century, but has now become a feature of most fire temples. Photo by Jenny Rose.

Curiously, this centrality of Zarathushtra to the religion is not reflected in the official religio-political discourse of imperial Iran. The name "Zarathushtra" does not appear in any Achaemenid, Parthian, or Sasanian inscriptions. Nor is "Zoroaster" found in the Greek accounts of the Persians provided by Herodotus, Xenophon, and Ctesias, the Greek physician of Artaxerxes II. This seems to indicate that, although Zarathushtra may have epitomized a religious ideal, in practice it was his words and actions, rather than his persona, that were the focus of faith.

Does the life-story of Zarathushtra resemble that of other founders of religion?

In so far as there can be said to be any biographical details concerning the person of Zarathushtra, there are three main sources: the *Gathas*, the *Videvdad*, and certain Middle Persian works, such as the *Denkard*, *Bundahishn*, and *Wizidagiha-i Zadspram*. The mantic text, *Zand-i Wahman Yasn* describes the visions of the cosmos and the afterlife experienced by Zarathushtra, while he was imbued with the "wisdom of all knowledge." A thirteenth-century New Persian hagiography, the *Zartosht Nameh* is also a significant and accessible source.

Although the *Gathas* do not present a biography of Zarathushtra, some attempts have been made, to connect each poem or section with moments in his life. Several people named in the *Gathas* seem to be in a familial relationship with Zarathushtra. His family name, or patronymic, Spitama, meaning "white" (Y. 29.8), is shared by Pouruchista, his youngest daughter (Y. 53.3), and by Maidyoimangha (Y. 51.19). In later texts, Maidyoimangha is named as the first member of the family (a "cousin") to accept the validity of the religion taught by Zarathushtra. Frashaoshtra and Jamaspa of the Hvo.gva lineage are also mentioned in the *Gathas* (Y. 46.16, 17).

Some of these dramatis personae recur in the *yashts*, but there is virtually nothing biographical about them. *Farvardin Yasht* (the hymn to the *fravashis*) refers to characters that existed within the framework of the mythical-to-actual history of the heroes of Iran. It also establishes the *fravashi* of Zarathushtra as authoritative, and as the paradigm for other humans (Yt. 13.87–95). He was the first to have good thoughts, speak good words, and perform good deeds.

Just as in the *Gathas*, the *Videvdad* presents Zarathushtra as asking ultimate questions of Ahura Mazda. Such dialogues are the means of disseminating the answers Zarathushtra receives. This is a literary technique that continues in subsequent Middle Persian settings. In the *Videvdad*, Zarathushtra is not the first to speak with Ahura Mazda, however—that is the privilege of Yima, who declares that he is not prepared to spread the religion (Vd. 2.1–3). So, Zarathushtra is the one who takes up the challenge to make the world of the living safe from the Lie and from Angra Mainyu, and to call down "the law for dispelling the false gods" the *vi-daeva-data* (Vd. 19.12, 16).

In the internal textual tradition, the Zarathushtra of the *Gathas* quickly develops into an archetypal figure. A well-known early twentieth-century theologian and high priest, Dastur Dr. Maneckji Nusserwanji Dhalla (1875–1956), maintained that, although the message and the mission of Zarathushtra had remained the same from the Gathic period to his own time, certain aspects of the prophet's life had been elaborated upon or added throughout history. In the Middle Persian books, Dastur Dhalla contended, the historical author of the *Gathas* was transformed into a myth, and his personality magnified by miracles and extravagant legends.[16] Middle Persian hagiographic representation of Zarathustra seems to have been based on much older material, however. The detail in *Denkard* Book 7 that Zarathushtra laughed when he was born (Dk. 7.3.2) was known to Pliny the Elder in the first century CE. Pliny wrote that Zoroaster was the only person he had heard of who laughed at his birth (*Natural History* 7.16.15.). This expression of happiness parallels the declaration in the Avesta that the entire creation rejoiced at the birth of Zarathushtra (Yt. 13.93).

Book 7 of the *Denkard* opens with the declaration that it is about the "wonders" of the greatest messenger of the religion, whose "miraculous power" (*varzavand*) derives through Ahura Mazda. In the *Denkard*, from the time of the first mortal, Gayomard, until the advent of Zarathushtra, humans were thought to have had conversations with Ahura Mazda through various means, and to have brought the word of the religion to others (Dk. 7.1.8–43). Zarathushtra, however, is said to have received the complete religion in all its parts, since his pre-soul (MP *frawahr*) was of the same essence as *asha* (Dk. 7.1.41, 43). According to the *Denkard*, this pre-soul of Zarathushtra was fashioned by the *amesha spentas* after the world had been created in its *menog* state and was on the point of becoming material (*getig*), but before the attack of the Lie (Dk. 7.2.15).

Even before his dialogues with Ahura Mazda, the capacity for thought of Zarathushtra was said to be larger than the whole world, superior to anything in material existence, and his intelligence capable of attaining everything (Dk. 7.2.46). The hymns (MP *niyayishn*) of Zarathushtra informed everyone about the religion (MP *den*), so there was no need for any further beings to teach it. The *Denkard* portrays Zarathushtra as embodying the perfect mixture of a physical body (*tan-gohr*), pre-soul (*frawahr*), and divine fortune (*xwarrah*), and as the ideal person of integrity. Zarathushtra's pre-eminence in intellect and body fit him for the task of reminding humanity of Ahura Mazda's creative activity in the world, and of the need to preserve its good creation from evil (Dk. 7.3.49). One of the tools that Zarathushtra brings to help his fellow humans in their task is the "marvel of the Avesta itself" (Dk. 7.5.11).

As the messenger of wisdom, Zarathushtra enters history through his physical birth at the end of the ninth millennium. In the periodization of 3000-year stages, Zarathushtra's reception of the religion at the beginning of the tenth millennium marks the "turning point" that brings in a period of intensified struggle between Ahura Mazda and Angra Mainyu (cf. Y. 43.6). This culminates in the moment of *wizarishn*—"separation and resolution." Both the *Denkard* and the *Wizidagiha-i Zadspram* detail the life of Zarathushtra and then incorporate material dealing with the future history of the faith until this final renovation (MP *frashegird*).

Zadspram expands on some of the events of Zarathushtra's life, including the character traits that enabled him to receive and disseminate the religion from the age of 30 (Zds. 21.1). Zarathushtra's disposition is said to have been one of compassion and generosity toward humans and animals, and he showed ritual reverence for fire and water (Zds. 20.16). These qualities are also celebrated in other Middle Persian texts, where Zarathushtra is recognized as the one who advocated "the right measure" (*payman*) in all things.

There is no mention of the death of Zarathushtra in the surviving Avesta, but the *Denkard* speaks of his departure (*wihez*) into "the best existence" aged 77 (Dk. 7.5.1). *Wihez* means "movement" or "progression." A current mystical understanding of this term is that Zarathushtra did not die but ascended to a higher plane of being beyond physical existence. A passage in the *Denkard* states that

Zarathushtra predicted his own death at the hand of a Turanian enemy, named Bratroresh (Dk. 5.3.2). *Zadspram* records the day of Zarathushtra's death at the age of 77, on the day Khorshid in the month Dae (Zds. 23.9). This event is commemorated annually by Zoroastrians at the holiday known to Parsis as *Zardosht no Diso* and to Zartoshtis as *Dargozasht-e Asho Zartosht.*

In Ferdowsi's *Shah Nameh*, the section narrating the story of Zarathushtra is thought to have been based on a composition by the tenth-century poet Daqiqi (d. ca. 976 CE), which in turn derived from a Middle Persian account. The *Shah Nameh* describes Zarathushtra as the one who brings the religion of goodness to King Goshtasp (Av. Vishtaspa), and as the king's wise mentor in the struggle between the forces of good and evil.

Another New Persian book, the *Zartosht Nameh*, was written within the Zoroastrian community in about 1278 CE. It seems to have been based on a Middle Persian original. This "Book of Zarathushtra" tells of the birth, childhood, and early teaching activity of Zarathushtra, and remains a central source for Zoroastrians concerning the eponymous founder of their religion. Again, the emphasis is on the divine mission of Zarathushtra, incorporating the notion that Ahura Mazda pre-ordained his birth as a means of freeing the world from the hold of evil. In the *Zartosht Nameh*, Zarathustra is a hero of spiritual agency who comes from the lineage of the mythical king Feridun. Several additional legends relating to his birth highlight his performance of miracles from infancy onward. This wonder-working includes an expanded account of his cure of Vishtaspa's black horse. The narrative culminates with Vishtaspa's conversion. Zarathushtra's thaumaturgic activity as is presented in this *Book of Zarathushtra* as a preliminary to the transformation of the world.

To what extent does the voice of Zarathushtra resonate through the centuries?

This transformative impact of Zarathushtra is understood to continue from his own time, beyond his death, and into the present. By the time of the *Persian Rivayats*, Zarathustra's *fravashi* was venerated on a daily basis through the liturgy. It was believed by some that Yasna offerings in the name of Zarathushtra could thwart the evil designs of hostile forces of demonic, human, or natural origin.

During the later period of the *Rivayats*, Parsi mystics in India composed several treatises in Persian, asserting that Zarathushtra had used allegorical and enigmatic language in his teachings to hide deeper truths of the religion from the ignorant. The seventeenth-century *Dabestan-e madaheb* summarizes such mystical teachings, which could be known only by adepts. The *Dasatir*, another "Parsi" mystical text, is now generally considered to reflect the influence of Iranian Illuminationist (*Ishraqi*) thought of the late sixteenth century.

The notion that the Avesta as a whole contains teachings integral to the spiritual progress of humanity became a feature of the early twentieth-century movement sometimes referred to as "Zoroastrian theosophy." The formal name for this esoteric philosophy is *Ilm-e Kshnoom*, meaning something like "the knowledge of spiritual satisfaction." Those who have a "khshnoomist" perspective may claim that the thaumaturgical abilities of Zarathustra show him to be not an ordinary mortal, but more like an incarnate *yazata*.

This understanding of Zarathushtra as near-divine contrasts with the view promoted in a Gujarati catechism where Zarathustra is presented as a wise man who had been admitted into the presence of the divine but was not himself divine in any way. Several Parsis translated this catechism into English in the late nineteenth and early twentieth centuries. J. J. Modi's translation, published in 1911, promotes Zarathushtra as having authority through his role as the great prophet who taught the Mazda-worshipping religion to the people of ancient Iran.[17] Modi, who wrote many books and articles on the religion, considered that Zarathushtra should not be thought of as the offshoot of Ahura Mazda, but as the model of a savior-figure whom everyone could follow through their own deeds.[18]

At around the same time, Dastur Dhalla, who had studied for a Master's and then a Ph.D. degree in Iranian Studies at Columbia University in New York, wrote his own analysis of Zoroastrian theology. He referred to Zarathushtra as a "paragon of reason" and a "practical common-sense thinker" clothed in divine wisdom.[19] This image of Zarathushtra as an enlightened teacher was also promoted by a contemporary Iranian nationalist named Ibrahim Pour-e Davoud (1886–1968). Pour-e Davoud had translated the *Gathas* into Persian, and understood Zarathushtra to be the ancient Iranian bearer of a momentous message to humanity that was still relevant to the modern world.

The idea that Zarathushtra was a great religious teacher whose ideas are not restricted to any single time or culture is still appealing for many modern Zoroastrians. There is, however, a diversity of opinion among Zoroastrians as to whether that "message of Zarathushtra" extends beyond the *Gathas*. Self-labeled "progressive Zarathushtis" tend to focus on the philosophical message of Zarathushtra as contained in the *Gathas*, and maintain that he was a monotheist who discarded most priestly ritual. This message, they claim, is applicable to all, regardless of ethnic or religious background. Traditionalists, on the other hand, view Zarathushtra as the original priestly authority for many of the religion's rites. They emphasize the continuing power of ritual and the role of the priesthood as being "like Zarathushtra" in sustaining knowledge of the religion and its ritual activity. From this traditionalist perspective, the *Gathas* are the core message of a broader group of sacred texts that have been passed on orally and which contain the totality of Zarathushtra's message.

WHO HOLDS RELIGIOUS AUTHORITY?

This question is about who has controlled the verbal transmission of the sacred word from the time of Zarathushtra to the present. It also asks:

Who has the authority to interpret the religion?

Priests as divine wordsmiths

In the *Gathas* there are references to some poets (*kavis*), who are bad, and to ritual practitioners who mumble (*karapans*) and who lack integrity (Y. 32.14–15; 51.14). The accusation of false authority or even deception to those in positions of religious authority suggests the existence of established "*manthran* schools" at this early stage. *Kavi* is the descriptive title that is also given to Vishtaspa, Zarathushtra's supporter.[20] Although in later Iranian mythology the term was applied to a ruler, in both Old Avestan and Old Indic *kavi* referred to an inspired poet. The negative references to some *kavis* in the *Gathas* suggests rival poets, some of whom generate good words, recited with best thought and concentration, and others whose words are mediocre and whose thoughts are unfocused (Y. 32.10, 14).

The *manthran*—the one who gives voice to the *manthra*—is the keeper of the sacred thought-word that is brought from the conceptual world into the material (Y. 33.5). This mediation between the two existences was through ritual action as well as verbal expression, although it is not entirely clear what the ritual relating to the Old Avestan *manthras* involved. The Gathic reciter refers to himself as a *zaotar*—literally, "one who offers libations" (Y. 33.6). Zarathushtra is described as such a priest in the *Farvardin Yasht* (Yt. 13.94). The term became *Zot* in Middle Persian, which is still the title for the presiding priest of the Yasna ceremony. In a couple of later Avestan texts, Zarathushtra is also referred to as *athravan*, a term used elsewhere in the generic context of a priest.[21]

Herodotus initially describes the *magi* as a Median people, but also uses the term for the religious experts of both the Medes and the Persians (cf. *Histories* 1.101, 107–8, 132). He states that the Persian *magi* would consecrate the sacrificial offerings of the laity through invocation. Herodotus notes that the prayer of the laity on this occasion did not take the form of an individual petition on the part of those making the offering, but was recited for the good of the king and the whole community. Xenophon presents the *magi* as a priestly order dating to the rule of Cyrus II (*Cyropaedia* 8.1.23.). According to Pliny, by the time of Plato, the Greeks considered the *magi* to be "the most famous and most beneficial of philosophical sects" (*Natural History* 30.3).

During the mid-Parthian period, Strabo wrote about a large "tribe of the *magi*" in Cappadocia, where there were "many sacred places of the Persian gods" (*Geographia* 15.3.15).[22] In Strabo's accounts, the *magi* control the whole ritual of sacrifice, during which they chant invocations for about an hour. Parthian ostraca (potsherds) mention different titles for priests, including the familiar western Iranian form, *magus*, and an *atarshpati*, whose function was apparently to tend the fire. A couple of fire temples that have been dated to the Parthian period have been excavated. One is in Mele Hairam in southeastern Turkmenistan, and the other, almost directly due south of there, is at Kuh-e Khajeh in Sistan, near the border with Afghanistan.

During Sasanian times some priests, such as Kerdir and Adurbad-i Mahraspandan, rose to prominence in both the religious and political spheres. Kerdir's four Middle Persian inscriptions provide some insight into his activity as a priest rising through the ranks. He records his promotion under at least four Sasanian monarchs from a teaching priest (*herbad*) to a high priest (*mowbed*) to "the high priest of Ahura Mazda". with control over both ritual and religious regulations at court and throughout the realm. Kerdir attributes his rise in religious authority to the fact that he promoted the Mazda-worshipping religion, served the *yazatas* well, lived in truthfulness, performed many religious services, established many *Wahram* ("victory") fires, and boosted the status of many priests.

We cannot be certain that the various titles of Kerdir held the same significance in the third century as they do in the ninth-century books. Most of our knowledge about the role of priests is found in these later texts, and so post-dates the Sasanians. A Middle Persian letter, which is accredited to Tosar the chief priest of Ardashir I, but which dates towards the end of Sasanian rule, presents its author as a figure whose advice and counsel in matters of state is sought by the king. This *Letter of Tosar* speaks of the clergy as the highest of the

Figure 2.3 Rock relief depiction of Kerdir, high priest under Bahram II. Sarab-e Bahram, Iran. Photo by Jenny Rose.

four social classes, and notes that there were many types of priest. The ecclesiastical hierarchy developed to include administrative, judicial, and teaching priests. Alongside the study and teaching of the Avesta and its *zand*, and the performance of ritual, the authority of the clergy extended into public affairs, including economic and legislative matters.

The modern priesthood still uses terms found in Middle Persian texts, although they do not necessarily have the same meaning:

Herbad/Ervad: from an Avestan *aethrapati*, which means a "teaching priest." It is now used for a priest who has been initiated in the *navar* ceremony, and who performs "outer" ceremonies, including *jashans*.

Mobed: from Old Persian **magupati*. In Sasanian times, this seems to have been the title of an administrative priest. Today, it signifies a fully qualified Zoroastrian priest in both Iranian and Indian contexts, who is authorized to perform both inner and outer ceremonies. In popular Iranian usage, the title is given to the officiant at any ritual, including a *mobedyar* (a lay "assistant priest").

Dastur: this term originally seems to have referred to a priest in authority, who acted in a supervisory capacity over other priests, and as an adjudicator in religious matters. It is now the title applied specifically to a high priest of one of the main fire temples, known as *Atash Bahrams*, in India. Some Parsis may use the term *dasturjis* generically in reference to a collective group of priests. The suffix "*ji*" is commonly used throughout India for someone who commands respect.

One Middle Persian term for a priest that is not now used is *andarz-bed*, which means "counsellor" or "wise man." Adurbad-i Mahraspandan is said to have composed many *andarz* or "wise sayings." This is a genre of religious teaching that has survived well, probably because it consists of short, easily memorized sayings. Such maxims can be read on contemporary Sasanian seals discovered in Iran. *Denkard* Book 6 also contains many *andarz*. These wise sayings are aimed at teaching right conduct, based on the ethic of good thoughts, good words, and good deeds. Some of Adurbad's aphorisms include:

1. *Do not hoard things, so that you may not feel need! For hoarding things does not lead to less need.*
2. *Strive only to store more Orderliness [or "rightness"], that is, in deeds and good works. For the only good thing you should store up is Orderliness*

16. *Receive traveling people well, so that you may be well received both here and there. For he who gives, receives, and he will grow thereby . . .*

23. *Be content in adversity, patient in misfortune, and do not trust life but good actions! For a person's good actions are his defenders, while a person's bad actions are his accusers. For of thoughts, words and actions, actions are best.*[23]

It is evident that these wise sayings were meant to apply to all members of the *weh den*—the "good religion." All were expected to exercise individual authority over their own thought, word, and action. Parallel to this emphasis on autonomy of ethical praxis was a structured priestly authority that acted as a formal arbiter of religious matters. This priesthood is portrayed as having been intimately linked with the monarchy from early on in the Sasanian period.

The relationship between religion and rule is found with Kerdir, the high priest who proclaims himself as having achieved material prosperity through his good, solid work on behalf of "the *yazatas*, the rulers and his own soul." Kerdir is followed a century later by Adurbad-i Mahraspandan, who epitomizes the priest who upholds the faith in both words and deeds, and so brings strength to both the religion and the kingdom. Tosar's letter, redacted around the sixth century CE, expresses the ideal relationship of priestly and royal authority to be as close as if they were "born of the one womb, joined together."[24] And a passage in the *Shah Nameh* concerning the very end of Sasanian rule provides the narrative of a model Zoroastrian priest in the eastern Iranian region of Merv. This priest, Zaruy, trying to protect the last Zoroastrian king, Yazdegerd III, argues that "kingship and prophethood are two gems set in the same ring" and that when one is broken, spirit and wisdom are both crushed.[25]

Priestly authority in a minority setting

After the arrival of Islam in the mid–seventh century it took some time for the authority of the Zoroastrian priesthood to diminish. In the ninth century, the religious affairs of the Zoroastrians were supervised by the *hudenan peshobay*—"the leader of those of the good religion." These religious leaders, such as Adurfarrobay Farroxzadan, exercised their positions of authority under the scrutiny of the Abbasid caliphate, which was now located in Baghdad. They were also responsible for writing down many of the Middle Persian Zoro-astrian books. It was not until in the tenth century CE that the chief priest Adurbad-i Emedan complained that the end of Iranian rule had finally occurred within Iran. From about this time on, Zoroastri-ans were a religious minority in their own homeland.

By then, however, the religion had arrived in India, where the priests continued to be guardians of both the fire and the sacred texts. Towards the end of the thirteenth century, a couple of hundred years before the writing of the *Qesse-ye Sanjan*, the Zoroastrian set-tlements on the Gujarati coastline had divided into five main districts (*panths*), each under the charge of a priestly family (*panthaki*). Descendants of these priestly families are still around and are known as *panthaks* even though they have often moved away from the origi-nal five districts. The reference to a *panthaki* today relates to a genea-logical line of ancestry through one of three original *mobeds*. *Panthakis* manage most of the fire temples in Mumbai. Many *pan-thaks* retain long-lasting associations with particular families in the

Figure 2.4 Ervad Parvez M. Bajan performs the *navjote* for his grandson Zerxes at the Seth Bomanji Merwanji Mevawala Agiary, Mumbai, October 20, 2009. Ervad Bajan is the sixth generation *panthak* to tend the fire in this agiary. Photo courtesy of Ervad Parvez Bajan.

lay community, and are asked to officiate at rites of passage for them and to provide counsel in social as well as religious matters.[26]

The *Qesse-ye Sanjan*, the narrative of the Zoroastrian religion's arrival on the shores of India, is told from a priestly perspective, but it involves the seminal role of a fifteenth-century lay leader from Navsari. This man, a farmer named Changa Asha, was said to have persuaded the lay council (*anjuman*) to move the sacred fire, which had been relocated to Navsari to preserve it from attack.

The input of Changa Asha indicates that by this time the institution of the priesthood in India was partly under the control of a wealthy, independent laity. This lay control increased as its mercantile power grew through dealings with the British East India Company. Changa Asha is thought to have been instrumental in sending a lay representative named Nariman Hoshang to Iran in 1478. From Nariman Hoshang's initial trip came the first of a series of Persian-language communications concerning the religion that chart the focus of priestly and lay concerns in both India and Iran through the following three centuries. These *Persian Rivayats* show that, until the mid–eighteenth century, Parsi priests looked to the Iranian priesthood as a source of religious authority.

By the time of the early *Persian Rivayats*, the term *mobed* seems to signify a priestly rank higher than a *herbad* and lower than a *dastur*. The *Rivayats*, as priestly commentaries on normative Zoroastrian belief and practice in Iran across almost four centuries, provide some insight into the theological beliefs, and priestly and lay observances, of both the Iranian Zoroastrian and Parsi communities. They consist of questions posed by the Parsis and answers supplied by Iranian priests. Although these *Rivayats* are not generally regarded as scriptures, they are often cited as authoritative in matters of praxis and behavior, especially as they address many of the same questions being asked today. They form part of the priestly tradition of interpretation and commentary on the religion. Selections of the *Persian Rivayats* were published in English at the beginning of the twentieth century, which made them accessible to a wider readership.

During Safavid rule in Iran (c. 1501–1736 CE) the country adopted Shi'a Islam. This period was marked by both religious and political upheaval for the Iranian Zoroastrians. Between the mid–seventeenth and early eighteenth centuries many Zoroastrians were relocated from Kerman and Yazd to work in the capital of Isfahan, and there were several attempts at forcible conversion. Some fire temples were converted into mosques, and *dakhmas* were desecrated, which presented a profound disruption in the ritual life of the religion. European visitors to Iran during the seventeenth century had described their encounters with Zoroastrian priests, who explained some of the beliefs of the religion. These Europeans also related their own experience of some of the outer rituals and practices of Zoroastrians. By the early eighteenth century, however, many Zoroastrian communities had been decimated, and their scriptures lost or destroyed. When Maneckji Limji Hataria reported back to the Parsis in Bombay about his visit to Iran in the mid–nineteenth century, the situation of the Zoroastrians there was miserable. Hataria noted that the priests in Iran appeared to have little understanding of their sacred texts, which he found troubling.

Throughout the last few decades of the nineteenth century and the beginning of the next, the Parsi Amelioration Society, represented initially by Hataria, aided its Iranian co-religionists to establish *anjumans* or "community councils." Parsis founded hospitals, medical clinics, and children's homes and helped to renovate or build fire temples, as well as community halls and *dakhmas* in Yazd, Kerman, and Tehran. Such close contact between Iranian Zoroastrians and Parsis led to the reinforcement of certain praxes considered authentic by Parsis, particularly those to do with ritual in the fire temples, and rites of passage. Hataria criticized certain aspects of Iranian Zoroastrian religious expression, such as animal sacrifice and polygamy, which he thought had been influenced by Islam. In fact, some of the differences in praxis that Hataria noted with concern were colored by the Hindu or British impact on his own Parsi upbringing.

Encouraged by Parsi support, some Iranian Zoroastrians migrated temporarily to India to work, to set up a business, or to train as priests. Some settled there permanently. By the mid–twentieth century, due to the decline in the number of sons born into priestly families in Iran, there were not enough practicing priests to serve the needs of the various Zoroastrian communities there. At this juncture, the Iranian Council of Mobeds in Tehran agreed to accept into the priesthood the sons of women from priestly families. Despite this shift from direct patrilineality, when the American anthropologist Michael Fischer was in Iran in the early 1970s, he noted that there were only six priests in Yazd and one in Sharifabad.[27] By 1996, there were only three priestly families in Yazd, of which only two had male heirs.[28]

The voice of the Zoroastrian priests was severely weakened by their loss of status in the last half of the twentieth century. The continued decline of a full-time hereditary priesthood led to a limitation on its ritual functionality and an erosion of its authority to speak for the community. Males from non-priestly families began to be trained as *mobedyars* ("assistant priests"), and in many Iranian Zoroastrian communities today the priest in charge of the religious affairs is no longer a *mobed* but a *mobedyar*. These *mobedyars* are regarded by the Zartoshtis as dedicated, spiritual, and capable of performing the various duties allocated to them. The ritual function of a *mobedyar* is limited: he cannot aid in the performance of the full Yasna ceremony, officiate at the induction ceremony for a fellow *mobedyar*, nor become a *mobed* himself.

In recent years, however, there has been a restoration of the rite of ordination into the priesthood in Iran, known as *nowzut*. The *nowzut* ceremony is the equivalent to the two stages of priestly initiation in Parsi praxis, known as *navar* and *martab* respectively. In Iran the new priest is called *navar* for a year after his *nowzut* ceremony, during which time he participates in religious ceremonies with a more senior *mobed*. After that year, the new priest automatically becomes *martab* without another ceremony. There were at least ten *nowzut* ceremonies in Tehran in the first decade of this century.

The number and status of priests in India, although higher than that in Iran, has experienced a similar drop, although the Parsi priesthood continues to be hereditary and patrilineal. There are several well-respected scholar-priests to whom the Parsi communities look for religious counsel, but the number of boys attending the *athornan* (priests') training schools in Mumbai has decreased sharply over the past 20 years.

Many young Parsi men consider a priest's salary insufficient to raise a family, and as a result, there are very few full-time priests, even in Mumbai. Since the job of a priest offers none of the financial rewards and social kudos of other professions—such as a lawyer, doctor, or engineer—there is little incentive to spend long hours training to become a *martab*, the second stage of initiation for a Parsi priest. Those who do attend a priests' training school or course often stop at the first ordination (*navar*) and then go to college to train for a full-time career in another profession. Many do not ever perform in any ritual capacity, although in Mumbai the infrastructure exists for young priests to be mentored with senior priests at local fire temples and to participate in prayer ceremonies, especially during the *Muktad* prayers just before New Year.

Figure 2.5 Ervad Burzin Balsara, age 9, performs his first *jashan* as assistant priest (*Raspi*) after his *navar* at the Vatcha Gandhi Agiary, Mumbai, December 25, 2008. Burzin lives in north Texas and, with other priests, has already officiated at several *navjotes* and *jashans* in his community. Photo courtesy of Poras Balsara.

WAPIZ has initiated two schemes to help *mobeds* financially and to ensure that rituals in the fire temples and at the *dakhmas* are maintained. This organization has set up a support system to relieve *mobeds* who need a temporary break, particularly in the communities outside Mumbai. It has also established a rotational program in which *mobeds* from the city undertake a three- to six-month tour of duty in places that have no permanent priest. These *mobeds* then return to their families, where they will do freelance work in a local fire temple, or for rituals held at the homes of individual families.

One newly elected member of the BPP had also set in motion a program to improve the financial situation of the priests. It remains to be seen what impact these initiatives will have.

Authority in the diaspora

At the beginning of the twenty-first century several different bases of authority for Zoroastrians exist, both priestly and lay. The attrition of numbers of initiated priests is felt keenly in Europe and North America, since all Zoroastrian priests, including those born and educated abroad, must be ordained in India or Iran. This is because a consecrated fire is a prerequisite for priestly ordination, and to date none exists outside the two homelands.

Ervad Dr. Jehan Bagli, a Parsi priest who now lives in Toronto, wrote about his view of priestly authority, which he feels is equally applicable in the new world: "To me being a priest is a commitment. It is an assignment to do all the things that help perpetuate the religion of Zarathushtra. A Zarathushti priest is duty bound to fill the spiritual needs of the members of Zarathushti community. It is incumbent upon the priest to find time to learn and understand the prayers that he recites. It is the responsibility of a priest to impart the knowledge of the Zarathushti tradition to the laity and to participate whenever possible in the ritual performances for the community and for an individual family when requested."[29]

Many Zoroastrians are painfully aware that the role of priests as perpetuators of the religion through counseling and teaching the laity, performing ritual, and mentoring and training other priests is challenged through lack of numbers. I recently heard a young Parsi woman, Shireen, who works in Washington, DC, speak eloquently on the need to sustain and develop the priesthood in North America. She wrote to me about how she envisaged this happening: "The Zoroastrian community in North America is enterprising, dynamic and visionary. A major part of that vision would constitute improving the situation for current and future priests. However the community lacks consensus in achieving that vision . . . Zoroastrian priests require strong monetary support complimented with respect and gratitude."

A lay priesthood

Outside Iran and India, priests and dedicated lay members work alongside each other in teaching religious education classes for local

Zoroastrian Associations. The introduction of a formal training for *mobedyars* was a natural extension of that co-operation. The North American Mobeds Council (NAMC) set up a *mobedyar* training program in 1995. NAMC was originally created as a Parsi organization, but seems now to have more or less merged with its Iranian equivalent, the Council of Iranian Mobeds of North America (CIMNA).

The Rustam Guiv Dar-i Mihr, which is one of the centers for Zoroastrians in southern California has two *mobeds*, and so is able to undertake both the training and the ordination ceremony for *mobedyars* in house. Elsewhere, the *mobedyar* has to find a *mobed* who is in good standing with the NAMC to act as mentor. At the ceremony of ordination, the North American *mobedyar* candidates officiate as the presiding priest (*Zot*) in the *jashan* ceremony. A *jashan* ceremony is held in celebration of festivals, rites of passage, and other special events. After qualifying, *mobedyars* are able to officiate as priests at *jashans*, other outer liturgical ceremonies, and bereavement services. They can assist at initiations and weddings, but cannot perform inner liturgical ceremonies such as the Yasna.

CAN WOMEN BECOME PRIESTS?

It has been suggested by some Zoroastrians that one of the ways to augment the priesthood is to accept anyone who feels called to be ordained—including women. The discussion that has arisen from this proposal is based on both scriptural interpretation and social norms. Similar factors have come into play for all the religions that have debated the ordination of female priests in the past half-century.

As is the case with many religions in which the transmission of sacred text and ritual has been male-driven, Zoroastrians have to look carefully to find evidence for women acting in a liturgical capacity. Although the *Gathas* present the concept of spiritual parity for both men and women, Zoroastrianism developed historically within a patriarchal structure in which the religious texts were composed and interpreted by male priests. In some cases, learned laymen also wrote theological treatises. In the past, women were largely excluded from positions of status within the religious organization and ritual life of the community.

In the history of the religion the main protagonists from Zarathushtra onwards were male. These include: the first convert Maidyoimangha;

Vishtaspa, the first patron of the religion; the end-time hero Peshyotan; and the three *saoshyants*. In Avestan mythology, the ancient rulers and heroic warriors who epitomize the "good religion" are also male, such as Yima, Thraetaona, and Keresaspa. The only female named in the *Gathas* is Pouruchista, the youngest daughter of Zarathushtra, who seems to encapsulate the ideal Mazda worshipper, promoting the religion through sustaining *asha* and the "sunny realm of good thought" (Y. 53.3–4). Pouruchista's dedication has a beneficial impact upon her immediate community, bringing rewards for her father, her husband, "herdsmen," and family. This resonates with the remark by Herodotus that the Ancient Persian laymen, when they performed a sacrifice, did not pray for themselves, but for the king and the community to which they belonged.

Although there is no evidence of female priests in Old Avestan texts, Young Avestan references are found to both men and women who were educated in the study of the religion and some of its rituals, including taking care of the fire. One passage reads: "we worship the departed souls [*fravashis*] of the teachers, of male and female students" (Y. 26.7). A section of the *Herbadestan* discusses the circumstances under which men, women, or children may leave home in order to teach the religion. Whoever in the family had the "highest esteem" for *asha* should represent the household, leaving the management of the family estate to whoever is more capable in that function.[30] A married woman could go, as long as a male escorted her. If she had the better management skills, however, then her husband should be the one to go (*Her.* 5.3–4). The word used to describe this activity of teaching—*athauruna*—is connected with *athravan*, a general Young Avestan word for priest.

The *Nerangestan* suggests that women and children could not only learn and recite the Yasna, but could also perform ritual. It states that any man, woman, or child who was able to recite the liturgy properly could make the offering to the waters, the *ab zohr*.[31] In this context, the word *zaothrada*, referring to the act of "pouring the libation," could be interpreted to mean that a woman or child is authorized to hold the office of a priest (*zaotar*). This reading is supported by the appearance of the word *Zotih*—the feminine form of *Zot*, the priest who presides at the Yasna—in the Middle Persian *Shayest ne Shayest* (10.35). The term could, however, relate just to the *zaothra* ritual, meaning that anyone who knows the Yasna by heart, including a layperson, could make the offering to the water.[32] A woman was, however, limited in such action during her time of menstruation. This regular monthly occurrence has been a key reason for excluding women from both public and private participation in any ritual involving fire.

A legal text compiled in late Sasanian times informs us that a daughter could inherit the family fire from her father, but that once she married, her husband would take on the responsibility for the fire (MHD 25.8–9). In the Middle Persian account of the vision of Arda Wiraz, his seven sisters, who "knew the religion by heart," kept watch around his body alongside the priests. These siblings kept the fire alight, burnt incense, and recited "the Avesta and Zand of the ritual" (AWN 2.2–3, 32–6).

Such textual references indicate that during the Sasanian period there was no gender barrier in terms of women being able to learn and recite religious litanies, nor to their performing certain rituals, except during menses. Although women's status with regard to ritual purity presents a challenge to the priests—and by extension to the lay community—in terms of their possible vitiation of ritual, their potential contribution to the existing structure of the priesthood looks set to be part of Zoroastrian discourse in the next few decades.

Female mobedyars

At times, Zoroastrian women who are respected for their religiosity and their versatility in memorizing and reciting prayers have been called upon to help out the male priesthood. It has been the custom in Iran since the late twentieth century that, on occasions when a qualified priest was unavailable, women would perform certain outer rituals. For instance, if the former full-time *mobed* appointed to the Isfahan fire temple was absent or unwell, he would ask a devout older woman, who was not from a priestly family, to attend the fire. Mobed Mehraban Firouzgary, a high-ranking Zartoshti priest in Tehran recently informed me: "Both my sisters have performed such jobs on various occasions, especially my elder sister Lal who passed away years back. My younger sister Shirin lives near London and single handedly or in the company of her husband Ardeshir has performed several ceremonies for friends and relatives around London."

Mobed Firouzgary also mentioned a woman whom the *Anjuman-e Mobedan* (the Council of Mobeds) had considered suitable to initiate several girls into *Sedreh Pushi* in a suburb of Tehran that had no resident priest. The Zartoshti women who perform such ritual activity are post-menopausal, and therefore not liable to the ritual pollution caused by the biological production of "dead matter" through menstruation or childbirth. In some of the villages in Iran such elderly women are appointed as "guardians" of local shrines.[33]

In February 2011, eight female *mobedyars* of varying ages were officially certified by the Council of Mobeds in Tehran. This was the first such initiation of women, and has caused some controversy.

Figure 2.6 This Zartoshti woman brings embers from her hearth fire to light an oil lamp in the shrine outside the fire temple in Cham, Iran. There is no resident priest in the village. Photo by Jenny Rose.

During the twenty-first AGM of the NAMC in 2008, Ervad Bagli proposed to open the *mobedyar* training program in North America to women in order to better meet the needs of the growing communities. Several women had raised the issue, and the Council unanimously agreed to amend the wording of the 1999 resolution concerning the *mobedyar* program from exclusively "male" to "all Zarathushtis."

In a subsequent *FEZANA Journal* article, one NAMC female *mobedyar* candidate, Houtoxi, outlined the reasons for deciding to become a *mobedyar*. She stated:

> As a young girl growing up in Ahmedabad, India, I loved watching my father . . . and his brother as they prayed at the changing of every Geh [time of prayer]. I remember hanging on to the ends of my father's *kusti* as I became lost in the melodious sounds of the Avesta . . . In India, we were surrounded by a Zarathushti way of life morning to night; in moving to the US, however, I realized that our children lack that same sense of immersion in the religion that my siblings and I enjoyed . . . I felt as though we were losing our beautiful religion because our youth were not being exposed to it in the same way.[34]

Houtoxi does not come from a priestly family, nor does her husband. In a personal e-mail, Houtoxi noted that she has received support from her family and friends regarding her decision to train as a *mobedyar*. She wrote: "the most comfortable ceremony for me to perform will be *Jashans* . . . since I listen to the prayers daily and have watched the ceremony being performed many, many times."

I know also of one Iranian Zoroastrian woman in southern California who has participated in a formal two-year class of *mobedyar* training that concluded in the spring of 2010. The Zoroastrian associations that form part of FEZANA appear to be generally supportive of women who are prepared to undertake the study and qualification process to become a *mobedyar*, but some traditionalists are vehemently opposed.

WHAT VOICE DO ZOROASTRIANS HAVE AS A MINORITY RELIGION?

The *Persian Rivayats* frequently discuss what should happen when "the Mazda worshippers" are in control and what happens when they are not. Zoroastrians have been a minority religious group in both

Iran and India for over a millennium, although the situation in each country is vastly different. In these two places, as elsewhere, the authority wielded by lay Zoroastrian organizations both reflects and affects the social and legal standing of the religion within the wider, non-Zoroastrian community. At present, there is no one authoritative, global Zoroastrian organization that can be said to represent all the various religious factions.

The Parsis remain a minority group numerically, but have had significant financial and political authority in India since the early eighteenth century. As the Parsis began to relocate to Bombay from Gujarat, and to build their own centers of worship, they felt the need for a formal body to represent Zoroastrians. They particularly wanted to formulate their own legislation concerning marriage and inheritance. The Parsi *Punchayat*—a "council of five"—was set up to regulate both social and religious affairs. In the early days, this *punchayat* often functioned as an internal disciplinary body, such as in cases when a man took a second wife, or when women went out unescorted at night. As a base of authority, this form of conciliar self-management has had a lasting impact on the way Parsis have defined themselves in the Indian subcontinent.

The initial Punchayat was reconstituted several times as the community grew and changed and as the British reform of law in India took effect. The Trust for the Bombay Parsi Punchayat (BPP) was established in 1851 at the instigation of Sir Jamsetjee Jejeebhoy. The BPP functioned as a central body of authority, and until recently consisted mostly of businessmen of high standing in the community. In 1936, the first female trustee of the BPP was elected, but a female president did not take the chair until 1974.[35] The assets of the BPP include a large parcel of land at Doongerwadi, on the top of Malabar Hill. This is where the *dakhmas*—the places of exposure of the dead—are located in Mumbai. The function of the BPP is mostly that of a charitable organization, providing scholarships and welfare programs, career guidance for the unemployed, and helping to finance various institutions including a home for the elderly, a student hostel, a few fire temples, a priests' training school, a healthcare unit, and a fertility clinic. Through such involvement, the BPP effectively controls several Parsi institutions, the most important of which is the *dakhmenashini* system (the exposure of the corpse in the *dakhma*) at Doongerwadi. More will be said about this practice in Chapter 3.

Following an earlier Bombay High Court Ruling, the BPP election in October 2008 was open to all Parsis over 18 years old, rather than to only the elected 3000-member Anjuman Committee. In that election, General Members had one vote, but Donor Members were allowed two votes each. The result of this exercise of universal adult franchise was that the elected board is now predominantly traditionalist. Of the seven BPP trustees, only three can be women. At present, the board includes two women, one elected on the initial ballot, and the other to replace her husband who died in office. The term of service is seven years. Parsi *anjumans* or *punchayats* also exist in other parts of India, including Calcutta (Kolkata), Delhi, Pune, Madras, Bangalore, Hyderabad, and Jamshedpur, as well as in some of the smaller, but important towns of Gujarat, such as Surat, Navsari, Udwada, Baroda, and Ahmedabad.

In Iran, Zoroastrians have the rights of a religious minority (*aqaliat*) according to the Constitution of the Islamic Republic.[36] The application of this term carries with it a degree of ambivalence: it affirms certain rights in theory, but institutionalizes the religious community as inferior, and therefore as liable to discrimination, particularly in terms of government employment and in social settings. Zoroastrians have one member of the Iranian parliament (*majles*), who is elected through a separate body of voters. Their religious freedom is legislated, in that they are allowed to perform ceremonies, to take time off for festival days, and to educate their children in the principles of the religion. Religious education is now usually taught at the weekend, out of school time. The curriculum of the few independent Zoroastrian schools has to include a textbook on religion published by the Ministry of Education and Training. There are Marriage Registration offices for Zoroastrians in Tehran, Yazd, and Kerman, with two licensed registrars in Tehran, four in Yazd, and three in Kerman. The license to register a Zoroastrian marriage is issued through the Ministry of Justice, which usually chooses priests, rather than laymen, to perform this function.

Some of the small village communities around Yazd have their own Zoroastrian associations, which are supported by the main *anjuman* in Yazd and by the Central Anjuman in Tehran. There are also *anjumans* active in the cities of Kerman, Isfahan, and Shiraz. In 1956, the Tehran *anjuman* extended its Council by two seats, and two women were accepted onto the Board.[37] The *anjumans* offer financial support towards the upkeep of fire temples, the celebration of *gahanbars* and *jashans*, festivals such as Nav Ruz and Mihragan, and rites of passage including initiations, weddings, and funerals. An annual National Conference of Zoroastrian *anjumans* and organizations is held, which helps to generate a sense of solidarity and common purpose.

Outside India and Iran, formal Zoroastrian associations exist in Europe, North America, Australia, New Zealand, Kuwait, Singapore, and Hong Kong. In all of these regions, although they are accorded the rights of any other minority group, Zoroastrians must obey the law of the land, which means that they could not build ever-burning fires in places of worship without the approval and oversight of a fire marshal, nor could they construct a place of exposure for the dead. The Zoroastrian community in Karachi, Pakistan, has been able to maintain its *dakhmenashini* system.

The oldest established Zoroastrian organization in Europe is the Zoroastrian Trust Funds of Europe, Inc. (ZTFE), which was founded in London in 1861. ZTFE manages a registered place of worship, the Zoroastrian Centre in London. Registrars appointed by the association are legally authorized to solemnize weddings and to issue certificates of marriages within that center. ZTFE defines itself as the "local *Anjuman* of the United Kingdom and [of] the Federation of Anjumans in Europe for Parsi and Irani Zarthushti members."

The Federation of Zoroastrian Associations of North America (FEZANA) is the largest umbrella group of Zoroastrian organizations. It was founded in 1986 and registered as a non-profit, religious and charitable organization in the State of Illinois the following year. FEZANA functions as a central nexus, or—as it terms itself—"a coordinating organization" for the 27 individual Zoroastrian Associations of North America. The main centers of Zoroastrian populations in America are, in numerical order: Los Angeles, the New York tri-state area, the Washington DC area, Houston and Dallas in Texas, and Chicago. In Canada, the cities of Toronto, Ottawa, Vancouver, and Montreal all have flourishing Zoroastrian associations. A few of these North American locations have two Zoroastrian organizations in the same neighborhood, one for Parsis, and one for Iranians. The division, although ostensibly along ethno-cultural lines, also relates to the differences in belief and praxis between "traditionalists" and "progressives," as described earlier.

Other lay organizations that hold significant power are the World Zoroastrian Organization (WZO), founded in London in 1980 in order to represent the many Iranian Zoroastrian refugees seeking asylum in other countries after the Iranian Revolution. A significant function of WZO is the practical aid that it provides to impoverished Parsi farmers in Gujarat, which includes digging wells, leveling land, providing bullocks and other animals, building houses or improving existing housing conditions, and supplying medical aid. In its bid to serve as a world body, rather than an offshoot of an existing organization, from the outset WZO permitted individual as well as group membership, including that of non-Zoroastrian spouses. This is a feature that traditionalists find unacceptable, since it could conceivably place control of what was intended to be a globally representative institution into the hands of "Zoroastrians by choice" or non-Zoroastrians. One of the reasons for the formation of the traditionalist organization WAPIZ was to counter this possibility.

WHO DETERMINES THE RELIGIOUS CALENDAR?

This question about the religious calendar may not seem to fit easily within the current focus on the "Word" and the authority associated with its recitation or interpretation. I have decided to mention it here, however, because whoever determines the religious calendar controls much of the ritual expression of the community. The religious calendar also reflects the predominant religious perspective. Just as when the Gregorian calendar replaced the Julian calendar in England in 1752, so changes in the Zoroastrian religious calendar at various points in the history of the religion have led to great internal turmoil.

There is no evidence that Zoroastrians have ever selected a particular day of the week to congregate to hear the sacred word. From early on there seem to have been five separate times of day to worship, which are referred to in Avestan prayers in the *Khordeh Avesta*. During each period, prayers are recited by both priests and laity, which include the praise of Ahura Mazda, the *amesha spentas*, the *fravashis*, and Zarathushtra. The times and the prayers are known as the five *gah* ("times"). These are:

1. *Havan gah*—the "time of [*haoma*] pressing"; from dawn to mid-morning.
2. *Rapithwin*—mid-morning to mid-afternoon; known as second *havan* in fall and winter.

3. *Uzayarin*—from mid-afternoon to sunset.
4. *Aiwisruthrim*—from sunset to midnight.
5. *Ushahin*—from midnight to dawn.

Greek authors tell us that the Achaemenid kings would get up at dawn to say prayers. Herodotus recounts that before crossing the Hellespont to do battle with the Greeks, Xerxes rose before dawn, and then faced the rising sun to say his prayers and to make an offering to the waters (*Histories* 7.54). In the *Cyropaedia*, which is probably based on the author's own experience as a mercenary under Cyrus the Younger, Xenophon describes how the king's tent faced to the east, and that as the dawn rose, Cyrus would chant a hymn, having summoned the *magi* to perform offerings (*Cyropaedia* 8.5.3; 8.1.23; 4.5.14).

A liturgical calendar

Herodotus also tangentially records the existence of a luni-solar calendar comprised of 12 months of 30 days, when he relates that the Cilicians paid tribute of 360 white horse to the Persians—one for each day in the year (*Histories* 3.90). During the Achaemenid period, this 360-day calendar was extended by five days to form an official religious calendar. This "Avestan" calendar, which is known to have operated in Cappadocia, included 12 months named after six *amesha spentas* and other *yazatas*, including Tishtrya and Mithra. One of the months was named after the "*fravashis* of the *ashavans*," which is also an Avestan term.

The Avestan calendar that is attested in Cappadocia is a model for the existing order of the liturgical calendar in use today. Ostraca found at Nisa, the eastern capital of the Parthians, provide evidence for the continuity of a calendrical system using Avestan month-names relating to the *amesha spentas*, such as Spenta Armaiti, Asha Vahishta, Haurvatat, and Ameretat. This Parthian use of a religious (Zoroastrian) almanac, rather than the Greek calendar, extends to the use of Avestan day names, such as the "day of Mithra." During the early Sasanian period, the Bactrian calendar of the Kushans also used such day-names from an Avestan original.

Clay tablets from Persepolis record offerings made to the *fravashis* of the *ashavans* (Elam. *Irtana-fruiritish*), which indicates a special time of recognition of these beings. Today, the liturgical calendar concludes the year with the celebration of Farvardigan ("of the *fravashis*"), a ten-day festival at the end of the month that leads into the New Year (Nav Ruz). This "all souls" commemoration at the end of the year is known as *Hamaspathmaedaya* in the Young Avesta (Yt. 13.49–52). It is thought that the Achaemenids also gathered to celebrate the festival of Mithra, held on the day dedicated to Mithra in the month bearing his name. This festival is alluded to by Strabo as "Mithrakana" (*Geographia* 11.14.9), and is celebrated by Iranian Zoroastrians today as Mihragan. (See Chapter 3, "Annual Festivals").

The Sasanians continued to use the Avestan calendar, but with some modifications. Under Hormizd I (272–273 CE) the five inserted days were dedicated to the *Gathas*. By the mid-first millennium CE, the calendar had become detached from the cycle of the natural year, and so was adjusted in order to realign Nav Ruz with the spring equinox, and to return the other festivals to their original seasonal placement. The term *gahanbar*—"the time of the *Gathas*"— for the five days before Nav Ruz was also used for the other seasonal festivals, which were likewise celebrated over five days, although Farvardigan, the last of the six *gahanbars*, was celebrated over ten days.

At around the end of Safavid rule in Iran, Zoroastrians immigrating to India brought with them the seeds of a controversy relating to the liturgical calendar. This confusion over the calendar is mentioned in the *Persian Rivayats* of the period and still reverberates today. The Iranian Zoroastrian calendar differed by a month from that of the Parsis. Assuming that their co-religionists from Iran had kept to an early, original form of the calendar, one group of Parsis chose to adopt the Iranian schema, which is referred to as the *Qadimi*, or "ancient," calendar. Most Parsis were unwilling to accept this new calendar, however, and they are known as *Rasmi*s ("traditionalists") or *Shehenshais* (often translated as "imperial").

The calendar dispute was largely focused on determining the proper time to celebrate the *gahanbars* and the days honoring the *yazatas*. It also involved a certain measure of lay dissatisfaction with the control of the religion by the priesthood. The confusion was further compounded at the beginning of the twentieth century, when K. R. Cama, a Parsi polymath and businessman, introduced the *Fasli* ("seasonal") calendar. This calendar, based on the lines of the

Gregorian calendar, retained the 365 days, but included a regulatory leap day every four years at the end of the year. Nav Ruz was placed once more on the spring equinox.

In India, there are now three different Parsi calendrical systems in operation, which affect the date of community observance of the seasonal festivals, particularly the New Year. The majority of Parsis follow the Shehenshai calendar, which observes *Muktad*—the Parsi equivalent of Farvardigan—and then the New Year in late summer. Many Parsis also celebrate March 21 as *Jamsheedi Nav Ruz*, along-side the Iranian celebration of the spring equinox. In Iran and among Iranian communities outside the country, Nav Ruz festivities take place on the spring equinox and are celebrated not only by Zoroastrians, but also Muslims, Jews, Christians, and Baha'is. Since the breakup of the Soviet Union, this celebration is now also common in parts of Central Asia and Azerbaijan.

All Zoroastrians date the beginning of their religious calendar to the same starting point—the accession year of Yazdegerd III, the last Sasanian king. This took place in 632 CE, and each year is referred to as *anno Yazdegerdi*. In Iran, on the accession of Reza Shah Pahlavi to the throne in 1925, a luni-solar calendar along the lines of the Fasli calendar, based on Zoroastrian month names, was introduced by the Iranian parliament. This is now the main calendar among Zoroastrians in Iran, although some older people in Yazd follow the *qadimi* calendar, since they felt that they could not abandon what they perceived as a traditional and authoritative ritual calendar.

The Zoroastrian calendar does not have a distinct week, with seven days that repeat during the course of the month. Instead, the 30 days of the month are named sequentially, beginning with Ahura Mazda, the six *amesha spentas* and 20 *yazatas*. Every eighth day is dedicated to Ahura Mazda (days 1, 8, 15, and 23). When the day and the month name are the same, it is a special time of celebration. Such days include *Mihragan* (the festival of Mithra), *Aban Yazad Jashan* (the festival of the waters), *Adargan* (the festival of fire), and *Tirgan* (the festival of Tishtrya). These now mostly last only one day, but Tirgan may extend over a longer period. Every month, *Behram Ruz* (the day of Verethragna, *yazata* of "victory") is the day that many lay Zoroastrians choose to visit the fire temple or a local shrine.

WHAT IS THE REASON FOR THE WESTERN
FASCINATION WITH ZARATHUSHTRA?

This is a question that relates to the authority that has been privileged to Zarathushtra/Zoroaster by non-Zoroastrians throughout the ages. Beyond the confines of the history of the Zoroastrian faith, the image of Zarathushtra has been portrayed in many disparate ways since the early Greeks first spoke of "Zoroaster." The founder of a religious tradition is always viewed differently by a believer than by an outside admirer or an interested academic. What is so appealing to the imagination about the figure of Zarathushtra that there should be such a recurrence of his image throughout "outsider" history?

The image of Zoroaster in external accounts usually coincides with the predilection of his "biographer." This provides one clue to his appeal—he is an emblem, a literary cipher for the message of the author who appropriates the authority of Zarathushtra. Certain classical Greek writers begin this process of transforming Zarathushtra into a figure of authority for some of their own philosophers. Instead of relegating the founder of the Persian religion to the role of "barbarian," these Greeks provide numerous reconstructions of Zoroaster as an historical individual who fits neatly into a succession of ancient thinkers and teachers. Greek texts from the fourth century BCE onward speak of Zoroaster variously as Pythagoras' teacher; an ancient precursor to Plato in the fight for the Good; the originator of the Chaldean Oracles; and the founder of magic, astrology, or alchemy. Such descriptions of the character and teaching of Zoroaster place him as an ancient "eastern" sage, whose wisdom informed Greek philosophy and so gave it authority. The attributes and persona ascribed to Zoroaster in these classical sources influenced the later European image of Zoroaster, leading eventually to his transmutation into such diverse characters as Sarastro in Mozart's *Zauberflöte* ("The Magic Flute") and Zarathustra in Nietzsche's eponymous work, *Also Sprach Zarathustra*.

The Greek appropriation of Zoroaster as a precursor to Pythagoras and Plato, and the attribution of arcane oracular sayings to him, later enabled Zoroaster to be commandeered by Christian Renaissance scholars to fulfill a similar role as the all-round primordial Wise Man—the first in a line of "Ancient Theologians." Indeed, it could be said that the only other figure that appears in a European context as such a powerful metaphor across the ages is that of Christ. The European portrayal of Zoroaster throughout history is developed in ways that both complement and confront the *imago Christi*: sometimes, Zoroaster is depicted as a great teacher who prefigures Christ, being identified with a character from the Hebrew Bible tradition; elsewhere, he is portrayed as the precursor of a deistic, rationalistic ideology that rebuts the uniqueness of Christianity.

Renaissance scholars relied on Latin translations of early Christian Syriac texts, in which Zoroaster was identified as the Mesopotamian king Nimrod, or a member of Nimrod's family, such as his father Cush, his grandfather Chaim, or his uncle Mesraim, all of whom were descended from Noah, via his son Ham. Syriac commentators on the passage in Matthew's Gospel about the journey of the *magi* recognize these figures as followers of Zoroaster, whose authority originated within the Hebrew tradition. In a couple of these commentaries, Zoroaster is identified as Baruch, the scribe of Jeremiah. The commentaries portray the *magi* as acknowledging the infant Jesus for what he is within Christianity, and so providing "outsider" validation for the Christian tradition. During the Renaissance a chain of continuity was perceived as stretching from Zoroaster through the Greek philosophers—particularly Plato—and Moses, directly to Jesus. In this manner, the person of Zoroaster became integrated into a chain of authoritative beings throughout history each of whom points to the truths of Christianity.

In contrast to this placement of Zoroaster as one of several ancient theologians who paved the way for Christ, later European deists elevated him as a symbol of the age of reason and enlightenment. Zoroaster's pre-Christian wisdom was seen as counteracting the intellectual stagnation and censorship of the Church. Enlightenment philosophers who challenged the authority of the Church were attracted to the distinctive message of Zoroaster that humans were good, and possessed the ability to make rational decisions between good and evil. This message fitted with the deists' own perception of the human condition and seemed to dispense with the problem of theodicy that arose within both Judaism and Christianity. In his *Philosophical Dictionary*, Voltaire stated that the morality of all the philosophers "from Zoroaster to Lord Shaftesbury" was "absolutely the same," but that Zoroaster took chronological precedence over all other moralists in teaching humans what they already knew in their hearts.[38]

A month prior to his death in 1778, Voltaire had been introduced into a Masonic lodge in Paris by a fellow freethinker, Benjamin Franklin, who by that time had been a Freemason for over 40 years. In 1772, Franklin had written a letter from London to a fellow amateur scientist named Ezra Stiles, who went on to became the president of Yale College. In the letter, Franklin encouraged Stiles to read a recently published work from Paris containing the "theological, philosophical and moral ideas" and religious ceremonies that an ancient "legislator" named Zoroaster had established. Both Benjamin Franklin and a contemporary young Freemason from Austria—an energetic musical prodigy named Wolfgang Amadeus Mozart—found great appeal in the ancient Iranian teacher.

Mozart went so far as to incorporate Zoroaster into his opera "The Magic Flute" in the form of Sarastro, the high priest of the Temple of Wisdom. In this overt appropriation of the person of Zoroaster as a 3D protagonist, Mozart was following the precedent of Jean-Philippe Rameau, whose French-style opera *Zoroastre* had introduced the figure of the *instituteur des Mages*—"the founder of the *Magi*"—onto the European stage for the first time in 1749. Such dramatic depictions placed Zoroaster in the limelight at a time of great intellectual ferment in Europe. This focus continued into the following century, as the authority of Zoroaster became augmented by the translation of texts ascribed to him and those that were about him.

As an academic philologist during this time of energetic textual discovery and translation, Nietzsche numbered several Iranists and Indologists among his friends. He seems to have deliberately replaced theology with philology, in terms of ascribing the origin of language and mythology to the product of human history rather than to a divine scheme. Nietzsche wrote: "What constitutes the tremendous uniqueness of that Persian in history is [that] Zarathustra was the first to see in the struggle between good and evil the actual wheel in the working of things."[39] Through his perception that it was Zarathushtra who had first spoken of morality as both cause and effect in the domain of metaphysics, Nietzsche unearthed Zarathushtra from under the pile of textual material and hermeneutic wrangling that was preoccupying contemporary European scholars. Nietzsche's own reinvention of Zarathushtra was an attempt to emancipate the modern world from the morality of "received religion", particularly Christianity. In April 1883, Nietzsche wrote to a female friend about his new philosophical poem, *Also Sprach Zarathustra*:

"It is a wonderful affair; I have challenged all religions and made a new 'Holy Book.'"[40]

Nietzsche openly tackles the parallels and differences between Zarathushtra and Christ as authoritative teachers, when he asks of Zarathushtra, "Who is this person to us?" This same question is now being posed by Zoroastrians of themselves. Alexander Baird, a Swedish author, artist, and a "Zoroastrian by choice," writes on his blog: "The point is to *get to know* a *person* called Zarathushtra . . . and then try to understand *how he thinks and why* and then *apply* that to our contemporary society and *our* lives . . . . . *The question is how would Zarathushtra think and act if he had been around with us here today?*"[41]

This statement—an echo of the "What Would Jesus Do?" challenge to action that is popular among Christians—presents a twenty-first century slant on the matter of defining who is "like Zarathushtra." It asks *how* to interpret—and, obliquely, *who* has the authority to interpret—the various elements of the message that bears the name of Zarathushtra. The question also invites Zoroastrians to consider how Zarathushtra may be an exemplary model for their personal faith and daily action. The focus of Chapter 3—the "Deeds"—is on the practical expressions and applications of the religion that relate to the model and the message.

CHAPTER 3

DEEDS, OR HOW ZOROASTRIANS PUT RELIGION INTO ACTION

This chapter explores the practical application of Thought and Word to Deed. The beliefs summarized in Chapter 1 of this book form the underlying basis for the ethical action of Zoroastrians. The putting-into-practice of that ethic both inside and outside the home and fire temple will be discussed here. The prayers and litanies referred to in Chapter 2 have been preserved through their recitation in ritual contexts, and some of these praxes are examined here within both domestic and priestly contexts. The following questions are addressed:

What does daily praxis involve?
Do Zoroastrians have special dietary rules?
What is the role of fire in Zoroastrian worship?
What do priests do?
What are the Zoroastrian rites of passage?
What festivals occur in the Zoroastrian calendar?
Are there gender differences with regard to praxis?
How do Zoroastrians put their ethics into practice?

No matter what one's religious and/or moral compass may be, putting belief into action is not easy. The conscious formulation of religious principle as the basis for behavior was expressed in the imperial propaganda of the Ancient Persian king, Darius I. As the self-proclaimed representative of Ahura Mazda on the earth, Darius claims, somewhat sanctimoniously, to desire always that which is right and not to "follow the lie"; nor has he done anything crooked, but has walked the straight path.[1] Darius asks that he, his family, and country may be protected from the "stink of evil," and that humanity in general may not stray from that straight path (DNa 51–60). These sentiments echo those of the *Gathas*, where those who follow the Lie are diverted from the right way and wander off the "paths of Order," but those who follow the straight path arrive at the place where Ahura Mazda is (Y. 51.13; 43.3).

In his inscriptions and some of his iconography, Darius promotes his role as king as affecting both the material and moral welfare of his subjects. As mentioned earlier, he considers it his duty to protect his people and their possessions from enemy attacks, famine, and the Lie. Darius states that his actions speak for themselves of his purpose, which derives from his "quickness in thought and comprehension" (DNb 16–32). In his capacity as one who should keep his country healthy, the king acts as moral arbiter, punishing those who side with evil and the Lie, or who act "crookedly"—in other words, those whose thoughts, words, and deeds are "bad" (DB 4.36–40, 67–69; 1.20–22; DNb 16–24). In contrast, Darius expresses his satisfaction with those who exert themselves to achieve their potential and to be effective in their own homeland. The impression from these official Achaemenid statements is that there is no middle ground in behavioral terms for the king and his people: they are either actively destructive ("crooked") or positively effective.

Such imperial propaganda from 2500 years ago represents an ancient Iranian ideal of the good rule of the Mazda-worshipping king. How does this royal Persian self-portrait relate to the daily praxis of Zoroastrians in the twenty-first century? The connection lies in the fact that, although the king does not announce himself to be "like Zarathushtra," his words and apparent actions signify that he adheres to the Avestan model of the *ashavan*, who worships Ahura Mazda and promotes that which is good and right while working towards removing the Lie. This model of behavior implies that as one detaches from evil, so one moves towards a state of health and happiness. The achievement of this increase of good is thought to occur through life-affirming actions, including personal and priest-conducted ritual, which give substance to the theoretical principles of the religion.

WHAT DOES DAILY PRAXIS INVOLVE?

The fact that there is no specific day of worship in their liturgical calendar means that nowadays most Zoroastrians only congregate for seasonal festivals, to celebrate a life-cycle ritual of one of their members, or for an educational program. Many groups try to meet more frequently, however, and there may be a regular program of study classes for adults and children on the weekend or in the evenings. To a large extent, however, the religion remains centered in the home and family. The form that domestic praxis takes varies according to the individual. For some Zoroastrians, it is enough just to say their prayers regularly. The prayers of the *Ahuna Vairya*, the *Ashem Vohu*, the *Yenghe Hatam*, and the *Airyaman Ishya* can serve as a focal point for personal daily worship. So also, the individual study of the *Gathas* may become an act of private devotion.

My Iranian Zoroastrian friend, Manijeh, gave me an example of one such individual religious act. Manijeh rises early each morning to stand on her balcony facing the sunrise. She looks to the sun as she says her morning prayers, which include the *Fravarane*, the statement of faith. This ancient creed is preceded by the words "*Jasa me avanghe*" recited three times. The phrase means "Come to my help, O Mazda." Manijeh maintains that, in beginning the morning this way, she reminds herself of the source of light, warmth, and creation, and commits herself to promote those same qualities throughout the day ahead.

Dr. Maneck S. Wadia, a Parsi who now lives in southern California, described how his father, Khanbahadur Sorabji Wadia, who was the shipping master of the port of Bombay, dealt with his highly stressful job: "Each night, before going to sleep, he said a short prayer, 'Yatha, tari mudad', leaving his problems to be resolved by 'God, your help'. He always slept soundly." According to Maneck, his father was a man who rarely lectured his family on values, but whose personal faith and professional integrity were both evidence of religion-in-action in his everyday life.

Many Zoroastrians, particularly those who might identify themselves as traditionalist, feel that a purely mental focus as one prays is insufficient. There needs to be a practical engagement of those thoughts and words in the material existence. It is for this reason that those Zoroastrians continue to wear the *sudreh* and *kusti*, and to say their *kusti* prayers on a regular basis. (For a depiction of these two garments, see Fig. 2.4)

Although such external action as untying and tying the *kusti* while saying prayers may be considered as perfunctory ritual or even as "superstitious" by some Zoroastrians, traditionalists maintain that it is a crucial means of upholding the good religion. The difference in perception is not so much across cultural lines, but based more on how the individual feels about the two garments. For some, they are just an outer symbol of the Zoroastrian religion worn at initiation to represent the adherent's intention to promote good and dispel evil. For others, the wearing of the garments is a way of actualizing that intention. Since evil has a real presence in the world, it must be dealt with through physical action in the form of ritual as well as ethical behavior. In untying and retying the *kusti* throughout the day, it is as if the individual weaves a protective barrier around the body as a defense mechanism against the onslaught of evil. In this sense, the actions of each individual as microcosm are thought to have wider macrocosmic repercussions.

Other examples of daily praxis that may be encountered in Zoroastrian homes around the world include the recitation of morning prayers in front of a fire. Rusi, a Parsi born in India, who now lives in northern California, describes his recollection of lighting the oil lamp (*divo*) in front of which his family would pray:

> The prayer table was where mom or dad, whosoever got ready first in the morning, would light the *divo*. The kids got their turns on their birthdays. The *divo* used to be a short glass partly filled with water topped with pure ghee [clarified butter] or cooking oil . . . with a long *kakrow* [wick], held by a metallic clip or a floating *kakrow* on a cork, or even a candle that was kept alight perpetually. As pure ghee became expensive, it was only used on festive occasions or on birthdays. In our uncle's house in Bombay the *divo* was suspended from the ceilings in all the main rooms, in an old-fashioned chandelier, like you find in some of the *Atash Bahrams*.

When relating the daily praxes that she grew up with, Ryna, a young Parsi woman, spoke of the ceremonial tray (*seis*) that was kept in one of the bedrooms of her grandmother and great-grandmother's homes:

> A *divo*, or small lamp, burned continuously, and small offerings of whole roasted *gram* (chickpeas), or sugar candy were kept on the silver tray with the fire. Pictures of Zoroaster the prophet and deceased family members were also set nearby on the table. In front of this *seis* was where all prayers were said in the home. At night, my grandmother would go through the entire house with burning sandalwood, perfuming the air with smoke. She told me it was to keep out mosquitoes, and to help us sleep. I learned later that the tradition was called *loban*, and that it is done in almost every Parsi household.

Figure 3.1 Anahita, a Parsi living in Dallas, Texas, takes the *loban* around the house. Photo by Jenny Rose.

A similar ritual still takes place in many homes in Iran, either in the morning or in the evening. In the Yazdi Zoroastrian ethnolect of Dari, this perfuming is called *tash o sven*, which means "fire and *esfand*." *Esfand* is the Persian name for the harmel plant. Up until about 30 years ago in traditional neighborhoods in Yazd, each morning the women of the household would sweep the area outside the home, and sprinkle water on the ground to keep the dust down, before placing some resinous incense on the portable fire holder and

taking it round the home. Mandana, a young Zartoshti woman born
and educated in Tehran, describes the practice:

> There are some, if not all, Zoroastrians who perfume the house
> in the mornings. In fact in my family, my father did it every
> morning . . . My grandparents also performed it. They emigrated
> from Yazd in their early 20s. I would say there are still people who
> will perfume the house off and on if not every morning.

In those urban families where both husband and wife go to work,
the *tash o sven* ritual is now only performed during weekends or on
festival days, such as Nav Ruz, the *gahanbars*, death ceremonies, or
name days for the *yazatas*. Here, too, the perfuming of the house is
regarded as both an act of physical disinfectant, aimed at keeping
away biting bugs, and one that disperses a fragrant and healthy atmo-
sphere throughout the home.

One custom that relates to keeping the house both ritually and
physically clean is that of wearing slippers or socks inside, rather
than padding around with bare feet. This practice is recommended in
the *Persian Rivayats* of the sixteenth century: the rationale seems to
be that one might inadvertently bring "dead matter" into the house
on bare feet and so pollute the ground, which is the domain of *spenta
armaiti*. Foot coverings such as slippers are considered to act as a
barrier for such matter.

DO ZOROASTRIANS HAVE SPECIAL DIETARY RULES?

Festival and social gatherings of Zoroastrians, wherever they are in
the world, always involve the blessing, sharing, and enjoyment of
food. Such activities attest to a positive view of the material world,
and to the fact that there has been little emphasis on asceticism in the
history of the religion. It was noted earlier that in Zoroastrian texts,
the way one lives one's life leads to a place that is either satisfying or
disappointing to the senses: acts of cruelty and corruption lead to the
"house of the lie," where the food is bad; but a sweet scented breeze
and a "house of song" meet the soul of the righteous person. The
aroma of freshly cooked food at communal gatherings is said to
remind the co-religionists of the good things that await them. So,
good food is a central part of most celebrations, acting as a welcome
and purposeful accompaniment to prayer.

The notion that sharing food together is more than just a social gathering, but a solemn occasion for giving thanks, is expressed in a Middle Persian text called *Sur i Saxwan*. This text dates to Sasanian times and records a dinnertime speech at a grand banquet. The Sasanian practice of keeping silent during meals was known as being "surrounded by *baj*." The Middle Persian *Menog-i Xrad* (1.33) and the later *Persian Rivayat*s consider the practice of eating while talking as contrary to the religion. My Parsi grandmother, Shereen, who grew up near Rawalpindi at the beginning of the twentieth century, told me how her mother, Meherbai, would pack her breakfast in a tiffin box, which she would take with her to the Irish Roman Catholic school that she attended. As the sun rose over the Himalayas, grandma would make her way in a pony and trap to the school, where she would eat her breakfast in silence, while the Christian girls celebrated Mass in the church. Today, this custom of eating in silence is mostly obsolete, although some devout priests and laity will only speak with muted voices after saying the blessing before a meal.

Zoroastrians do not have a set of dietary codes but are admonished not to eat the miscreations of Angra Mainyu—the "creeping animals" (*xraftsra*) of the Avestan texts. One Young Avestan passage states clearly that living beings cannot survive without nourishment, and that humans should only consume things that are beneficial to them (Vd. 3.33). There are no foods that are particular to either gender. Additions to a woman's diet during pregnancy are to keep her healthy, and after birth, to help her milk production, but have no particular religious significance. The notion of dietary deprivation over an extended period does not fit with the Zoroastrian understanding of humanity's role in creation. But humans are not supposed to overindulge to the extent that they become unhealthy. Xenophon refers to the Persian custom of exercising self-restraint during meals (*Cyropaedia* I.2.8), and Ammianus Marcellinus (c. 330–395 CE) later claims that Persians avoid both extravagant feasting and excessive drinking, but only eat moderately, as much as they need (*Histories* 23.6.76–8). This approach anticipates the later notion of *payman*, the "right measure" in all things: one should not eat an excess of food, nor food that is bad for health, nor should one have a diet deficient in healthy food.

The traditional cuisine of both Parsis and Iranian Zoroastrians favors meat from herbivores or poultry. In India, beef and pork are often avoided out of deference to Hindu or Muslim neighbors respectively, and this sensibility is retained by some older Parsis living elsewhere. Fish remains a favorite at birth celebrations and weddings for Parsis, and at the New Year (Nav Ruz) for Iranians. Dried fruit and nuts are also staples of religious celebrations. Grapes, apricots, mulberries, and pistachios are still grown in family alotments in the region of Yazd, and are donated to the community to form the *lork*, a ceremonial food consisting of seven types of dried fruits, dates, chickpeas, and nuts, which is shared among the community at the end of the recitation of festival or celebratory prayers. These foods are thought to represent the beneficent activity of Ahura Mazda in their immediate environment. In Parsi celebrations, the dried fruits and nuts are incorporated into the festive foods of *Ravo*, a sweet dairy dish of milk, semolina, and ghee, or *Sev*, which consists of vermicelli fried in ghee and then cooked gently in sugar water, and topped with fried nuts and raisins.

At a recent culinary demonstration by a Parsi priest's wife in Chicago, I learnt that many younger women have never been taught how to make *Malido*, the special dish prepared for the prayer ceremony at a death anniversary and for *Muktad*, the annual "all souls" festival at the end of the year. *Malido* is another sweet dish, made with ghee, wheat flour, semolina, nuts, milk, sugar, spices, and dried fruit. Those who do know how to cook the dish each have their own preference as to how it should taste. Such familiar dishes can act as both a mnemonic of past family events, and also bring comfort to those gathered together.

At the beginning of the twentieth century, the Parsee Vegetarian and Temperance Society was formed. This movement was partly influenced by the Theosophical movement, which had been introduced to Bombay by Madame Blavatsky and Colonel Olcott in 1879. It was also motivated by the intention of bringing the world nearer to *frasho.kereti*. Middle Persian texts explain that just as the first pair of humans consumed water, then plants, then milk, then meat, so in the final millennia, humanity will progressively forego each of these food in reverse until the final "world benefactor" arrives and the earth is established as wholly good and undying (Bd. 34.1–3).

A similar rationale probably lies behind the abstention from meat, poultry, and sometimes also eggs, during the eleventh month of the calendar, dedicated to Bahman (Vohu Manah). The vegetarian diet can last the whole month, or for just the four days of the month relating to the animal kingdom, the particular care of Vohu Manah. Those four days are: Bahman, Gosh (Av. *Geush Urvan*—the "soul of the cow"), Mah (moon), and Ram (joy, air). Some regard it as a religious duty not to eat "flesh foods" for those same four days every month.

One Zartoshti women described this "animal appreciation day" in her childhood with this recollection: "I remember one occasion when I was at a cinema in Tehran with friends. During the interval I was eating a meat sandwich. Halfway through I suddenly remembered it was Bahman Rooz [Bahman Day]! The others continued eating, but I went hungry until the next day!"[2]

Most Zoroastrians also abstain from eating meat for three days after the death of a family member or loved one, when the soul is believed to linger nearby, until the time of reckoning on the morning of the fourth day.

In keeping with the idea that life is supposed to be enjoyed, there is no restriction on the consumption of alcohol, unless it impairs one's judgment. As a religious minority in Muslim-dominant Iran, Zoroastrians are permitted to include a glass of wine among the items spread out on the *sofreh* or table at community festivals.

Although some Zoroastrians do smoke, some refrain because they feel it involves the pollution of fire through the saliva on the cigarette or pipe, the smoke produced, and the extinction of the match. Others choose not to smoke for health reasons.

WHAT IS THE ROLE OF FIRE IN ZOROASTRIAN WORSHIP?

The matter of smoking raises the question of the central role of fire in Zoroastrian ritual. The significance of fire as a symbol of Ahura Mazda was addressed in Chapter 1, but it is appropriate here to expand the discussion to consider how reverence is shown to this element.

My student, Ryna, remarked that many of her friends first came into contact with the fact that she was a Zoroastrian, as they were toasting marshmallows together over a campfire. She related:

My marshmallow caught on fire—a common occurrence. My reaction, however, wasn"t quite so ordinary. I turned to the friend next to me yelping, "Help! Blow this out for me!" With a confused look, he complied. The problem, I explained, with blowing out my own marshmallow was that, as a Zoroastrian, I revere fire as a symbol of Ahura Mazda, our God. We believe that to blow out fire would be to pollute it with our breath—thus, blowing out a small fire is forbidden.

The question concerning the importance of fire, when considered within the context of how Zoroastrians put their beliefs into practice, leads to questions about what fire temples are, and what happens inside a fire temple.

Fire temples

"Fire temple" is the generic Zoroastrian term for a structure that houses either a consecrated fire or, in a few cases, an unconsecrated fire. Most fire temples consist of an assembly hall for general gathering, a place for washing and performing *kusti* prayers, and a prayer room that has access to the fire. The fire itself is placed on a square plinth, known as a *takht*, or "throne," which may be enclosed. The fire sanctuary is called the *gombad* (see Fig. 3.2 on p. 132).

Some Zoroastrians in urban India or Iran live close enough to a fire temple to be able to visit it on their way to or from work, or in their lunch hour. Certain fires are considered to be particularly holy by Parsis. These fires are mostly located in the more important fire temples, and are visited by large numbers on auspicious days, as well as being the focus of individual worship throughout the year. For those who live some distance away from a fire temple—which includes most Zoroastrians living in countries outside India or Iran—the only time that they might attend a fire temple is for the congregational celebration of a *jashan* (a ceremony of praise and thanksgiving), a seasonal or annual festival, or for an initiation, wedding, or memorial service.

There are three main types of fire temple with permanently burning fires. Each fire temple is defined by the type of fire that it holds.

1. *Atash Bahram*
The *Atash Bahram*, meaning "victory fire", is often popularly known as the "cathedral fire." It is the most important or "highest grade" fire, comprising 16 different types of fire, such as fire caused by lightning, a hearth fire, the fire of a potter and of a goldsmith (Cf. PRDd. 18e6–20). After all the fires have been collected, they are purified and consecrated separately. This is a lengthy process that can last up to a

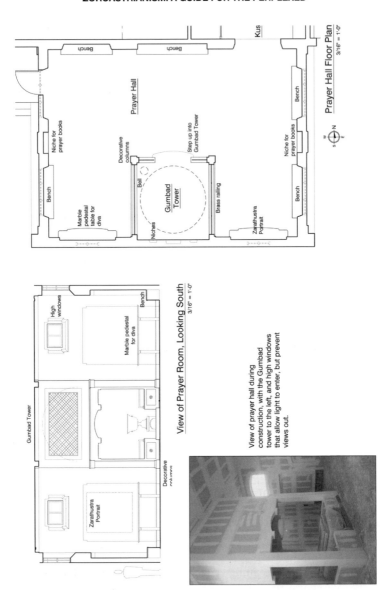

Figure 3.2 Views of the Prayer Room of the Zoroastrian Center now under construction in Dallas, Texas, for the Zoroastrian Association of North Texas. Architectural plan and photo courtesy of Cyrus Rivetna of Rivetna Architects Inc. © Rivetna Architects Inc.

year, and requires the services of many priests. The fires are then combined together. Then follows a series of ceremonies conducted over several days by the priests, before the "victory" fire is eventually enthroned and consecrated. India has eight such fires, four of which are located in Mumbai, the rest in the northwestern state of Gujarat, where Zoroastrians emigrating from Iran after the Arab conquest first landed. The oldest existing Atash Bahram in India was established in a temple building in Udvada, Gujarat, in 1742 CE. The fire it contains is known as *Iranshah* ("King of Iran") and is believed to have been transported from Iran to Sanjan on the northwest coast of India a thousand years earlier.

In Iran, an Atash Bahram is located in the city of Yazd, although local Zoroastrians do not commonly use this designation. A building was first constructed there with Parsi funding in the late nineteenth century, and reconstructed in the 1930s, but the fire it contains is said to be very ancient, having been preserved in secret by the priests in Yazd since Sasanian times. The oldest *atash bahram* fire in the world is said to be located at Sharifabad, a village to the north of Yazd.

Figure 3.3 The *Atash Bahram*, Yazd, Iran. Photo by Jenny Rose.

2. *Atash Adaran*

Atash Adaran means "fire of fires." An *Adaran* fire includes four different types of fire, which come from hearthfires belonging to the four classes named in Yasna 19.17. These are: priests; warriors or rulers; farmers; and artisans or craftsmen. The majority of fires in Iran and India belong to this category, and are housed in a building referred to as an *atashkadeh* or *agiary* respectively. There are 16 *ateshkadehs* in Iran with Adaran fires and about 200 *agiaries* throughout India, with 50 in Mumbai, the city where the majority of India's Parsis reside. The Adaran fire does not need a high priest (*dastur*) to supervise the priests serving the fire, which can be looked after by a *mobed*. In Iran, due to the lack of trained priests, both the fire and the ritual life of the *atashkadeh* is often now the responsiblity of a *mobedyar*, a trained layperson.

3. *Atash Dadgah*

The third type of fire is known as a Dadgah fire. Dadgah means "a lawful place." The name derives from the Avestan term *daityo gatu*, which seems to refer to a specific place for fire in the *Videvdad*. The Dadgah fire comprises a single fire, which, once consecrated through the recitation of the Yasna by two priests, is supposed to be kept burning at all times. It may be tended by a *para-mobed* or *mobedyar* (a layman trained as a priest). In the days when most homes had an ever-burning hearth fire, this was also considered to be a Dadgah fire. The *dar-i mihrs* outside Iran and India have unconsecrated Dadgah fires.

Dar-i Mihr

The term *Dar-i Mihr* is probably most accurately translated as the "gate or door of Mithra," but is often popularly interpreted as "house of devotion or light." This phrase, or its more colloquial version *dar-be mehr*, is used generically in Iran to refer to any fire temple and its precincts. It is now applied to the model of fire temple that came into existence when Zoroastrian communities began to establish themselves outside the two homelands. The *dar-i mihr* as a place of worship outside Iran and India usually has an assembly hall and a prayer room, where the fire is located. This Dadgah fire is not kept perpetually burning, but is allowed to "grow cold" naturally or, if it is gas fired, is turned off, and lit again when needed. Even for a fire that is not constantly burning, there are consecration rituals for the building that houses the fire, as well as for its installation.

Figure 3.4 Mobed Dr. Rostam Vahidi demonstrates the offering of sandal-wood to the fire at the Rustam Guiv Dar-i Mihr, Westminster, California. Photo courtesy of Jaehyung Cho.

The first Zoroastrian places of worship to be established in North America—in Toronto, Chicago, New York, Vancouver, southern and northern California, and Washington DC—were funded through a trust established by the Iranian Zoroastrian philanthropists Arbab Rustam and Morvarid Guiv. There is also a *dar-i mihr* in Sydney, Australia. The Zoroastrian association in Hong Kong owns a building that has a priest's accommodation, a library, and a prayer room with a fire that is lit for rituals.

Although to date, none of the diaspora fire temples has a consecrated fire, there has been discussion for the past decade or so—mostly among Parsis—about the possibility of consecrating a Dadgah fire. The London Zoroastrian community was the first to undertake a study to determine whether this was a feasible proposal for their newly acquired center in Harrow. A detailed report was prepared in early 2001 by Malcolm Deboo and Paurushasp Jila, who were then honorary joint secretaries of the ZTFE.[3] In Mumbai, they consulted the retired high priest of the Wadia Atash Bahram, Dastur Firoze Kotwal, along with several other senior priests (*Ervads*), an art historian, and an architect.

Dastur Kotwal has consecrated several fire temples, and responded to the report in a positive manner, recommending that a team of full-time *mobeds* could be employed from seminaries in India, but that if necessary *para-mobeds* (lay assistant priests) could tend the fire on a temporary basis. The compilers of the report suggested that an ever-burning, consecrated fire would receive more respect from the Zoro-astrian community in London. Dastur Kotwal stipulated that access to the fire should be restricted exclusively to Zoroastrians (that is, as in India, to those born of two Zarathushti parents), who have per-formed their *padyab kusti* before approaching the fire.

Before a Dadgah fire can be consecrated, a certain infrastructure needs to be in place, including the construction of a consecrated well with running water, the application of unconsecrated bull's urine (MP *gomez*) to ritually purify the site, a sufficient supply of hardwood to feed the fire, and the special implements to perform the various cere-monies connected with maintaining the fire. Zoroastrian associations would also have to find financing for at least two full-time trained priests or to establish a rota of volunteer *mobeds* or *mobedyars* to tend the fire at all times with due reverence. In London, these practicalities have proved difficult to resolve. The project itself has been somewhat divisive, and so has been shelved for the time being.

At a recent conference in Chicago, sponsored by the local Zoroastrian Association and the Society of Scholars of Zoroastrianism (SSZ), simi-lar plans for consecrated fires in Toronto, Chicago, and Houston were displayed and discussed. These, and several other Zoroastrian Associa-tions throughout North America have aquired properties of sufficient acreage to be able to construct a separate *ateshkadeh* or *agiary* apart from a communal prayer hall. Pallan Ichaporia, one of the co-founders of the SSZ, posted this statement online after the Chicago conference: "There is a possibility that *in the near future an Atash Dadgah will be enthroned in North America*, as the community of faithful has the will, and resources to do so."[4] Dr. Ichaporia realized that the tricky question about admission of non-Zoroastrians to the consecrated Atash Dadgah might well be raised, but thought it best resolved by those who had financed and therefore "owned" the fire.

This comment relates to one of the key discussion points whenever the notion of building a temple with a consecrated fire is raised. Apart from the practicalities of the consecration itself and the subse-quent maintenance of the fire, is the question concerning who will have access to the fire sanctuary. Would it be open to all? Or only to those of Zarathushti parents, or to paid-up members of a Zoroastrian association?

In India, all fire temples are officially restricted to those who are "Parsi" according to the definition provided earlier. In twentitieth-century Iran, as the numbers of priests dwindled, so fire temples were opened, to an extent, to anyone who wanted to visit. In most Iranian fire temples, however, the visitor can only view the fire through glass. An alternative—and apparently ancient—floorplan is retained in several of the fire temples in Yazd, where the main everburning fire is placed to one side out of sight of the casual visitor, and a fire holder placed in the center of the temple is lit on occasions of congregational worship.

The journalist Brian Murphy describes a visit with a Zoroastrian community leader to a fire temple in Yazd, where an ancient fire had, according to local lore, been kept burning in secret for centuries following the Sasanian overthrow:

> The door creaked open. We were immediately hit with the smell of burning wood from deep below . . . He opened a metal door to a tiny chamber. Inside, a fifteen-hundred-year-old fire smoldered in a metal cauldron. Everything in the room was covered with a shiny black resin from the smoke. "Breathe deeply," Yazdani said. "It's good for you."[5]

Inside a fire temple

The custom on entering a fire temple varies according to the individual and the setting. In Iran at the beginning of the last century, the laity began to abandon some of the practices of the religion, such as wearing the *sedreh-kusti*, or the ritual washing (*padyab*) before entering the fire temple, but these now seem to be observed more keenly. Bahman, a young Zoroastrian man from Yazd, told me:

> *Padyab* . . . is performed by washing one's hands and face before entering the fire temple. This is done in designated places in the yard of the building. Of course people would take a shower beforehand at their homes before travelling to the fire temple, but still washing face and hands are practiced.

At the *atashkadeh* those Zoroastrians who do not wear a *kusti* on a daily basis may bring one with them to tie over their *sudreh*. There are caps provided at the fire temple for worshippers to cover their heads before they enter the prayer hall where the fire is located.

Parsis also cover their heads and perform the *padyab kusti*—the ritual wash accompanied by the untying and retying of the *kusti* with the relevant prayers, before entering the the sacred area which holds the fire. Those Parsis who visit the fire temple straight from home will also usually bathe before setting out. Before entering the prayer hall to recite prayers in front of the fire, Parsi adherents will "greet" any representations of Zarathushtra or other holy persons in the temple precinct. The length of time spent in prayer depends on the occasion. Shehnaz Munshi, a Parsi woman who has documented the oral traditions and religious praxes of her community remarked: "Those who visit the fire temple regularly may just offer sandalwood, recite a short prayer and leave, while others may pray longer."[6]

In his short story, "Auspicious Occasions," Rohinton Mistry describes how praying in the fire temple has been a significant element in the life of the main character, Mehroo, since she was young:

> In high school she would visit the fire-temple before exam week. Her offering of a sandalwood stick would be deposited in the silver tray at the door of the inner sanctuary, and she would reverently smear her forehead with the grey ash left in the tray for this purpose. *Dustoor* Dhunjisha, in his flowing white robe, would always be there to greet her . . . The smell of his robe would remind her of mother's sari, fragrant with sandalwood. Serene and fortified, she would go to write her exam.[7]

This short scene, penned by a Mumbai-born Parsi living in Canada, suggests both the sensory experience and the spiritual resonance of this act of worship.

WHAT DO PRIESTS DO?

One of the main functions of Zoroastrian priests since early times has been to feed the fire. In the middle of the Parthian period, the geographer Strabo described the contemporary *magi* in Cappadocia whose fire sanctuaries each had a fireholder containing a large quantity of ashes, where they "keep the fire ever burning."[8] Strabo mentions that the Persians bring "dry pieces of wood without the bark" to place on the fire, which remains the practice today. The laity provides the hardwood, preferably sandalwood, which the priest offers to the fire. This occurs even when the fire is lit by gas, as some are in Iran, and most in diaspora (see Fig. 3.4).

Priests are also responsible for orchestrating the ritual life of the community in terms of both the "higher" or "inner" rituals that take place within the temple precincts, and the "lower" or "outer" rituals that can be conducted in a community setting, such as an assembly hall or private home. In this function they are "both performer and audience": they are both inside the ritual in terms of their words and actions, and also outside the ritual looking in on the "visual virtual space" that they are creating.[9] From this "inside and outside" perspective, the priest's actions serve to create and negotiate an additional level of religious activity that they understand to reverberate through both the conceptual and material worlds.

As *manthran* in the tradition of Zarathushtra, the words the priests utter encapsulate the "sacred thought" and make it resound in both existences, as do the physical actions of the accompanying ritual. In the Yasna ceremony, when the priest strikes the metal mortar with the pestle four times, it is thought not only to resonate across all points of the compass, but also in the "thought world." It acts as a warning for evil to disperse and for good to prevail.

According to Dastur Kotwal, a priest must be a principled person "whose conduct and manner is disciplined and exact, one who abstains from and avoids the superfluous and inessential."[10] When a range of Parsi priests in India was recently asked what they thought constituted the ideal features of a good priest, many indicated that the primary qualities of a priest were that he should act as a guide, providing intelligent responses to the questions of the laity, and showing concern for others and the wellbeing of the community.[11] Sincerity, honesty, and dedication were all thought to be important qualities, especially in terms of validating the performance of ritual. Not every priest, however, placed the proper performance of ritual at the top of the list of ideal qualities.

Priestly rituals

The value accorded by the laity to the role of priestly ritual in the religion varies. Some feel that ritual is the bedrock of the religion in terms of its function in keeping the world ticking over, and ensuring that good prevails. Rituals conducted by priests are particularly important, especially those that take place in the fire temple such as the Yasna, purification rituals, and the rites of passage that demarcate the stages of a Zoroastrian's life. Zoroastrians who hold a more sociological view of the role of religion maintain that rituals such as *jashans* and initiations bring community cohesion and may have symbolic value, but have no "cosmic reverberations."

The Yasna

In Iran, the limited number of priests has led to the modification and simplification of most priestly rituals, including the inner rituals that only ordained *mobeds* can perform. The 72-section Yasna is no longer performed regularly, nor in its longer version in conjunction with the *Videvdad* and *Visperad*. A *Yasna khani*—a full Yasna celebration—is, however, still part of the installation of a newly initiated *nowzut*. In India the entire Yasna is regularly celebrated by two priests (the *Zot* and *Raspi*) in the morning in the main fire temples. It seems that at an earlier point in history, eight priests were required for the liturgy. The full ceremony takes at least two-and-a-half hours to perform, much longer if the preparatory ceremonies are also counted.

In their book *Ritual Art and Knowledge*, Ron Williams and James Boyd discuss the aesthetics of the Yasna as a way into interpreting the ritual in terms of its use of liturgical language, the relationship between different dimensions of the ritual, and the function of the performance. Dr. Boyd has co-authored several monographs on Zoroastrian ritual with Dastur Kotwal. The authors discern three types of space that operate within the setting of the Yasna:

1. the physical space—the place of ritual, and its tangible implements
2. the "meaning" space—the multi-layered significance of the place and objects
3. the "virtual" space—the "new matrix of significance" of the ritual, that is more than the physical setting and its symbolism.[12]

They identify these three spaces as being intertwined throughout the performance of the Yasna, just as the priests move between their roles as "performers and audience."

The liturgy takes place within a specially demarcated sacred space, within which the various aspects of the cosmos are represented. One of the terms for this area, where the priests and implements are situated throughout the ceremony, is the *urwisgah*, "the place of the turning point" (Av. *urvaesa*). The *urwisgah* functions as a performance stage for the cosmic drama that is enacted through the Yasna and that marks progress towards the final renovation. Even though the Yasna, as an inner ritual, is not a congregational activity, it is thought to bring benefit to the whole community and to have macrocosmic repercussions. For traditionalists, the ceremony is of the utmost importance in that it is believed not only to symbolize but also to actualize the regulation and regeneration of the cosmos.

The priests' initial function is to ensure that all the material elements of the Yasna are ritually and physically clean, including themselves. The ritual purity of a priest is established through a nine nights' *barashnum* ritual prior to ordination and should be retained and occasionally renewed for the priest to perform the Yasna and other inner ceremonies. This state can be compromised through any contact with "dead matter" (*nasu*), such as a flow of blood from the body or a nocturnal emission (Vd. 18.46). Generally, ritual purity can be reinstated through a ritual bath and prayer. There are no longer any *barashnum* facilities anywhere in Iran, so this ritual purification is now not a practice followed by Iranian *mobeds*.

The two officiating priests wear crisp, clean white clothes, and head covering, and keep a *padan*—the white cloth worn across the mouth so that the officiant's saliva will not pollute the implements, particularly the fire—tucked into their cap or turban until needed. They both perform *padyab-kusti* before entering the demarcated area, then cleanse the whole area with water and consecrate everything in it. The status of ritual purity also extends to the intentionality of the priests, who should be utterly focused. In a passage, concerning priestly recitation of the *paragna* ceremony that precedes the Yasna, Dastur Kotwal declared:

> The manner of recitation by the priest is also important . . . . [He] must recite the holy words with utter devotion and attentiveness. He must concentrate and engross himself in the speech itself, not in the conceptual meanings given the Avestan words in interpretive translations.[13]

The correct recitation of the words and proper performance of action are also considered crucial to the effectiveness of the *manthras* of the liturgy. Words from the Avesta are spoken in a normal, audible voice, but Middle Persian formulae are uttered in a soft voice, so that they can barely be heard.

The *paragna* ritual before the Yasna consists of the consecration and preparation of the twigs of the *hom* (Av. *haoma*: now usually ephedra), and pomegranate, and the metal *barsom* twigs. The *hom* and pomegranate are mixed with water to be ritually consumed during the ceremony. A similar *hom* offering is prepared during the course of the Yasna, but this time mixed with milk. At the end of the Yasna, the two priests take this consecrated liquid offering and, exiting the sacred space, pour it into flowing water, to revitalize all the life-giving waters of the world (cf. Y. 65, 68).

The time (daylight), the place, the elements of the performance and the performers are all co-ordinated and consecrated to ensure that the Yasna is effective at all levels. The liturgy is said to re-enact the original Yasna performed at creation by Ahura Mazda and the *amesha spentas* (Bd. 3.23); it re-energizes the cosmos in the present time; and it rehearses for the last Yasna that will be officiated by Ahura Mazda as *Zot* and Sraosha as *Raspi* to mark the final defeat of evil (Bd. 34.29–32).

The *Jashan*

The priestly Yasna allows no active role for the lay community apart from sponsorship. Sometimes the sponsors are permitted to watch the ceremony. There are several community celebrations, however, in which the laity can actively participate. Such outer rituals are not as circumscribed as inner rituals, and are more flexible in their implementation. As communities became more urbanized, priests in Iran and India began to preside over *jashans*, death anniversaries, seasonal celebrations (*gahanbars*), and other outer ceremonies in the community hall of the fire temple. It is still common in India, however, for these outer ceremonies to be held in people's houses. In other countries, *mobeds* and *mobedyars* will often travel quite a distance to conduct these services for Zoroastrian families in their homes. When a *jashan* take place in a person's home, it provides a sense of connectedness for the family members and friends who participate.

Ryna, one of my Parsi students, remembered as young child hearing the *Dasturjis* (ordained priests) praying in her family home in Mumbai:

Several times, my grandmother or another relative would hold a *jashan* while we were visiting. Relatives and family friends would come from around Parsi colony, each person bringing some food, or a small gift for the family. Two priests from the *agiary* would come over, and perform the ceremony. As I was a child, my most clear memory of the ceremony itself was sitting and breathing in the thick sandalwood smoke, looking forward to the traditional *jashan* food ahead.

A *jashan* is regarded by many Zoroastrians as transformative in that it helps to bring a family or community closer together in times of sadness as well as times of joy. Central to a *jashan* or *gahanbar* is the *afrinagan* ceremony of blessing. *Jashans* are celebrated on various significant occasions that include blessing a new home; honoring a dead person; celebrating the investiture of a new *dastur* or *mobed*; giving thanks for success in passing an exam, or graduating; praying for rains to relieve a drought; or welcoming the birth of a baby. During the ceremony, Zoroastrians give thanks to Ahura Mazda for all the blessings they and their families have received.

A Parsi acquaintance, Rusi Sorabji, described his earliest memories of a *jashan* in Delhi in the 1930s:

> The place is a raised piece of land some 6- or 7-feet high about 100-feet wide and maybe 200-feet long . . . While my father is helping the priest arrange the *Jashan* items, the gardener is arranging the rented chairs in rows, my mother takes me and her baby sister Roshan (who is a little older than me) . . . More people have arrived and are settling down, covering their heads and opening their prayer books. Between the *Ashem Vohus*, my gaze wonders off from the *jashan* ceremony towards the city of Delhi. I see the soft light of the setting sun fall along the city wall that leads to the Delhi Gate . . . For several years I attended *jashans* here, under the shade of the trees.

The form of the *jashan* does not vary greatly between India, Iran, and other countries, since it is conducted by priests who have all trained in a similar manner. Those gathered sit on chairs or on the floor a little distance away from a large white cotton cloth set out on the ground or sometimes on a table. On the cloth, known as a *sofreh*, are several objects with a symbolic connection to the seven elements of creation. (See Fig. 3.8). The ritual—like that of the Yasna—is believed to recreate the world in microcosm:

The **Sky** is represented by a metal container such as a copper bowl and other implements made of metal, including fire tongs. In the Avesta, the sky is said to be made of a hard substance, either stone or metal.

The **Waters** are present in the beaker full of water.

The **Earth** is the ground on which the ceremony takes place.

Plantlife is present in trays of fresh or dried fruit, and vases of fresh flowers, as well as in the leafy twigs or flowers held by the Iranian and Parsi priests respectively. In Iranian Zoroastrian celebrations, there is generally a tray of sprouted grass (*sabzeh*) as well as stalks of cypress or myrtle. **Plants** are also represented by the rounds of flat-fried wheatbread set out on the *sofre*, and the sandalwood sticks and incense used to fuel the fire.

Animals are represented by a beaker of milk. In Iran cow's milk is used, but Parsis in India use goat's milk.

Humanity is present in the priests and those gathered to celebrate.

Fire in an urn (*afargan*) or censer made of metal is also present, and there is also often an oil lamp.

The main priest sits close to the *afargan* so that he can feed the wood and incense to the fire using the metal tongs.

The first part of the *jashan* ceremony is the *afrinagan*. In the Parsi form of the *afrinagan*, the officiating priest (*Zot*) picks up eight flowers in succession from the tray, taking two flowers at a time. He chants prayers while holding one flower in each hand. The words he chants praise all the good thoughts, good words, and good deeds, both here and in any other place, that have already been performed, and those that are being performed. The *Zot* transfers each flower to the right-hand palm of the assistant priest (*Raspi*). In the Iranian version of the *afrinagan* ceremony, sprigs of greenery, such as myrtle are used instead of flowers, and the priest may take up two of the leafy twigs four times. This circle of connection generated between the priest and plant reminds participants that the ritual looks toward a time of returning to the original perfection of the world and a state of incorruptibility and immortality (*ameratat*), which the plant symbolizes.

Rusi described what happened at the end of the *jashan* prayers: "We had to remove the shoes, line up to put offerings of a stick or two of Sukhar [sandalwood] on the glowing fire on the *afargan* and recite an *Ashem Vohu.*" He remembers that the officiating priest would bring a long handled, flat spoon (PGuj. *chamach*) with ash from the fire on it to each person, and that his mother would put a mark of the ash on his forehead. This is known as the *teelo* and seems to be a purely Parsi custom, which has been influenced by Hindu practice.

The *jashan* ends with the sharing of the food that has been set out on the *sofreh*, including the wheatbread, and the fresh fruit that has been chopped up. In an Iranian context, the dried fruits and nuts of the *lork* are served first as part of the ceremonial food (*chashni*). When the ceremony is performed in the home, the priests will supply the ritual implements for the occasion including the *afargan*, fire tongs and sandalwood, but the lay participants provide the *chashni* and any main meal afterwards. After the *jashan*, Parsis will carefully pour the water over nearby plants. Rusi remembers that "if a dog was to be found in the vicinity, the dog was fed the milk." In Iran, the milk, wine, and water are sometimes combined with some of the bread and dried fruit or flowers, to offer to the waters as "a meal for the fishes."[14]

Hamazor

At the conclusion of the *jashan*, as the main officiating priest (*Zot*) recites the benedictions, the assistant priest (*Raspi*) may clasp hands with those who are present, both priests and laity. This action serves as a bridge between the sacred zone of ritual and the mundane. It is thought to galvanize everyone present with the energy of the *jashan*, and to encourage them to promote harmony and righteousness as they move back into the everyday world. The handclasp is called *hamazor*, after the words that are recited. *Hama* means "together" or "all"; and *zor* means "strength" in both a physical and inner sense.

In former times, a similar handshake was a common custom at festive occasions such as Nav Ruz, when it would be exchanged among friends and family as a sign of deep friendship. In a Nav Ruz prayer book produced by FEZANA, Ervad Soli Dastur describes the *hama-zor* ritual, which is being reintroduced at community gatherings:

1. Two participants face each other with their hands outstretched side by side vertically.
2. Reciting first the words: "Hamā Zor," both look into each other's eyes and place right hand between the two hands of the other simultaneously, join all hands and slide them out slowly.
3. Continuing on, reciting "Hamā Asho Bade," both continue looking into each other's eyes and now place left hand between the two hands of the other simultaneously, join all hands and slide them out slowly
4. "Hamā Zor" means "Let us be united."
5. "Hamā Asho Bade" means "Let us be righteous."
6. Together, "Hamā Zor, Hamā Asho Bade" means "Let us be united in righteousness"![15]

Dastur Kotwal suggests that the integration of such religious practice into the day-to-day activity of Zoroastrians can have a profound impact on their lives: "Religious discipline teaches you to regulate life . . . While sitting, standing, washing, eating or drinking, a Zoroastrian has to keep in front of him God and religion . . . religious practice produces excellent influences on the everyday life of a Zoroastrian."[16]

WHAT ARE THE ZOROASTRIAN RITES OF PASSAGE?

Birth

A period of isolation after birth is still maintained by some Zoroastrian mothers, especially those from priestly families. The "observant" mother of a newborn child customarily remains away from the fire temple and does not attend any funeral or other formal religious ceremony until 40 days later, or after postpartum bleeding has ceased. This length of time, advocated in the *Persian Rivayats*, corresponds to the six weeks considered optimum for women to recover from childbirth, and to be signed off by their doctor to resume a normal pattern of daily activity. When a baby is born some Parsis keep a *divo* burning for between 3 to 40 days.

The new Parsi mother may be symbolically reintegrated into the community by means of a ritual bath (*nahn*) at the end of this time. The Iranian equivalent is called *sar shostan* ("washing the head"). The format for the ritual bath is similar to that prescribed for men and women before initiation or marriage, and afterwards the individual is considered free from *nasu* ("dead matter"). In traditionalist Parsi families, the priest comes to the house to pray over the new mother and touches her lips with *nirang* (consecrated bull's urine), and a mix of ephedra (*hom*) and well water. She then chews a pomegranate leaf. In less conservative families, these items are replaced with a few drops of pomegranate juice. The *Hom Yasht* states that *haoma* (MP *hom*) ensures bright children and offspring full of integrity (Y. 9.22).

On the sixth day after birth, some Parsi families observe the custom of placing a tray containing a sheet of blank paper, ink, a pen, a coconut, and *kumkum* (red turmeric powder) beside the new mother's bed, in order to promote the child's good fortune and success. At this time, a name may also be chosen for the child.

Iranian Zoroastrians have no formal naming ceremony, but often choose traditional names from the Avesta, or one of the heroes of the *Shah Nameh*, or from a living member of the family whose qualities it is hoped that the child will emulate.

Initiation

One important aspect of Zoroastrian identity that is emphasized in modern discourse is that both women and men are equally capable of religious insight and wisdom, and of taking responsibility for their thoughts, words, and actions. The rite of initiation is the same for both girls and boys.

The *kusti* has been worn by Zoroastrians for centuries, if not millennia. It marks the arrival at adulthood of the Zoroastrian child, which is traditionally the age of fifteen (Vd. 18.54). The format of the ceremony of initiation for both boys and girls, and the symbolism of the sacred shirt and thread seem to date back at least to Sasanian times (Dd. 39). The ritual of initiation is called *navjote* by the Parsis, probably referring originally to a "offerer of libations" and now interpreted along the lines of a "new religiously-responsible adherent." Some translate the term as "new birth." Iranian Zoroastrians refer to the ritual as *sedreh pushi* or *pushun*, which means "putting on the *sudreh*." Traditionally, the age of maturity was 15, but nowadays, a child's initiation occurs before puberty, usually between 7 to 11 years old. Parsis tend to be initiated at the earlier age, and Iranian Zoroastrians somewhat later.

The *sudreh* is a white undervest made of cotton. This natural vegetable fiber is said to represent "continuity of life" (*ameretat*), the beneficent quality inherent in plants. The *kusti* is woven of wool made from lamb, goat, or camel hair, into a hollow tube of 72 strands symbolizing the 72 sections of the Yasna. The *Persian Rivayats* refer to the weaving of the *kusti* as the task of the priests, but in the nineteenth century the Parsi priests' wives assumed this responsibility. In Iran, laywomen took over *kusti* weaving early in the twentieth century. The *kusti* thread is blessed by a priest, and must be woven by women who are post-menopausal, and therefore ritually pure.

The *kusti* is worn wrapped around the waist three times, which reminds the wearer to generate only good thoughts, good words, and good deeds. A popular interpretation of the tying of the *kusti* is that the knot in the front signifies the importance of performing good actions, and the knot in the back affirms that the wearer will champion the cause of *asha*. The *sudreh* has a pocket at the front, called the *gireban* or the *kisse-ye kerfeh*, which is for the storing of good deeds. Wearing the *sudreh* and *kusti* is said to keep the faithful on the straight and beneficent path of Ahura Mazda.

Before the ceremony, the initiate takes a bath or shower, accompanied by prayer. The Iranian *sedreh pushi* is similar to that of the Parsi *navjote*, with some differences in format of the prayers. In Parsi initiation ceremonies, the mother and another female relative of the initiand will carry a tray (*seis*) containing some or all of these items: a sugar cone, rosewater, *kumkum*, a coconut, pomegranate, a flower garland, a raw egg, and a new set of clothes. They rotate the tray seven times clockwise around the initiate's head. If there is an egg, it will be smashed on the ground in a gesture of dismissing all bad things. A coconut might also be broken. This ceremony with the *seis* is known as the *Achu Michu*.

In both an Iranian Zoroastrian and Parsi setting, the initiand takes his or her place in a clean area set aside for the ceremony. Parsis wear white trousers, a cap on the head and a shawl around the top, ready to discreetly put on the *sudreh*, which is worn like a vest. Iranian Zoroastrians wear white tops over their *sedreh*. It is now common practice in Iran for several young Zoroastrians to be initiated at the same time. The initiand faces the officiating priest, and they recite the *Ahuna Vairya* as the sacred shirt is invested. The priest and initiand both face the fire in its container, and the initiate ties the *kusti* while reciting the *kusti* prayers. (See Fig. 2.4). For Parsis, these prayers include the *Ahuna Vairya* while tying the knot at the front, the *Ashem Vohu* while tying the knot at the back, and conclude with the *Fravarane*. Iranian Zoroastrian initiates recite from memory the *Srosh Baj* (prayer to Sraosha) at the investiture; the *Avestaye Koshti* (Avestan *kusti* prayers) while the priest ties the *kusti* around their waist; and then the *Peymane Din* (PGuj. *Din no kalmo*), a statement of faith. At every initiation, the presiding priest recites a blessing known as the *Tandorosti*—or "good health." The ceremony is followed by a meal provided by the family of the new initiate for all the guests.

The *sudreh* and *kusti* are removed before having a bath. The *kusti* has to be untied and tied again, with the recital of certain prayers, several times a day: after getting out of bed in the morning; before and after using the bathroom; before meals; before beginning any prayer; and before going to bed. Both *sudreh* and *kusti* are replaced when they become worn out. Traditionalist Parsis will wear the *sudreh* and *kusti* at all times, except when bathing. Iranian Zoroastrians might only put on their *sedreh* and *kusti* when attending the *dar-i mihr* or special ceremonies at which the fire will be present. Some Zoroastrians, particularly those living outside Iran and India, choose not to wear the garments at all after the initiation ceremony.

For some youngsters, the daily wearing of the *sudreh* and *kusti* can be a cause of embarrassment, and it is often at this stage that they may adapt the garments, or decide to stop wearing them. One young Parsi woman, who grew up in America, and who is now in her early twenties told me:

> After my *Navjote*, I wore the traditional garment and thread of Zoroastrians every day until middle school. The combination of questions in the locker room and occasionally "having a tail" when my *kusti* slipped out made me decide to stop the tradition. I know in India, where Parsis are a substantive minority rather than a complete rarity, people have modified rather than discarded traditions. My friends there wear "tube-top" *sudrehs* with their clothing so that the garments do not show through fashionable tops; *kustis* are tied and then pinned with safety pins to clothing so they can't come out.

Marriage

The model of marriage is thought to be exemplified in the last of the five *Gathas*, Yasna 53. The setting for this song is said to be the wedding of Zarathushtra's daughter Pouruchista. From a Zoroastrian perspective marriage serves to propagate humanity, in order to contribute to the ultimate victory of good. The *Videvdad* recommends marriage and having children as the prefered state (Vd. 4.47), as does the Middle Persian *Chidag Andarz-i Poryotkeshan* (CAP 5). In other Middle Persian Zoroastrian texts, getting married is one of the expected good deeds for the initate to perform.

In the *Persian Rivayats*, a father is encouraged to make sure that his daughter is married as soon after menarche as possible, so that she will bring life—in the form of more babies—rather than "not-life" in the form of the pollution of menstruation. As mentioned earlier, one of the dilemmas facing Zoroastrians worldwide in current times is that of the increase in interfaith marriages, and the decrease in number of births into the religion. The statistics point to an apparent tension between the religious ideal and actual behavior.

Traditional Zoroastrian weddings take place over several days, and involve many ceremonies that formalize the connections between the two families involved and that are also to do with fertility and longevity. In Iran, the bride may be welcomed to the groom's house with silver coins, sugared fruit, and sweets. She may also be greeted by family and friends waving green leaves of marjoram and myrtle. Before a Parsi marriage in India, it is a custom for members of the families of both the bride and groom to plant a mango tree sapling in a pot, along with a few grains of rice and wheat, some small pieces of gold and silver, and a spoonful of curd, symbolizing the fruitfulness that it is hoped the marriage will bring.

In the Iranian Zoroastrian wedding ceremony, the bride and groom sit on chairs next to each other facing the *mobed*, who asks them whether they freely accept each other in marriage. (See Fig. 0.3). He offers nine points of advice (*Andarz-i Gavah*) including the need to offer charity, and to seek a mediator if there are any marital problems. Then he advises the couple to live according to the attributes of the *amesha spentas*.[17] At the end of the ceremony, while reciting the *Tandorosti* blessing for health and wellbeing, the priest showers the newlyweds with rice, flower petals, and marjoram.

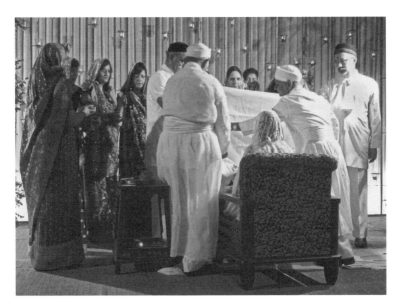

Figure 3.5 The cloth separates Anahita and Nauzad, during their wedding ceremony at the Colaba Jeejeebhoy Dadabhoy Agiary, January, 2010. Ervads Palanji and Soli Dastur officiated. Photo courtesy of Ervad Soli Dastur.

In a Parsi wedding, the couple sits opposite each other, with a sheet between them, which is held up by their relatives (see Fig. 3.5). Their right hands are held together under the sheet, and encircled three times by a piece of cotton. They hold grains of rice in their left hands. The couple is then encircled clockwise seven times by the priest who wraps a cotton thread around them as he walks, chanting the *Ahuna Vairya* on each round. When the priest has finished his circling and recitation, he knots the seven threads together. Then the cloth is removed quicly and the bride and groom each tries to be the first to throw the rice over the other.

The couple, now sitting side by side, may then receive a blessing from the priest that begins with the words:

May you be brilliant
Try to do good deeds.
Be increasing.

Be victorious.
Learn to do deeds of piety.
Be worthy to do good deeds.
Think of nothing but the truth.
Speak nothing but the truth.
Do nothing but what is proper.[18]

In each Zoroastrian marriage, the consent of both partners is required in a pledge of affirmation before winesses, but no vows are made. The officiating priest admonishes the couple to acknowledge Ahura Mazda and to follow the spiritual guidance of Zarathushtra. They are also encouraged to help each other to pursue good in all elements of their life together, so that they will be blessed with many children and grandchildren, a good livelihood and a long life.

Most discussions of sexual relations in Zoroastrian texts concern whether it results in "life" or "not-life." Does it generate new life through the conception of a child? Or is it a union that will not produce children to further the good religion, such as in the case of infertility? The *Persian Rivayats* refer to a woman's barrenness as a viable cause for a man to take a second wife. The impossibility of reproduction may have been the reason that male homosexuality was classified as an act introduced by Angra Mainyu (Vd. 1.11). According to the *Videvdad*, one of the greatest sins was for a menstruating woman to have sexual intercourse with her husband (Vd. 15.7, 13–16), since not only would there be no possibility of reproduction taking place, but she would also pollute him. Nowadays, some take a bath or shower after sexual intercourse, since they consider spent semen also to be "dead matter."[19]

Death

If possible, a person should die with a prayer on his or her lips at the last breath. Many Zoroastrians feel that some kind of light in the form of a candle, or even a bedside lamp, should be placed near the dying person's head to illuminate the way for the soul as it leaves the body.

At death, the body is said to fall under the polluting influence of the *Druj Nasu*, sometimes referred to as the "corpse demon." In India and Iran, the family may wash the body and clothe it in an old *sudreh* and *kusti* but will then refrain from touching it again. The funeral ceremonies are held as quickly as possible after death, preferably within 24 hours. Any organ and tissue donation occurs during this period, and, if necessary, an autopsy.

A custom that is still practiced in India relates to a description in the *Videvdad* of dogs awaiting the soul of a dead person as it arrives at the Chinvat crossing (Vd. 19.30). A dog with a mark just above each eye—making it "four eyed"—is brought in to see the corpse. This is known as the *sagdid* ritual, literally the act of "seeing by the dog." In the spring of 2009, I met a former resident of Shiraz, Iran, who told me that when he was young, a local Zartoshti man was appointed to look after the dog who performed the *sagdid* after the death of his co-religionists in the city. Food would be placed on the chest of the deceased, and if the dog ate it, then the family was assured that the person was truly dead.

Mobed Firouzgary, writing from Tehran, provided a rationale for this custom:

> The practice of *sagdid* was very useful in the days when sensitive instruments and the knowledge of determining a definite biological death were not perfected. The dog had the instinct and special sensory advantages . . . and the purpose was to find out if the corpse had any amount of life remaining in that body, a murmur of a heartbeat or warmness of body for which they had no means for detection in those days. The dog had been trained not to touch food placed over a live, sleeping body, while it could eat it if placed over a dead body. Nowadays death is ascertained with little chances of a mistake. As such the practice of *sagdid* is not followed, anywhere in Iran.

In most Zoroastrian homes where bereavement has occurred, family members who participate in the funeral will bathe after the body has been removed. Many will eat no meat for three days, which is the period when ceremonies are performed for the benefit of the soul. In the Avesta, it is said that the soul of the dead person remains within the world for three days, under the protection of Sraosha (Y. 57.25).

If the body is consigned to the *dakhma* in India, a fire is kept burning in a small adjacent building for these three days. A fire may also be kept alight for three days in the room where the person died. The room is then thoroughly washed, but may not be used for some time afterwards.

Disposal of the dead

For centuries, the ancient Zoroastrian method of disposal of the dead has been a source of curiosity among outsiders: from Herodotus and Strabo in ancient Anatolia, to European travelers through Iran and India in the medieval and colonial periods. An early fourteenth-century description of a *dakhma*—the hilltop enclosure in which a corpse is placed to be consumed by vultures—is found in the writings of a French Dominican friar named Jordanus. Jordanus wrote that the Parsis he encountered in Gujarat did not burn or bury their dead, but exposed them in a "roofless tower" to the birds of the sky. Excavations at Sanjan that began in 2002 have unearthed a *dakhma* that seems to have been in use from the eleventh to the mid–fifteenth century.

Around three-and-a-half centuries after Jordanus, the French merchant Jean Chardin described a *dakhma* located in an isolated spot some distance away from the city of Isfahan.[20] Much of his account seems to be based on firsthand observation. Chardin remarked that there was no door to the *dakhma*, and that the corpse-bearers used ladders to scale the walls and ropes to raise the corpse over the wall, which they descended via projecting steps on the interior.

In 1672–73, at about the same time of Chardin's account, a *dakhma* was the first building to be erected by the Parsi community in Bombay. Fifty-seven acres of land on Malabar Hill had been donated by the British East India Company to provide an incentive for Parsis to move from Gujarat, and it was here that the first *dakhma* was constructed in Mumbai. Since then, four more have been built on the site. In the early nineteenth century, a British official named Sir Robert Murphy is attributed with coining the euphemistic term "Tower of Silence" for the place of exposure.

The actual word *dakhma* has been derived from two different roots, one meaning "to bury," the other "to burn." The word is used in various ways in the *Videvdad*, where it variously seems describe a tomb (Vd. 3.13), an open place of exposure (Vd. 8.2, 5.14), or a place of pollution (Vd. 7.56–58, 3.18). It is not known when the first enclosed *dakhma* was constructed. One theory is that makeshift enclosures on

Figure 3.6 Exterior and interior of the old *dakhma*, Yazd, Iran. Photo by Jenny Rose.

mountains close to battlefields were constructed during Achaemenid times for the remains of soldiers. Recent archaeological finds in the region of Karakalpakstan in northwestern Uzbekistan, indicate the existence of purpose-built *dakhmas* dating from perhaps as early as the second century CE. This is the region of ancient Chorasmia. The exposure of the dead continued in Chorasmia and Sogdiana (modern southeastern Uzbekistan and western Tajikistan) until after the arrival of Islam in the region. This is evidenced by the discovery of many ossuaries, or "bone-holders," dating from the fifth- to the eighth-centuries CE. These held the collected sun-dried bones of an individual, which were then placed in family vaults.

The practice of exposure of the corpse to animals is mentioned in the accounts of Wei-jie, a Chinese ambassador to Sogdiana in the early seventh century CE. There seem to be no ossuaries after the mid–eighth century. But there is a record of a letter sent in the ninth century CE by a priest in Iran to the Zoroastrians of Samarkand, telling them what to do with a dead body while they constructed a new *dakhma* to replace the damaged one. The advice was to place the corpse on a pile of flat stones to one side of the old *dakhma*, and then to move the remains to the new *dakhma* when it was completed.

Dakhmas are round structures built on elevated ground some distance away from human habitation, so that they cannot be seen into. They are round so that there will be no corners to hold pollution, and are made of stone so as to protect the earth. In India and Karachi, Pakistan, the body of a person who opted for consignment to the *dakhma* is carried on an iron bier by official corpse-bearers called *nasasalars*. The *dakhmas* constructed in the eighteenth or nineteenth centuries have steps or a sloped path from the ground up to an iron gate in the wall, which opens onto a circular platform of solid stone, divided into rows of large stone slabs for men, women, and children, with a well in the center into which the dry bones, bleached by the sun, are deposited. Any rainfall that falls on the bodies is channeled into drains that connect, via a filter of charcoal and sandstone, to underground wells so that the clean water is not polluted.

In Iran, burial in the ground is now the norm for Zoroastrians. They first began to bury their dead in purpose-built cemeteries in the late 1930s, when an *aramgah* (literally, a "place of peace") was constructed in Tehran and another in Kerman. The *dakhma* at Yazd was still in use until the early 1970s. Since then, all Zoroastrians in Iran have been buried in separate cemeteries. At burial, the base of the grave is lined with rocks, and the tomb is lined with slabs of concrete. Such burials take place in diaspora communities including those in Sri Lanka, England, Canada, the United States, and Australia.

Interment in tombs cut from stone or in living rock are known from the time of the Ancient Persian kings onward. Cyrus the Great was buried in a freestanding stone mausoleum at Pasargadae, at which Alexander of Macedon paid his respects after his conquest of the Persians. Darius I, Xerxes, Darius II, and Artaxerxes I, II, and III were all buried in cliff-face tombs at Naqsh-e Rostam or Persepolis. Herodotus relates that the custom of exposure was practiced by the Persians at the same time as burial: the former may have been an eastern Iranian rite, which became the predominant Zoroastrian practice until the mid–twentieth century.

After death
On the morning of the fourth day, as the sun's rays touch the earth, the soul is thought to begin its ascent. The family celebrates the departure of the soul with an *afrinagan* ceremony known as *sobhe chaharom* ("fourth morning") by the Zartoshtis and *uthamna* ("last") by the Parsis. Nowadays, the *chaharom* ceremony in Iran is performed at dawn on the day following death. At the ceremony *dron* (fried wheatbread) is consecrated, and food is blessed. After the ceremony, the mourners share the consecrated bread and food. The consecrated food of the Zartoshti *chaharom* consists of seven boiled eggs, pieces of boiled potato, and the leaves of herbal plants, such as mint. Originally, there were 33 eggs, to represent Ahura Mazda and all the

yazatas. Those gathered will then eat a funerary meal together. The prefered dish of the Parsis on this occasion is *dhansak*, traditionally made with mutton, lentils, chopped vegetables and spices. At this time, food is often also distributed to the poor, and an endowment may be announced on behalf of the deceased.

The *fravashi* of a righteous person is believed to remain involved with the welfare of family members so long as they pursue good thoughts, words and deeds, including the performance of meritorious charitable acts. On death anniversaries, the living may give food and clothing to the poor of the community and money to charity in the name of the deceased relative. Endowments in memory of the departed range from community feasts intended to be held at the time of the *gahanbars* (seasonal festivals) to the establishment of charitable foundations, such as hospitals or schools.

In Iran, a ceremony is held at the death anniversary for several years—thirty is the traditional length of time, but this is not always possible. Most families remember the dead at the annual festival of Farvardigan (of the "*fravashis*"), which is referred to as Muktad by the Parsis.

WHAT FESTIVALS OCCUR IN THE ZOROASTRIAN CALENDAR?

Such seasonal festivals and gatherings are an important element of Zoroastrian community life.

Farvardigan

The festival of Farvardigan, or Muktad, is thought to date back to a kind of All Souls' festival mentioned in the Avesta as taking place at the end of the year, at the time of the vernal equinox (Yt. 13.49). This festival, known as *Hamaspathmaedaya*, was dedicated to the collective souls of the living, the dead, and those yet to be born. It was thought to bring increase and blessing to the world. The Ancient Persians commemorated this occasion in the springtime, and it came to be known as *Farvardigan*, dedicated to the *fravashis*.

Farvardigan is still celebrated today by Iranian Zoroastrians on the last ten days of the year. The time of year varies according to which of the three calendars is used (Qadimi, Fasli, or Shehenshai). On each of the last five days , which are known as the "*Gatha* days," the *Gathas* are recited. Among Iranian Zoroastrians, the festival is sometimes called *Panji* meaning "five," as it is divided into two five-day parts, the first being the "lesser *panji*," and the second (the *Gatha* days), the "greater *panji*."

Throughout the ten days, *afrinagans* and other ceremonies are held in honor of the souls of the dead, who are thought by some to come and visit their terrestrial dwelling place. Iranian Zoroastrians visit the cemetery, carrying bunches of fresh flowers and foliage to place in vases next to the tombs. Parsis set up Muktad tables, usually in a room of the fire temple, but sometimes in the home. Silver vases holding sweet-smelling flowers are set up on the tables, and the flowers are often changed daily. In both cultures, the plants, and the water that keeps them alive symbolize the combined aspects of "wholeness" (*haurvatat*) and "immortality" (*ameretat*) that are qualities associated with *frasho.kereti*.

At dawn on the morning of the last day of Panji, residents in some of the Zoroastrian villages of Yazd will light a fire on the flat roof of their house, and fathers and sons will recite Avestan prayers. The women of the household cook a farewell meal for the *fravashis*, and sprinkle water and marjoram leaves on the rooftop as the sun rises, to greet the New Year. On the last day of Muktad, known as *Pateti*, or "repentance," Parsis repent of any bad thoughts, words or deeds, and then, in a similar gesture, empty the vases and invert them, having said their farewells to the collective *fravashis* for another year.

Nav Ruz

Nav Ruz means "New Day" in Persian. It is celebrated at the spring equinox in Iran and marks the start of the liturgical and calendrical New Year. One of the most important preparations for Nav Ruz, takes place around the beginning of Farvardigan, ten days earlier. This is the planting of wheat, barley, or lentil seeds in clay pots in time for them to germinate and sprout into a bunch of lush green grass. The sprouted seed is called *sabzeh* in Persian, which means "greenery." At Nav Ruz, *sabzeh* is a word that symbolizes the very essence of life.

The notion that it is a beneficial act to grow plants is found in the Avesta (Vd. 3.23). This connects with the identification of all plants, whether twigs, leafy branches, flowers, or seeds as representing not only the force of life itself, but the possibility of continuity of life—that is, "immortality" (*ameretat*). The belief that the end of death and the regeneration of life is possible remains central to the celebration of Nav Ruz, which offers hope that a New Day will dawn, when evil will be dispelled, good will triumph and the world will be made wonderful again.

Alongside the *sabzeh*—the green sprouts—there are always at least six other items on the Iranian Nav Ruz table beginning with the letter "s." These are known as the *Haft Sin*—the Seven "S"s. It is thought that the seven items on the *Haft Sin* table today originally represented the seven elements of creation associated with the *amesha spentas*. The table itself is sometimes understood to be a microcosm of the whole world. The practice of arranging seven propitious items on a special table at Nav Ruz dates back at least a thousand years. One source from that time describes that, as seven grains, seven branches from fruit trees, or seven shiny new coins were arranged, prayers would be said for long life, happiness, and blessings.[21] The same wishes are still expressed at Nav Ruz today, wherever it is celebrated.

One of the other items on the Haft Sin table that does not begin with an "s" is a mirror: this is said to encourage individuals to reflect on their thoughts, words, and deeds of the previous year, so that they may determine to do better in the months ahead. Nav Ruz is also, then, about personal growth.

Jamsheedi Nav Ruz

Those Parsis who do not keep to the same seasonally linked calendar as the Iranians observe their New Year somewhat later in the year. But many Parsis celebrate a festival known as Jamsheedi Nav Ruz at the spring equinox. Outside India, communal festival activities are usually scheduled for all groups on this occasion.

In March 2010, the Children's CBeebies Team of the BBC worked with the ZTFE Children's Educational Club to film the Jamsheedi Nav Ruz celebrations at the Zoroastrian Centre in London. This was an occasion at which both Iranian Zoroastrian and Parsi customs relating to the New Year celebrations were intertwined. Berzin and Binaifer, two Parsi children from the London community explained how their family prepares for and participates in the festival.[22] They began by helping their mother to springclean the house, and then planted seeds for the *sabzeh*. On Jamsheedi Nav Ruz they made colorful chalk stencil patterns on the pavement outside the house, put

Figure 3.7 Ervad Zubin P. Writer teaching the extra young Zoroastrians (XYZ) at the Zoroastrian Center in London in preparation for Jamsheedi Nav Ruz on March 21, 2010. Photo courtesy of ZTFE President, Malcolm Deboo.

on their new clothes, and took their *sabzeh* and painted eggs to display on the Haft Sin table. The two children and their parents prayed in the prayer room (*setayash gah*) of the fire temple, and watched the senior priest, Ervad Bhedwar, performing the *maachi* ceremony, as he fed the fire with pieces of sandalwood stacked to resemble a throne.

Sometimes to prepare for this day, teachers will tell their class of Zoroastrian children the story of Jamsheed, who is called Yima in the Avesta. According to tradition, King Jamsheed was the royal protector of Ahura Mazda's good creation, under whom the world and all living things flourished. Nav Ruz looks forward to such a golden age in the future.

Gahanbars

The springtime Nav Ruz in Iran is the first of the seasonal festivals of the Zoroastrian liturgical calendar. Six festivals, ending with Farvardigan, derive from an ancient agricultural calendar and are known collectively as *gahanbars*. Each *gahanbar* is said to celebrate one of the creations connected with the *amesha spentas*.

Maidyoizaremaya	mid-spring	sky
Maidyoishema	mid-summer	waters
Paitishahya	fall corn harvest	earth
Ayathrima	bringing herds home	plants
Maidyairya	"mid-year"/winter	animals
Hamaspathmaedaya/		
Farvardigan	pre-spring	humans

Fire, the seventh element of creation, is associated with Nav Ruz, when the sun at the spring equinox is celebrated as bringing warmth and life after the cold of winter, and reminding humans of the creativity activity of Ahura Mazda that energizes all of creation.

Figure 3.8 The ritual *sofreh* for the *Maidyoizaremaya gahanbar*. Community hall, Mazra-ye Kalantar, Yazd. Photo by Jenny Rose.

Apart from Farvardigan, each *gahanbar* lasts five days. There may be community feasts on each of the five days, following the recitation of *gahanbar* prayers. Both the ritual recitations and the congregational meals that follow are often financed by charitable endowments in remembrance of departed souls.

The *gahanbar* prayers are read or recited next to a ritual *sofreh* on which are placed items representing the various elements of creation, such as at a *jashan*. During the *gahanbar* ceremony, Ahura Mazda is praised for all the blessings given to those present. The participants also pray for blessings in the future, not just for themselves but for the world as a whole. These seasonal festivals provide Zoroastrians with a sense that they are part of an unbroken chain of devotional activity that is intended to revitalize the elements of the created world, including the humans who have gathered together to celebrate. One Zartoshti described her memory of a *gahanbar* during Farvardigan:

> Everone sat in silence listening to the Zoroastrian priest (*mobed*) who was dressed in traditional white gown and cap . . . . The ceremony lasted about an hour and ended with the *mobed* blessing members of the family and all those present. Then there was a sudden burst of activity, laughter would fill the air and the tray of nuts and sweets (*lork*) would be offered round to everyone.[23]

Annual festivals

Dedicated days

There are also some annual festivals that celebrate individual *yazatas* or particular aspects of creation. Zoroastrians in Iran have celebrated the festivals of Mihragan and Tirgan for centuries, although the current form and seasonal placement of contemporary observation has been impacted by certain reorganizations that occurred in the mid–twentieth century. This was the result of an attempt to align the Iranian Zoroastrian liturgical calendar—as well as the form of celebration of festivals, religious ceremonies, and rites of passage—with that of the Parsis. It was introduced by *mobeds* who had trained or pursued higher studies in Mumbai.

Some non-Zoroastrians in Iran, partly as a sociopolitical critique of the current government, have sought to join in some of these Zoroastrian ceremonies. The *anjumans* have implemented several strategies to prevent the co-opting of their festivals, such as holding public events away from the fire temple, requiring pre-registration for the festival, or employing security police to keep non-Zoroastrians away during times of congregational worship at shrines, such as Pir-e Sabz.

Mihragan

Mihragan, or Mehregan, is the festival dedicated to Mithra, which falls on the sixteenth day, Mihr (Mithra), in the seventh month, Mihr. In the fourth century BCE, Xenophon mentions an official celebration in honor of Mithra, and Strabo later calls this festival *Mithrakana* (*Geographia* 11.14.9). A festival is mentioned as being held in honor of Mithra by the tenth-century Persian Muslim historian Al-Biruni, who connected the day with the story of the hero Feridun's defeat of the evil king Zohak. Various external texts describe the day of Mithra as a day on which a sacrifice was made, and until the mid–twentieth century, the feast included a sheep that had been ceremonially killed for the occasion. Shirin Simmons describes how the festival was celebrated in Yazd when she was young:

> On the morning of Mehregan, Bahman the old Zoroastrian baker would call at our house to make bread (*nan*) in our traditional oven (*tanoor*) and would make at least a hundred loaves. A whole lamb was roasted and cut into portions to cool, then garnished . . . The lamb and garnish were sandwiched together between *nan* and distributed amongst the Zoroastrian community, rich and poor alike.[24]

The idea of a "sacrifice" is thought by some to be contrary to the religion, and often the community *sofreh* will include no meat for that reason.[25] Some may cook a sheep for the festival, but will avoid the use of the word "sacrifice" (*qorban*). Most now observe the festival according to the *fasli* calendar at harvest time, but there are a few Yazdis who still hold to the *qadimi* (old) calendar in which the month of Mihr is much earlier in the year. Mihragan is one of the official religious holidays for Iranian Zoroastrians, but is not commonly celebrated by Parsis. In Yazd it is a cultural event, with speeches, music, and performances following the *jashan* prayers.

Tirgan

Tirgan is dedicated to Tishtrya, falling on the day Tir (Tishtrya) in the month Tir. It is identified as an Iranian festival in the Babylonian

Talmud. Two weeks before the midsummer festival of Tirgan, Zartoshtis
in Iran have taken to making a "pilgrimage" to the shrine of Pir-e
Sabz, located in northwestern Yazd on the borders of the desert.
They travel from across the country to stay overnight in the hilltop
shelters next to the shrine, where they celebrate with prayer, food,
music, and dance. Security police prevent non-Zoroastrians from
attending these celebrations, although anyone can visit the shrine
during the rest of the year. Such informal gatherings provide the
opportunity for members of the community to relax some of the
restrictions on social interaction that operate within the majority
Shi'a Muslim norm.

Avan Yazad Jashan
Although Parsis do not celebrate Mihragan or Tirgan as major festivals, they do celebrate the "birthdays" of water and fire. The eighth
month of the year is dedicated to the waters (Pers. *aban*, PGuj. *avan*)
and the tenth day of that month is the day of the waters. On that day,
known as *Avan Yazad Jashan* or *Avanu parab*, Parsis may decorate the
well in the fire temple precinct, and offer flowers and a preparation of
Dar-ni-Pori, a sweetened lentil mixture in pastry, to the water after
reciting a *kusti* prayer by the well, the sea, or a river. The *seis* for this
occasion may also include a lit *divo* or *afargan* and *loban*, a coconut,
sugar crystals, and rice. The coconut may be broken over the water.

Men also observe the festival, but the offering is particularly associated with women, perhaps because of the belief that the source and
sustenance of all the rivers—and by extension, of all life—is the
beneficent female *yazata* Aredvi Sura Anahita. In the *Aban Yasht*—
the "hymn to the waters"—Anahita is praised for the increase and
well-being of the community, and for making "the seed of all males
pure" and "childbirth easy for all females" (Yt. 5. 2).

In the past decade, celebration at a well on *Aban Ruz,* the day of the
month dedicated to the waters, has become popular among Zartoshti
women in Iran. Susan, a female participant at such a celebration at
the Parseshgah well in Yazd that took place in December 2004
remarked to me: "The women prayed and danced at that well with
perhaps more devotion than I have seen at other sacred sites since."
On this day of the month, Zoroastrian women wherever they live,
may make an excursion to a natural source of water to invoke Anahita's beneficent action, by reciting the the prayer to the waters, the
Aban Niyayishn.

Adargan

Parsis also celebrate the "birthday" of the fire on the ninth day (*Adar*) of the ninth month (*Adar*), known as *Adargan* or *Atashnu Parab*. They often decorate the area of their home where the fire stands in the *afargan*, which is usually in the kitchen. Those households that still have a hearth fire may keep it burning through the night. Many who live in urban apartments will visit a fire temple instead, and make an offering of sandalwood for the fire there.

Khordad Sal

On the sixth day, known as *Khordad* (Haurvatat), of the first month of the year (Farvardin), the birth of Zarathushtra is commemorated. This is another of the official Zoroastrian religious holidays in Iran. A festival is thought to have been celebrated on this day during Sasanian times, supported by reference in the Babylonian Talmud to an Iranian festival of *Nausard* that was distinct from Nav Ruz. The day is sometimes called the "Greater Nav Ruz." Those who are able to, will go to the fire temple during the day. On this day in Parsi fire temples or homes, images of Zarathushtra may be decorated with garlands of fresh flowers.

Zardosht No Diso

The *Persian Rivayats* record that each year the whole community commemorated the anniversary of Zarathustra's death on the eleventh day (*Khorshed*) of the tenth month (*Dae*). This festival is called *Zardosht No Diso* by Parsis, and *Dargozasht-e Asho Zartosht* by Iranian Zoroastrians. The holiday is marked by adherents visiting the fire temple to contemplate the life of Zarathushtra as a model for their own lives. In Iran, a ceremony is also held in the cemeteries, which serves as a *memento mori* for the living.

Jashne Sadeh

Jashne Sadeh, or Sadeh, is one of the five official Zoroastrian festivals celebrated in Iran. *Sadeh* means the "hundreth" and is celebrated on the hundredth day after Ayathrima *gahanbar*, that is, on the tenth day of the month Bahman, which falls at the end of January. The festival is connected with the story of the legendary king Hushang, who threw a flint rock at a serpentine beast, which missed its mark, but struck the stony ground and sparked a flame. This story of the defeat of evil and the discovery of fire is included in the *Shah Nameh*.

The festival, which is particularly celebrated in Kerman, has been reintroduced to the Yazd region in recent years. It is commemorated with the building of a large bonfire by the local Zoroastrian community. After the fire is lit, the priests will say prayers facing the fire, including the *Atash Niyayishn*.

ARE THERE GENDER DIFFERENCES WITH REGARD TO PRAXIS?

While all members of the community may participate in these regular collective celebrations, there are a few lay rituals that involve only women. Such praxes are sometimes shrugged off as peripheral, or belonging to local folklore, rather than as viable expressions of women's worship. This is perhaps due to the fact that these rituals are enacted by women independent of priestly supervision.

Chak o duleh

Zoroastrian women in Yazd, Iran, perform a ceremony known as the *chak o duleh* ("pot of fate") that is linked with the festival of Tirgan. A ceramic pot (*duleh*) is filled with water into which a group of women from the same family or village place a small personal possession made of a waterproof material. Objects might include a ring, a bracelet, or a key. The pot, covered with a cloth, is placed overnight under a green leafy tree such as a myrtle or box bush. The group gathers together the following day, and while a young unmarried girl retrieves each item from the water, the older women recite verses of poetry relating to the future of the item's owner. The ritual, which is held in the heat of the summer, is intended to bring good fortune to the participants, and to keep away drought and disease. In Montreal in the fall of 2009, I met a Canadian Zartoshti woman, originally from Kerman, who recalled that her grandma from Yazd knew many such poems, but that to her regret she herself knew none. Such practices—and their poetry—are now not found outside Yazd.

Sofreh rituals

Certain shrines in Iran are both the locus and focus of independent female praxis. Some of these shrines are relatively new, or have been newly refurbished. Women's visits to these shrines often involve votive actions, including the setting up of a ritual *sofreh*. These stand-alone *sofrehs* relate to a personal pledge or petition and are usually entirely women-led and women-oriented.[26] Some of the votive *sofrehs*, such as for *Bibi se shanbeh* ("the Tuesday lady") or *Shah Pari* revolve around folktales about poor or unfortunate individuals, who are helped by supernatural beings, and who are then restored to health and good fortune. These supernatural beings are not identified as Zoroastrian *yazatas*, although Shah Pari has been linked with Feridun (Av. Thraetaona), who became one of the kings of ancient Iranian myth. The *sofreh* ritual enacted by the women is intended to bring wellbeing to themselves and their families through the retelling of the story.

There are no similar, separate shrines among Parsi religious institutions, but on special days of the month it is now popular for Parsi women and men to attend a couple of the fire temples in Mumbai that have a reputation for being particularly sacred places. These are the Aslaji Bhikhaji Agiary and the Cowasji Behramji Banaji Atash Bahram.[27] In a more domestic setting, Parsi women may be said to create their own ritual arena in the form of the *seis*, or metal tray, on which they place the various elements used in family celebrations, particularly relating to pregnancy, birth, initiations, and weddings. The *Achu Michu* ceremony mentioned earlier in relation to the *navjote* is a rite of welcoming used on these occasions.

A problem-solving ritual

One ritual activity that is common to both Parsi and Iranian Zoroastrian women occurs on the day of the month dedicated to Bahram (Verethragna), the *yazata* of victory. On this day, Zoroastrian women perform a ritual known in Yazd as *nokhud-e moshgel gosha*, and among Parsis as *mushkil asan*. Both terms refer to the "overcoming of something that is difficult"—the resolution of a problem. The ritual is generally observed by older women in fulfilment of a vow. In both Iran and India, men will sometimes sit in on the *moshgel gosha*/ *mushkil asan* ceremony, but do not generally participate. In Yazd, the ceremony takes place at a nearby shrine or in the home, and may precede or follow that of the *chak o duleh*.

The ritual involves two or more women, who get together to sort chickpeas from a large tray. As they husk the chickpeas, one of them narrates or reads a long story about a poor woodcutter and his daughter, whose consecration of chickpeas every Friday enables them to overcome their adversity. The tale ends with an Avestan prayer, and the chickpeas are then distributed among the women and their neighbors. In Iran, the chickpeas are often left at a shrine for others to share. The story implies that in order to resolve one's own problems, one has to engage in acts of kindness or generosity to others.

Purity

Perhaps the most obvious gender difference in terms of lay praxis is the separation that comes into effect when an individual is considered to be "polluted" by contact with "dead matter" of any kind. The designation of something as "dead matter" (Av. *nasu*) from the Avesta onward relates to the corpse of a human or animal or anything that is excreted from the body. This includes one's breath, saliva, urine, blood, nail, and hair clippings. The most polluting substance of all is a dead body. According to this definition, all humans become "unclean" at some point. The Zoroastrian textual tradition includes many stipulations through the ages as to how this situation might be managed and negated, so that the boundaries between "life" and "not-life" can be maintained.

Loose or trimmed hair and nail clippings are still treated as "unclean" (*na pak*) by many Zoroastrians, and are disposed of by being flushed down the toilet or placed in the bathroom dustbin. In many households, the bathroom is the only place where the hair is combed or nails cut, and such activity will not take place during the night, when the influence of evil is thought to be greatest. Some will take a bath or shower after the haircut for a ritual as well as physical cleansing.

Whereas priests and most laymen are only occasionally—and temporarily—unclean, two groups within the Zoroastrian community are constantly subjected to segregation through their "polluted" state: the *nasasalars* (corpse-bearers) of India and Pakistan; and women, through the occurrence of regular menstruation or childbirth.

Due to their profession, the *nasasalars* are perpetually polluted. They are provided accommodation separately from the community and sit apart to eat food at religious or social events held in public gathering places. Traditionalist Parsis do not shake their hands. At congregational events outside the fire temple, n*asasalars* will not come near the fire, and they will not enter the fire temple itself until they have purified themselves with the nine-day *barashnum* ritual.

It has been suggested in recent years that the *nasasalars* should not be treated as "second-class Zoroastrians" in this way, and that volunteer pallbearers should be used instead of, or as well as, the *nasasalars*, but should stop short of the *dakhma*. Such discussion arises from a desire to integrate the role of the *nasasalar* into the general community, but does not get around the traditionalist notion that the pollution brought by death must be controlled, so that the community at large is not negatively affected.

According to this traditionalist perspective, death and the defilement of dead matter comes through the agency of Angra Mainyu and the *daevas* (MP *dewan*). In Chapter 1, it was noted that in the texts, Druj Nasu is a female hypostasis of dead matter and menstruation is the domain of a female *daeva* named Jahi.

Pollution through dead matter is referred to in terms of an evil that has physical repercussions in terms of defiling or harming the elements of creation. Although washing with water is recommended before any ritual activity, the Avestan and then Middle Persian texts state there were certain levels of pollution that were thought to contaminate the water. In those cases, cattle urine (MP *gomez*) was used as a "cleansing" agent that was wiped over the person or object that was "unclean" before washing with water (Vd. 5.54, 56). Sometimes sand was used to dry the *gomez* first. Recitation of parts of the Avesta, particularly the prayer of dedication to Sraosha (the *Srosh baj*), was also used in the case of humans, to let loose the purifying power of the *manthra*. *Gomez* and consecrated bull's urine, *nirang*, is still used in some traditionalist Parsi rituals today, such as the ritual bath (*nahn*) before initiation or after childbirth (see "Birth," above). These elements are no longer part of any Iranian Zoroastrian practice, which has replaced the *nirang* with pomegranate juice.

The *Videvdad* contains injunctions to women to contain and control their monthly "pollution" (Vd. 16). This seems to have involved a formal separation of menstruating women from the community, so that they would not convey the corruption of death to others, or to the good creations of fire and water. Although we assume that these strictures and those of later texts were devised and elaborated by men, many women still choose to segregate themselves to a certain extent during menses. They no longer isolate themselves to the degree stipulated in the *Persian Rivayats*, which in Zoroastrian villages in Iran meant sequestration in an outbuilding away from water or fire. In India by the early twentieth century, when my own grandmother was a girl, women would be secluded in one part of the house, using only metal or glass utensils for eating. Metal, particularly iron, is non-porous, and therefore thought to be immune from the pollution of *nasu*.

A retired Parsi friend of mine, Behram, who grew up in Navsari, tells me that in his grandmother's time, for several days after the birth of a child, some mothers would not hand the baby directly to another person, but would place the swaddled baby carefully on a mat on the floor for the other person to pick up. Other mothers would pass the baby gently to his grandma without touching her hands with theirs. This was so the "uncleanness" of the mother's childbirth would not be passed on to anyone else. As an indication of how perceptions and practices have changed in the past century, it did not occur to Behram to expect his wife to follow such customs—nor would she have agreed. But prior to menopause, she voluntarily kept her distance from fire at any outer ritual when on her cycle, and did not enter the fire temple during that time.

Many Zoroastrian women engage in modern rationalist discourse about definitions of "purity" and "pollution," and regard the regulations of the *Videvdad* as antiquated and gender-biased. For many, the concept of "purity" is more to do with hygiene, or a "clear and spotless mind," than the maintenance of physical boundaries. Despite an intellectual scepticism about the practice of segregation, those same women may regard it as either a religious duty or an act of sensitivity to others to isolate themselves for a few days after the birth of a child or during menses. Some see this time as a welcome respite from the daily grind. And, as one of my Parsi female friends, who lives with her husband and young children in America, confided: "They don't want to take any chances (like me)!"

Most women on their cycle do not go near fire in the fire temple or at public ceremonies. Those who are more traditional may choose not to perform any domestic activity that involves fire, such as lighting the lamp for the daily prayers. They may also take a ritual bath (PGuj. *nahn;* Pers. *sar shostan*) after menstruation and forty days after childbirth. After this, the woman is considered to be free of *nasu*. A few Parsi women from priestly families may undergo the ritual purification of the *barashnum* ceremony after menopause. The women least likely to follow praxes relating to purity regulations are those younger Zoroastrians who were born or raised outside Iran or India.

HOW DO ZOROASTRIANS PUT THEIR ETHICS INTO PRACTICE?

The trifold Zoroastrian ethic—Good Thoughts, Good Words, Good Deeds—is similar to the ethical base of most religions. As someone said to me recently, "Whoever heard of a religion based on bad thoughts or actions?" The modernist Zoroastrian interpretation of the maxim emphasizes the exercise of personal responsibility in terms of living a good, ethical life, which shows that one has "chosen for" Ahura Mazda.

One of Adurbad-i Mahraspandan's precepts cited earlier states that out of thoughts, words, and actions, actions are best. The idea of actualizing ethical beliefs through lay and priestly praxis, including rituals to do with purity, has already been discussed. This last question is about how an ethic of "Good Deeds" has shaped and continues to shape the social and environmental awareness and activity of Zoroastrians.

From the *Gathas* and onward, the religion has been referred to internally as the "good religion" (Av. *daena vanguhi*). In Middle Persian books, the practitioners of the religion spoke of themselves as *weh denan*—"those of the good religion": the New Persian form is *beh dinan*. The question about how Zoroastrians put their ethics into practice is about the mandate of the good religion to be a person of integrity, truthfulness, and "doing the right thing" in both one's dealings with other people and one's impact on the material world.

A social ethic

In the *Gathas*, the concept of the *ashavan*—the person of integrity who upholds Order, Right, Justice, and Truth—is equally applicable to both men and women. They are both expected to promote—and to walk—the straight path at all times. Gathic terminology describes the forces of confusion and deception that can twist this path into an obstacle course. These forces represent an Old Iranian equivalent to contemporary social evils, which might be expressed in today's terms as the tyranny and corruption of unjust rule, the loss of self-control that leads to violence, the struggle of the needy, and the lack of protection for those who are most vulnerable. According to the *Gathas*, women and men should address such issues because they have chosen the good religion and are therefore bound by the directive to "do good" and "bring benefit." Also, they will be held accountable for their actions in life at the place of reckoning (Y. 46.10). Whatever is done today will have future repercussions.

In this manner, the pursuit of what might now be termed "social justice" is perceived as being woven into both the guiding principles and the individual eschatology of the *Gathas*. When Zoroastrians today recite the ancient *manthra* the *Ashem Vohu*, they feel that they are being reminded of their obligation to promote the "best good" and "happiness." Each human who chooses to follow the straight path is said to be imbued with a *fravashi*—a "pre-soul" that at creation chose to engage in the business of counteracting evil at all levels in order to bring about the future restoration of the world (Bd. 3.23–4). This scenario provides the Zoroastrian paradigm for decisive ethical action. The choice facing all humans at all times is whether to think, speak, and act beneficently or not; whether to bring healing or hurt (Y. 30.3, 9, 6). There can be no standing on the sidelines as a passive onlooker. This relates to the concept of maintaining the "right measure" that was referred to in Chapter 1.

The notion of "being strong in one's future action" is expressed in the Gathic concept of the *saoshyant*. Zoroastrians look to the example of Zarathushtra in the past and toward the *saoshyants* who will come in the future, and consider that they are positioned to bring benefit in the here and now. The individual, strengthened through personal prayer (which may involve the tying of the *kusti*), or through participation in community ritual, is empowered to do good in the wider world. The *gireban*—the small pocket sewn into the front of the *sudreh*, in which the good deeds of the individual are "stored," is cut out and burnt once the *sudreh* becomes worn out. Since this part of the garment represents the enactment of the religion it does not pollute the fire, but is seen as an offering. Sometimes, the sewn borders and the pocket at the back for potential good deeds are also cut out and burnt.

The wish to bring benefit to all living creatures is found in many prayers of the religion. The *Yenghe Hatam* prayer is about upholding Ahura Mazda's creation, and basing one's thought and action on the good model established by Ahura Mazda, who is "pastor for the poor" (Y. 27.13). The *hamazor* ritual described earlier is intended to encourage a sense of community responsibility that integrates practical acts of goodness into everyday life. The custom of sharing the bounties of life with others, particularly those who are in need, is evident at times of community celebration, when food is kept aside for anyone who is unable to attend the festivities due to illness or incapacity.

Another "wise saying" of Adurbad relates to the crucial role of such hospitality. Adurbad tells his co-religionists that when it comes to doing good deeds, they should keep their door open to whoever should turn up. In other words, they should not pick and choose the recipients of their benevolence, because anyone in need is deserving of aid. Adurbad admonished that if the person doing good deeds did not keep the door open to everyone, then the door to the "best existence" would be closed to him. I witnessed the application of this principle, when, in the spring of 2009, I attended a *gahanbar* in the village of Mazra-ye Kalantar, Yazd. There were a couple of elderly Muslim men from the village, sitting in the shade outside the community hall while the *gahanbar* was in progress. At the end of the ceremony, they were invited into the vestibule to share the food with their Zoroastrian neighbors.

Food is an obvious way of relieving the immediate distress of hunger, but also of bringing people into social contact with each other, which can address another form of human need. It is customary for Iranian Zoroastrians to celebrate any occasion of good fortune and blessing, such as the successful outcome of a medical procedure, the passing of an important exam, or the safe return of a member of the family from a long journey, by making a nourishing soup to share with friends and neighbors, regardless of status or religion. The soup is known as *ash-e khayirat*, or "Charity Soup." The favorite kinds of soup for this are *ash-e reshteh* (noodle soup, made with lots of beans and chick peas) or *ab gushte sonati* (a thick meat and bean soup). In former times, the preparation and offering of this soup took place frequently, often in fulfillment of a personal vow to distribute the soup on an annual or even monthly basis.

A Middle Persian text lists the best qualities for humans to nurture. These include:

for the soul, generosity . . .
for the body, wisdom,

[and] for all works, right-mindedness . . .
generosity is the greatest good deed (MX 2.2, 6; 3. 2, 4).

The exercise of generosity, wisdom, and compassion in bringing practical relief from distress was reiterated in a letter from Dr. Homi Dhalla in a letter to the magazine *Parsiana*:

> The Zoroastrian ideals of self-control, moderation and kindness are useful guideposts for [the] prevention and care [of AIDS] . . . Who are we to judge and condemn? Instead of rejecting AIDS victims, we should not only accept them but also show compassion.[28]

Dr. Dhalla placed the mandate for such altruistic behavior on the part of Zoroastrians as being the particular duty of those who have the financial means. He went on to describe the pragmatic initiative against AIDS that has been implemented by the Godrej group, a Parsi-owned corporation. This involves the implementation of education and prevention strategies as well as welfare programs for Godrej company workers and their families that include free screening for HIV, and free counseling and anti-retroviral treatment for those who test positive.

The preservation of honesty and integrity by Zoroastrians in their business dealings and company policies has been a proverbial aspect of the religion. Michael Fischer noted, during his time in Yazd in the early 1970s, that "[P]eople remember how bags of money would be left with such-and-such a merchant without being counted. And still today, Zoroastrians are hired in banks, as accountants, and in offices on the theory that they are more honest."[29] In a similar vein, he remarks that "the word of a Parsi sufficed as security for transactions involving large sums of money."[30] Self-promotion as a member of a religion that encourages such upright behavior does not in itself indicate scrupulousness in all matters. Nor can a general reputation for integrity be indiscriminately applied to an entire group, but, as Fischer points out, a minority religious community would soon lose its reputation for honesty and would suffer the social and legal consequences if they cheated, especially against non-Zoroastrians.

In one version of the Parsi story of the Sugar and Milk, the *dastur* does not place sugar, but a gold ring in the bowl of milk, signifying both the brightness and the material benefit that the Parsis will bring.

The accrual of wealth through honest work is considered to be a positive attribute, but it carries with it the social obligation to share that wealth with those who are in need. Such social responsibilities have been taken seriously, as evidenced by the number of hospitals, orphanages, schools, fire temples, and housing complexes in both Iran and India that bear Zoroastrian names. This model of philanthropy is one that also embraces non-Zoroastrians. For instance, Arbab Rustam Guiv, the president of the Tehran *anjuman* in the 1940s and 1950s, and his wife, Morvarid Khanum, founded low-income housing for Zoroastrians in Tehran with an *atashkadeh* and a community center, but also built a water reservoir (Pers. *ab anbar*) in Yazd, that benefitted all.

At around this time, the sons of Ardeshir Godarz Jahanian founded a hospital in Yazd, to which a maternity clinic and training school for nurses were later annexed. The family set up endowments to treat any patient in need, and during the Iran-Iraq war in the 1980s the hospital cared for many wounded Iranian soldiers. Other Zoroastrian families established water reservoirs and schools open to all in or near the city of Yazd. Two brothers from Yazd, Mehraban and Faridoon Zartoshty, whose family had always set aside part of their business profits for charity, have helped to fund Zoroastrian educational and philanthropical ventures, as well as religious institutions, around the world. Most recently, their support partially financed the renovation of the Zoroastrian Centre in London, and the establishment of a Chair in Zoroastrian Studies at the School of Oriental and African Studies, University of London.

The Parsis of India provide similar examples of philanthropy that have far-reaching benefits beyond the immediate Zoroastrian community. For instance, apart from founding an Atash Bahram in Mumbai, Dr. Maneck Wadia's ancestors also established a college, an Institute of Technology and an Institute of Cardiology, along with numerous other educational and medical foundations. One Parsi company that is renowned for creating a supportive work environment for all its employees is the Tata Motors plant at Jamshedpur, founded in 1945. This corporation branch operates community support centers for those who live and work in the region, and has implemented the introduction of water supplies and road construction, the sustainable development of land and of rural industries, rural health and education institutions, and family planning.[31]

This kind of holistic approach has become a model for other Parsi enterprises and for non-Zoroastrian companies in India. Such a model not only serves the immediate physical and psychological needs of employees and local residents, but it is also intended to have a positive impact on the surrounding environment.

An environmental ethic

Adurbad-i Mahraspandan—not surprisingly—also had something to say about this relationship between humans and the environment. He is attributed with the statement that it is important to cultivate the earth and to do good things, because all humans are nourished through such activity. The idea of being nourished in both a literal and figurative way through cultivation of the soil is found in the *Videvdad*: those who plant grain are said to plant *asha* and those who share the produce of the earth with others also bring joy to the earth (Vd. 3.31, 34). Adurbad goes on to warn people not to harm water, fire, cattle, sheep, or dogs. These admonitions echo those in the *Gathas* and the *Yasna Haptanghaiti* to care for the cow and the ox, and to provide peaceful pasturage for cattle.

In this age of competitive "greenness," Zoroastrians often make the claim that theirs is the first ecologically-aware religion. This claim derives from the early connection that is made between the *amesha spentas* and their correlate elements in the material world. It is partly supported by the fact that injunctions to "gladden the earth"—particularly through the growing of cereal crop, grass, and food-bearing plants (Vd. 3.4, 23)—actually seem to have been put into practice at an early stage. From the Ancient Persian period onward, documents from Persepolis and elsewhere tell us that Zoroastrians were engaged in the cultivation of farms, orchards, and produce-bearing gardens on both crown lands and private estates. Darius I's specific request for the prevention of a "bad harvest" denotes an imperial ideology coherent with the Avestan worldview that a harmonious and orderly existence was marked by the thriving of both the land and its people.

The trope of nurturing the land as part of a divine mandate was observed by Jean Chardin, the French merchant and travel writer who visited Iran in the mid–seventeenth century. Chardin remarked that the Zoroastrians—whom he called *Guèbres*—considered that planting trees, and reclaiming barren fields to grow grain or fruit was "meritorious and noble . . . the first of all vocations, that for which the Sovereign God and the Lesser Gods [the *yazatas*] as they say, have the most satisfaction and which they reward most amply."[32] Today, many Zoroastrian-owned or operated companies keep up such environmentally friendly activity. Tata Motors, for example, is a signatory to the United Nations Global Compact, an initiative that consists of ten principles to which businesses pledge to align their operations and strategies. These principles cover the fields of human rights protection, labor standards, environmental issues, and anti-corruption guidelines.

One "homegrown" environmental problem that the Zoroastrians of the Indian subcontinent have had to confront in recent years relates to the *dakhmenashini* system—the consignment of the corpse to the *dakhma*. As mentioned earlier, this practice is still in use in India and Karachi, Pakistan, but in the last two decades it has been challenged as a viable system. There are various factors behind these challenges of which the two prime causes are the increased proximity of high-rise residences overlooking the *dakhmas*, and the decimation of the vulture population in the region. The former problem—more a social than environmental one—has been addressed by not using the visible *dakhmas* and by planting more trees to shield the "towers of silence" from outside eyes and vice versa.

The decline of the Southeast Asian vultures is a global issue, but in the case of the Parsis it has also led to public health concerns regarding the length of time it now takes for the disposal of a corpse. Parsis have been active in addressing the problem at both worldwide and local levels. They have supported research into the cause of the vulture decline, which has now been attributed to the consumption of biochemical toxins, particularly diclofenac, used by vets to treat livestock. Diclofenac was banned in India and Pakistan in 2006, and in Nepal in 2009, and an alternate treatment for livestock found, but some farmers still use the toxic drugs.

Before the cause of the loss of vultures was known, the BPP began to discuss alternative options for disposal of the dead. Some opted for the method of stone-encased burial. Others felt that the practice of cremation used by the majority of the Hindu population was acceptable as a "cleaner" way of disposal of the body. Traditionalists, however, are set on preserving the *dakhmenashini* system as the most religiously sanctioned. To this end, they have helped to promote a vulture-breeding program. Several years ago, one of the *dakhmas* was adapted for solar concentrators intended to speed up the decomposition of the corpse, but these only work in sunny weather. There continues to be internal debate as to whether this method is in keeping with the ancient tenets of the religion, and also, whether it is a "clean" way to dispose of the body.

The environmental concerns raised by this issue highlight the paradoxical nature of trying to correlate some ancient practices with those of modern ecological conservationism. For instance, the ancient Zoroastrian care to keep the waters of rivers and streams clean from urine, spit, or "dead matter" is a sound practice, but is religiously based on the concern that the waters themselves should not be polluted through contact with dead matter. Middle Persian legal texts stipulated that it was unlawful for Zoroastrians to visit bathhouses run by or frequented by Muslims for this reason. It was not until recent times that this apotropaic rationale for keeping the waters pure was reinterpreted as a safeguarding from harm in ecological terms.

It would be misleading, however, to suggest that the Zoroastrian approach to nature has only been concerned with preserving the ritual purity of the elements of earth, fire, and water, rather than the ecosystem as a whole. The passages from the *Videvdad* that praise the cultivation of the earth display an understanding that humans can either have a "good" and productive impact on the environment, or a "bad" and destructive impact. This dual taxonomy of "good" or "bad"—as with all Zoroastrians categorization—operates at both a physical and ethical level.

As Dr. Richard Foltz, a professor of Religion at the University of Concordia, Montreal, has pointed out in a recent paper, such categorization does not always cohere with modern thinking on environmental issues.[33] This is particularly true with regard to the teaching that although certain animals, such as the cow and the dog are beneficent, other animals are the miscreations of Angra Mainyu, such as flies, snakes, frogs, and other creepy-crawlies (Vd. 14.5–6). The *Videvdad* states that such noxious creatures (*xrafstra*) should be killed, an action that Herodotus indicates was put into practice (*Histories* 1.140). Agathias records a day known as the "Removal of Evil" when Zoroastrians killed serpents, and other wild animals in the belief that they were increasing good and combatting evil.[34] A thousand years later, Tavernier described a similar list of harmful animals to Herodotus, and a festival when the

Zoroastrian women went out to kill all the frogs they could find in the fields.[35] In these accounts, the extermination of such animals is presented as undertaken from a moral rather than an ecological or biological motive, and based on the notion that they are evil.

Foltz notes:

> [F]or contemporary ecologists concerned with maintaining the overall integrity of ecosystems, the reverence for nature that is undeniably to be found in the Zoroastrian tradition would nevertheless be seen as unacceptably selective . . . Contrary to the Zoroastrian tradition, nature does not distinguish between "good" and "bad" species, and all organisms are dependent on the waste, death, and decay of other organisms.[36]

The differing perspectives between many ancient religious teachings and the contemporary scientific understanding of the world often stimulate a degree of reinterpretation of the former, in order for the religion to retain its relevance. Although the binary classification of "good" and "evil" remains at the core of the Zoroastrian religion, the ancient stipulations to keep the natural elements "clean" are now often reconstructed as relating less to ritual purity than to a wider ethic of renewal for the self and the world.

EPILOGUE: ENDLESS LIGHTS AND LIMITLESS TIME

One dictionary definition of an Epilogue is that it is a short speech addressed by one of the protagonists of a play to the audience. That speech provides a summary of what has occurred as well as a hint at what the future holds. Because there are so many voices claiming to represent the Zoroastrian religion, I felt that it would be too biased for me to choose one voice above all others to provide the closing statement—and to choose all would mean that the book would never be completed. Although my own biases have been at work in the compilation and arrangement of the material presented here, I hope that I have allowed Zoroastrians who hold different perspectives on the religion to speak out in their own voices throughout the book. Some will no doubt tell me that their particular voice was not loud enough or properly represented. Such critique will, I hope, lead to further dialogue, both within the various factions of Zoroastrianism, and also between academics aiming to produce a qualitative analysis of the religion and those claiming to adhere to it.

My own summation of the contents of the book is as follows: The baseline questions at the front of this book and at the beginning of each of the three main sections indicate that the queries of outsiders and some insiders concerning Zoroastrianism are, for the most part, the kind of questions that are asked of all religions. The conceptual questions relate to the nature and essence of the divine, the problem of evil, the purpose of human existence, what happens at the end of life for the individual, and whether there is an end of time in universal terms. The questions to do with sacred text are about its authority in terms both of divine guidance and of human transmission and interpretation. And then there are all those matters concerning the nitty-gritty of religious practice—to do with the symbols, artifacts, rituals, places of worship, rites of passage, and ethical practices. This book highlights some of the responses of the Good Religion to these three areas of discussion and attempts to show how they have evolved through the millennia.

An Epilogue can also be the section at the end of a literary work that deals with the fate of its characters. As humans continue to evolve, perhaps we will move collectively closer to the light, where some of the questions we ask concerning our place in the world and the nature of that world will be blindingly clear. In the present, however, there remains a set of questions that have been asked for generations, but that relate to matters that only "limitless time" will resolve. They concern the sustained connection between religion and ethnicity, the relationship between religion and gender, the preservation of identity in a religiously plural society, the cost and compromise involved in the survival of a minority religion, and the persistence of ancient beliefs and praxes in a predominantly rationalist and materialist world. Since this is not a novel, I do not have a free hand to construct the future of the religion that has been the focus of these pages. Any prediction as to what might happen to Zoroastrianism as a discrete religious system in years to come is an area of conjecture that is the prerogative and problem of Zoroastrians, rather than within the purview of this book.

Although Zoroastrians do speculate on the fate—or destiny—of their religion, the most common questions that they ask of themselves do not seem to relate to what will happen in the long run. Instead, my impression is that they ask the same Ultimate Questions about life as others, albeit from a specifically Zoroastrian mindset. These self-examinations are found in one of the sections of the *Gathas*, Yasna 44, which is often aptly called the "Yasna of Questions." They include:

v.1. "How shall I venerate Mazda?"
v.2. "What is the source of the Best Existence?"
v.6. "Is what I speak really the truth?"
v.8. "What is the teaching of Mazda concerning enlightenment?"
v.9. "How shall I fully realize my insight into religion?"
v.12. "Among the people that I speak with, who is righteous and who is a liar?"

v.13. "How shall we get rid of the Spirit of Untruth from among us?"

v.17. "How can I reach your perfection, Mazda, and make my voice effective?"[1]

The answers to these ancient but ever-pertinent personal challenges encompass all levels of understanding and awareness of the religion.

GLOSSARY OF TERMS AND NAMES

ab zohr "libation to the waters"

Achu Michu (PGuj.) a welcoming ceremony

Adargan (PGuj. *Atashnu parab*) the "birthday" of fire, the ninth day of the ninth month

Adurbad-i Mahraspandan high priest under the Sasanian king, Shapur II

aeshma "wrath"

afargan fire vase

afrinagan a ceremony of blessing

agiary (PGuj.) fire temple

Ahuna Vairya an Old Avestan *manthra*

Ahura Mazda the "Wise Lord"

Airyaman ishya an Old Avestan *manthra*

Ameretat "immortality"; one of the *Amesha Spentas*

Amesha Spentas the "beneficent immortals"

Anahita female *yazata* of the beneficent waters

Angra Mainyu (MP *Ahriman*) the "destructive impulse/spirit"

anjuman "association," "organization"

aramgah "place of peace"; cemetery

Armaiti "right-mindedness"; one of the *Amesha Spentas*

Asha "order," "right," "truth"; one of the *Amesha Spentas*

ashavan "one who follows *asha*"

Ashem Vohu an ancient prayer

astvant "boney," "corporeal"

Astvat.ereta "he who embodies *asha*"; the name of the final *saoshyant*

Atash Adaran "fire of fires"; second grade of fire

Atash Bahram "victory fire"; highest grade of fire

Atash Dadgah "fire in a lawful place"; third and lowest grade of fire

atashkadeh (Pers.) "house of fire"; fire temple

atashparast (Pers.) "fire-worshipper"; misnomer for Zoroastrians

Avan Yazad Jashan (PGuj. *Avanu Parab*) the "birthday" of the waters; the tenth day of the eighth month

Avesta corpus of sacred texts of the Zoroastrians

bareshnum nine-night ritual of ablution and purification

barsom bundle of metal rods or twigs held by the priests in ritual

behdin (Pers.) someone of the "good religion"

Bundahishn "Creation"; Middle Persian Zoroastrian text

chinvat peretu "crossing-place of the account-keeper," where the soul is judged at death

daena "[religious] insight"; religion
daeva false/erroneous god
dakhma site of exposure of the dead; also known as a "tower of silence"
dakhmenashini system of exposure in a *dakhma*
dar-i mihr fire temple; prayer hall
dastur highest rank of priest
Denkard "Acts of the Religion"; Middle Persian Zoroastrian text
divo oil lamp
dregvant "one who follows *druj*"; a "liemonger"
druj the Lie; deceit, chaos, confusion
Farvardigan festival commemorating the *fravashis*
Farvardin month name
Ferdowsi composer of *Shah Nameh*
Feridun (Av. *Thraetaona*) Iranian mythical hero
frasha (Av.) "wonderful," "perfect"; (OP) "excellent"
frasho.kereti (MP *frashegird*) "the making wonderful/perfect" of the world
fravashi the "pre-soul" that pre-exists and post-exists the individual
gah "time"; also "place"
gahanbar one of six seasonal festivals
Gathas the Old Avestan *manthras* of Zarathushtra
getig "living" existence
gomez cattle urine, used as a ritual cleansing agent
Haft Sin the "seven s's"; seven items beginning with 's' on the Nav Ruz table
haiti (sg. *ha*) "sections"of the *Gathas* or *Yasna Haptanghaiti*
hamazor "united in strength"; a ritual handshake
haoma (MP *hom*) the beneficent plant pressed during the *Yasna*, and offered
    with milk and water as *ab zohr* at the end of the liturgy
Haurvatat "wholeness,""health,"; one of the *Amesha Spentas*
herbad "religious teacher"; now, priest (*erbad*) who is initiated as *navar*
Ilm-i Khshnoom "knowledge of *khshnoom*": an esoteric interpretation of
    Zoroastrian texts and rituals
jashan ceremony of praise and thanksgiving
Kerdir a powerful priest under several early Sasanian monarchs
Khordad Sal sixth day of Farvardin month, birthday of Asho Zarathushtra
Khordeh Avesta prayer book
kusti woven cord of wool, worn over the *sudreh* after initiation
loban (PGuj.) incense
lork (Pers.) festival food of seven kinds of dried fruits, chickpeas, and nuts
magi ancient term for Zoroastrian priests
manthra sacred "thought-word"
Mazdayasna "Mazda worship"
Mihragan a seasonal (fall) celebration in honor of *Mithra*
Mithra "bond", "contract"; male *yazata*
menog "conceptual" existence
mobed ordained priest
mobedyar lay "helper to the priest"
Muktad Parsi celebration before *Nav Ruz* (similar to Iranian *Farvardigan*)
nasasalar "corpse-bearer"

nask "bundle"; one of the 21 parts of the Avesta

nasu "dead matter"

navar first grade of ordination as a priest

navjote Parsi term for initiation

Nav Ruz "New Day"; New Year's Day

Nerangestan an Avestan text on priestly ritual, with Middle Persian commentary

nirang i. a powerful prayer; ii. consecrated bull's urine

niyayishn "praises"; five Avestan prayers to the sun, Mithra, the moon, the waters, and fire

nowzut rite of ordination into the priesthood in Iran

padan mouth-covering white cloth worn by priest while facing the fire

padyab ritual washing of hands and face (Parsis may also wash the feet)

panthak (PGuj.) jurisdiction of Parsi priest

panthaki Parsi priest responsible for a *panthak*

Persian Rivayats correspondence concerning the religion sent from Iranian Zoroastrians to Parsis between the fifteenth and eighteenth centuries

saoshyant "one who will be strong"; a future benefactor of the religion

sedreh pushi Iranian Zoroastrian term for initiation

seis silver tray used in Parsi ceremonies

Shah Nameh Iranian national epic, composed by Ferdowsi

siroza "thirty days"; prayers for the 30 *yazatas* presiding over the days of the month

spenta "bringing increase," "beneficent"

Spenta Mainyu "beneficent inspiration/spirit"; one of the *Amesha Spentas*

Sraosha "readiness to listen"; a *yazata*

sudreh (Pers. *sedreh*) white cotton shirt invested during initiation

Tandorosti a prayer for health and wellbeing

Tirgan a seasonal (midsummer) festival dedicated to *Tishtrya*

Tishtrya yazata of water and fertility

Tosar priest under the Sasanian king, Ardashir I

urvan "soul"

urwisgah place where the Yasna ceremony is performed

Videvdad/ Vendidad "law dispelling the *daevas*"; a Young Avestan text

Vohu Manah "good thought"; one of the *Amesha Spentas*

Xshathra Vairya "desired rule"; one of the *Amesha Spentas*

yasht Young Avestan "hymn" to the *yazatas*

Yasna "worship/consecration"; the liturgy and its Avestan text

Yasna Haptanghaiti "worship of the seven sections"; Old Avestan liturgy

yazata a "being worthy of worship"

Yenghe Hatam an ancient prayer

zand "exegesis," commentary on the Avesta

zaotar (MP *zot*) "one who pours"; a priest

zaothra (MP *zohr*) "libation"

Zarathushtri "like Zarathushtra"

Zardosht no Diso (PGuj.)/*Dargozasht-e Asho Zartosht* (Pers.) the death anniversary of Zarathushtra, on the eleventh day of the tenth month

A HISTORICAL TIMELINE

c. 1500 BCE Iranians in the region of the modern Central Asian republics?
Old Avestan oral texts: mid–late 2nd millennium BCE
Young Avestan oral texts: early to mid–1st millennium BCE

9th century BCE Persians and Medes in (north)western Iran
669–c. 630 Neo-Assyrian Assurbanipal rules from Nineveh

c. 550–330 BCE The Ancient Persian /Achaemenid Empire
539 Cyrus II (the Great) captures Babylon
522–486 Darius I rules the Achaemenid Empire
Old Persian cuneiform inscriptions: late 6th—4th centuries BCE
509–494 *Persepolis Fortification Tablets*
516 Second Temple dedicated in Jerusalem
472 Aeschylus' play *The Persians* staged in Athens
486–465 Xerxes rules
465–424 Artaxerxes I rules: Nehemiah and Ezra (?) at the Achaemenid court
c. 430–425 Herodotus' *Histories*
404–358 Artaxerxes II rules
c. 430–354 Xenophon: *Anabasis, Cyropaedia*
384–322 Aristotle
c. 378–320 Theopompus: *Philippika*

334–330 BCE Alexander of Macedon overthrows Ancient Persians

312 Seleucid Dynasty founded
305–280 Seleucus, king of Persia

c. 270–231 Ashoka, ruler of Buddhist Maurya Empire

c. 250 BCE–224 CE Arsacid (Parthian) Empire

206 BCE–222 CE Han Dynasty, China

1st–4th centuries CE: Kushan Empire predominated in the region of Gandhara

c. 63–24 CE Strabo: *Geography*
23/24–79 Pliny the Elder: *Natural History*
c. 37–100 Josephus: *Antiquities*
46–120 Plutarch: *On Isis and Osiris*
216 Mani was born

224–651 CE Sasanian Empire
Middle Persian inscriptions and texts: 300–1000 CE
224–c. 240 Ardashir I rules; Tosar is high priest
c. 240–272 Shapur I rules; the priest Kerdir rises to power
c. 273–276 Bahram I rules
c. 276–293 Bahram II rules; Kerdir at the peak of his power
293–302 Narseh rules
301 Armenia converts to Christianity
309–379 Shapur II rules: Adurbad-i Mahraspandan is high priest
4th century: Syriac texts concerning Persian (Christian) martyrs
438–457 Yazdegerd II rules: Mihr Narseh is prime minister
mid–5th century: Elishe Vardapet's *History of Vardan and the Armenian War*
489 Byzantine Emperor Zeno closes the "Nestorian" School of Edessa
529 Byzantine Emperor Justinian closes the Neoplatonic Academy in Athens
531–579 Khosrow I rules
6th/7th centuries CE: corpus of *Avesta* written down
591–628 Khosrow II rules
632–651 Yazdegerd III rules

661–750 Umayyads rule Iran
750–1258 Abbasids rule Iran
Zoroastrians ("Parsis") emigrate to the Gujarat region of India
9th–10th centuries CE: *Middle Persian Zoroastrian books* compiled and written
New Persian texts: 1000 CE onward
1010 Ferdowsi completes the *Shah Nameh*
1135–1204 Moses Maimonides: *Guide for the Perplexed*
1258–1368 Mongols dominate Eurasia
c. 1278 *Zartosht Nameh* ("the Book of Zarathushtra")
1368–1506 Timurid dynasty in Central Asia and Iran
1502–1524 Safavid dynasty based in Isfahan, Iran

1526–1707 Mughal Rule in India
1612–1757 British East India Company active in India
1670s first Bombay Parsi Punchayat founded
1757–1857 BEIC rule in India
1851 Rahnumae Mazdayasnan Sabha ("Religious Reform Association")
  founded

1779–1924 Qajar dynasty, Iran

1858–1947 British Raj in India

1861 Zoroastrian Trust Funds of Europe (now ZTFE, Inc.) established in London

1947 Indian independence

1925–1979 Pahlavi dynasty, Iran

1979 Islamic Republic of Iran formed

1980 World Zoroastrian Organization (WZO) founded
1987 Federation of Zoroastrian Associations of North America (FEZANA) registered as an organization
2004 Association for the Revival of Zoroastrianism (ARZ) founded
2005 World Alliance of Parsi and Irani Zarthoshtis (WAPIZ) founded

NOTES

INTRODUCTION

1 To overcome any difficulty in articulating the word "Zoroastrianism," readers might consider listening to a phonetic pronunciation online. The *Oxford English Dictionary*—apparently the first place to record the name of the religion as such—uses the phonetic transcription "zɒrəʊ'astriənizəm." In the *American Heritage Dictionary*, the word is respelled in the more easily readable form "zôrō-ăstrē-ə-nĭzəm."

2 Y. 4.11, 59.18.

3 See http://www.wapiz.com/whoare.htm

4 J. K. Choksy, "Despite Shāhs and Mollās: Minority Sociopolitics in Premodern and Modern Iran," *JAH 40/2* (2006): 129–84; 176.

5 Ibid., 136.

6 N. Kotwal, "History of the North American Mobeds Council (NAMC)," *FEZANA Journal* (Spring 2010): 90–2; 91.

7 See, for example, Kreyenbroek and Munshi (2001), 47.

8 S. Taraporewala, *Parsis: The Zoroastrians of India: A Photographic Journey 1980–2004* (Woodstock, New York and London: Overlook Duckworth, 2004), 21.

9 W. M. Braun, "Zoroastrian Bioethics: The Evolution of An Ancient Ethic to a Code for Modern Science and Medicine," unpublished M.A. paper, Claremont Graduate University, 2009.

10 Mobed M. Firouzgary, "Zarathushtis in Iran—a demographic profile," *FEZANA Journal* (Winter 2004): 26–8; 27.

11 A. Ariane, "From the desk of an Iranian immigrant," *Parsiana* (August 2004), 185.

12 See Palsetia (2001), 158–64.

13 Ibid., 185, 272.

14 J. K. Choksy, "Zoroastrianism," in B. R. Taylor, ed., *The Encyclopaedia of Religion and Nature* (Bristol: Thoemmes Continuum, 2005): 1811–15; 1811.

15 See http://zoroastrian.ru/en/node/14.

16 As reported in *Bombay Samachar* August 22, 2010.

17 M. Stausberg, "Para-Zoroastrianisms," in Hinnells and Williams (2007): 236–54.

18 M. M. J. Fischer, *Zoroastrian Iran Between Myth and Praxis*, unpublished Ph.D. dissertation, University of Chicago, 1975, 9.

19 See J. Cribb, "Das Pantheon der Kushana-Könige," in C. Luczanits (ed.), *Gandhara: das Buddhistische Erbe Pakistans– Legenden, Kloster und Paradiese* (Mainz, Bonn: Zabern, 2008): 122–5.
20 See J. R. Russell, *Zoroastrianism in Armenia* (Cambridge, MA: Harvard University Press, 1987).

CHAPTER 1

1 A. Hintze, "The Migrations of the Indo-Iranians and the Iranian Sound-Change s>h," in W. Meid, ed., *Sprache und Kultur der Indogermanen* (Innsbruck: Innsbrucker Beiträge zur Sprachwissenschaft, 1998): 140–53; 147–8.
2 J. Kellens, *Essays on Zarathustra and Zoroastrianism*, trans. and ed., P. O. Skjaervø (Costa Mesa, CA: Mazda, 2000), 51.
3 W. H. T. Gairdner, trans., *Al-Ghazzali's Mishkât Al-Anwar* ("The Niche of Lights") (Lahore: Shaykh Muhammad Ashraf, reprint 1952), 166.
4 P. O. Skjaervø, "The Achaemenids in the Avesta," in Curtis and Stewart (2005), 57. Identical statements are found on a statue of Darius I carved in Egypt, then transferred to Susa, the Persian capital in Elam; on a cliff inscription by Darius in the Elwand Gorge, near Hamadan; and at Persepolis at the beginning of one of Xerxes' inscriptions.
5 B. Lincoln, "A la recherche du paradis perdu," *History of Religions 43/2* (2003): 139–54; 148.
6 For a detailed discussion of this verse, see A. Hintze, *A Zoroastrian Liturgy: The Worship in Seven Chapters (Yasna 35–41)* (Wiesbaden: Harrassowitz, 2007), 147–54.
7 Vasunia (2007), 144.
8 Vd. 3.7–11; 7.25; 8.6–7.
9 Hintze, *A Zoroastrian Liturgy*, 230–2
10 Clement of Alexandria, *Protreptikos* 5.65.3.
11 For an introduction to the use of "progressive" in a Zoroastrian context, see above, pp. 10, 13, 16.
12 Mehr (2003), 33–4.
13 *FEZANA Journal* (Summer 2001), 61.
14 Adapted from R. G. Kent, *Old Persian Grammar, Texts, Lexicon* (New Haven, CT: American Oriental Society, second ed. rev., 1953), 148.
15 P. O. Skjaervø, www.fas.harvard.edu/~iranian/Zoroastrianism/Zoroastrianism3_Texts_II.pdf, 167.
16 R. W. Thomson, trans. and comm., *Elishē: History of Vardan and the Armenian War* (Cambridge, MA: Harvard University Press, 1982), 78–9.
17 Gairdner, *Al-Ghazali's Mishkât al-Anwar*, 167.
18 J. W. Boyd and D. A. Crosby, "Is Zoroastrianism Dualistic or Monotheistic?" *JAAR 47/4* (December 1979): 557–88; 558.
19 M. Stausberg, "Zoroastrianism," in P. B. Clarke and P. Beyer, eds., *The World's Religions: Continuities and Transformations* (London, New York: Routledge, 2009): 721–36; 732.
20 P. O. Skjaervø, "Truth and Deception in Ancient Iran," in F. Vajifdar and C. Cereti, eds., *Jamshid Soroush Soroushian Commemorative Volume*,

vol. II: *Taš-e dorun: The Fire Within* (Bloomington, IN: 1st Books Library, 2003): 383–434; 423.

21 Y.26.4; Yt. 13.149.

22 Cf. PRDd. 48.55; see A. V. Williams, *The Pahlavi Rivāyat Accompanying the Dādestān ī Dēnīg, Part II: Translation, Commentary and Pahlavi Text*, Copenhagen: Munksgaard (1990), 83, and 234 n.35.

23 Rivetna (2002), 56.

24 S. Shaked, trans., *The Wisdom of the Sasanian Sages (Denkard VI)* (Costa Mesa, CA: Mazda, 1979), 17.

25 Skjaervø, "Achaemenids and the Avesta," 74.

26 Fr.W. 4.3: see Y. Vevaina, "Resurrecting the Resurrection: Eschatology and Exegesis in Late Antique Zoroastrianism," *BAI 19* ([2005] 2010): 215–23; 217.

27 See, for instance: www.frashogard.com; http://tenets.zoroastrianism.com; www.indiayellowpages.com/zoroastrian.

28 See Williams, *The Pahlavi Rivāyat*, 63, 191.

29 Cf. Vevaina, "Resurrecting the Resurrection," 217–18.

30 P.O. Skjaervø, www.fas.harvard.edu/~iranian/Zoroastrianism/Zoroastrianism3_Texts_II.pdf, 167.

31 *Anabasis* 5.3.9–12; 1.2.7; *Hellenika* 4.1.14; *Oikonomikos* 4.13

32 See J. R. Russell, "Ezekiel and Iran," in A. Netzer and S. Shaked, eds., *Irano-Judaica V* (Jerusalem: Ben-Zvi Insititute, 2003): 1–15.

33 See, for instance, Isa. 27.1–3, 26.19–21.

34 *Natural History* 30.3: cited in Vasunia (2007), 70. A discussion of this and other connections between the Greek philosophers and Zoroastrians may be found in de Jong (1997), especially pages 205–12.

35 See Rose (2000); Stausberg (1998), vol. 1.

36 There is still a small, but active Jewish community in Iran, and sizeable Jewish Iranian populations on both the east and west coasts of America—in Los Angeles, California, and on Long Island, New York.

CHAPTER 2

1 F. M. Kotwal and J. W. Boyd, "The Zoroastrian *paragnā* ritual", *Journal of Mithraic Studies 2/1* (1977): 18–53; 37.

2 S. Simmons, *Entertaining the Persian Way* (Harpenden: Lennard, 1991), 35–6.

3 P. O. Skjaervø, "The Importance of Orality for the Study of Old Iranian Literature and Myth," *Nāme-ye Irān-e Bāstān 5/1&2* (2005–6): 9–31; 21.

4 PRDd 17b1; see A. V. Williams, *The Pahlavi Rivāyat Accompanying the Dādestān ī Dēnīg, Part II: Translation Commentary and Pahlavi Text* (Copenhagen: Munksgaard, 1990), 32.

5 See A. Hintze, "On the Literary Structure of the Older Avesta," *BSOAS 65/1* (2002): 31–51; 46–50.

6 M. Shaki, "The Denkard Account of the History of the Zoroastrian Scriptures," *Archiv Orientalni 49* (1981): 114–25; 124, 119.

7 *Zandik* is sometimes translated as "Manichaean": the latter were known as *zindiq* in early Islamic texts.

8 M. M. Noshirwani, "9th World Zoroastrian Congress, Dubai 28th—31st December 2009," *Hamazor* I (2010): 19–25; 24.

9 B. Murphy, *The Root of Wild Madder: Chasing the History, Mystery, and Lore of the Persian Carpet* (New York: Simon & Shuster, 2005), 151–2.

10 cf. Y. 2.13, Dk. 7.1.41,

11 M. L. West, *The Hymns of Zoroaster: A New Translation of the Most Ancient Sacred Texts of Iran* (London: I.B. Tauris, 2010), 3–4.

12 J. Kellens and E. Pirart, *Les Textes Vieil-Avestiques* I: *Introduction, texte et traduction* (Wiesbaden: Dr. Ludwig Reichert Verlag, 1988), 18.

13 A. Hintze, "On the Literary Structure," 48–9, 35.

14 Kellens and Pirart, "Les textes," 20, my translation.

15 See Rose (2000), 176, 190 n. 17.

16 M. N. Dhalla, *History of Zoroastrianism* (Bombay: K. R. Cama Oriental Institute, repr. 1994), 322.

17 J. J. Modi, *A Catechism of the Zoroastrian Religion* (Bombay, 1911), 4.

18 Ibid., 15.

19 Dhalla, *History of Zoroastrianism*, 13; M. N. Dhalla, *Zoroastrian Theology from the Earliest Times to the Present Day* (New York: 1914), 16

20 Y. 46.14; 51.16; 53.2.

21 Yt 13.88, 94; Yt. 19.53; Vd 8.19, 18.

22 See De Jong (1997), 126

23 P.O. Skjaervø, www.fas.harvard.edu/~iranian/Zoroastrianism/Zoroastrianism3_Texts_II.pdf, 150.

24 M. Boyce, *The Letter of Tansar* (Rome: IsMEO, 1968), 33.

25 R. Levy, trans., A. Banini, rev., *The Epic of the Kings* (London: Routledge & Kegan Paul, 1985), 419.

26 See Ervad P. M. Bajan, "Panthaks: Their Historic Evolution and Modern Day Functions," *FEZANA Journal* (Spring 2010): 57–9.

27 Fischer (2004), 26.

28 N. Green, "The Survival of Zoroastrianism in Yazd," *Iran: Journal of Persian Studies* 38 (2000): 115–22; 119.

29 Cited in A. S. Wadia, "Religious Education and the Future of Young Mobeds in North America . . . and Beyond," *FEZANA Journal* 23/3 (Fall/ September 2009): 60–1; 60.

30 A. Hintze, "Disseminating the Mazdayasnian Religion," in W. Sundermann, A. Hintze and F. de Blois eds., *Existi Monumenta: Festschrift in Honour of Nicholas Sims-Williams* Iranica 17 (Wiesbaden: Harrassowitz, 2009):171–90; 172–3, 179.

31 Ner. 22.1–5; see F. M. Kotwal and P. G. Kreyenbroek, ed. & trans., *The Hērbedestān and Nērangestān, Vol. II: Nērangestān, Fragard 1* Studia Iranica 16 (Paris: Association pour l'avancement des études iraniennes, 1995), 19, 121–3.

32 Ibid., 121 n. 430.

33 Langer (2008), 91.

34 *FEZANA Journal* (Spring 2010), 98.

35 Stausberg (2002), 2: 408.

36 See E. Sanasarian, *Religious Minorities in Iran* (Cambridge: Cambridge University Press, 2000), 154.

37 Stausberg (2002), 2: 421.
38 F. M. A. Voltaire, *Essai sur les Moeurs, Oeuvres complètes de Voltaire* (Paris: Pourrat Frères, 1831), 1: 467.
39 F. Nietsche, *Ecce Homo*, trans. R. J. Hollingdale (Harmondsworth: Penguin, 1979), 127f.
40 *Friedrich Nietzsche* 3 vols., Karl Schlechta, ed. (Munich: Carl Hanser, 1954–56), 3: 1206.
41 http://alexanderbard.blogspot.com January 24, 2010: my italics, replacing capitalization in the original.

CHAPTER 3

1 DSf 15–18; DNb 5–12; DB 4.61–65.
2 S. Simmons, *Entertaining the Persian Way* (Harpenden: Lennard, 1991), 34.
3 M. M. Deboo and P. B. Jila, *Consecrated Atash Dadgah: The first traditionally consecrated Zoroastrian Fire Temple in the West, enthroning an ever-burning fire*, (London: ZTFE (Inc.), 2001)
4 http://tenets.zoroastrianism.com/dadgah33.html
5 B. Murphy, *The Root of Wild Madder: Chasing the History, Mystery, and Lore of the Persian Carpet* (New York: Simon & Shuster, 2005), 154–5.
6 Kreyenbroek and Munshi, (2001), 18.
7 R. Mistry, *Tales from Firozsha Baag*, (London and Boston: Penguin/ Faber and Faber, 1998), 13
8 *Geographia* 15.3.13–15, cited in De Jong (1997), 126.
9 Williams and Boyd (1993), 35.
10 F. M. Kotwal and J. W. Boyd, "The Zoroastrian *paragnā* ritual," *Journal of Mithraic Studies 2/1* (1977): 18–53; 38
11 This information was provided by Dr. Michael Stausberg in a paper entitled "Qualities of the Ideal Priest: Contemporary Priestly Interpretations," presented at the SSZ Conference, Chicago, June 26, 2010. It forms part of an ongoing research project on the Parsi priesthood.
12 Williams and Boyd (1993), 26–9.
13 Kotwal and Boyd, "The Zoroastrian *paragnā* ritual," 38.
14 Cf. Ner. 49.11; also Boyce (1989), 44.
15 Ervad S. P. Dastur, *Hamā Anjuman Prayers for Naurooz in English, Farsi and Gujarati* (Hinsdale, IL: FEZANA, 2010), 50.
16 Williams and Boyd (1993), 53.
17 See Mistree and Shahzadi (1998), 48–9. Michael Stausberg (2004) provides extensive descriptions of these and other ceremonies.
18 See D. F. Karaka, *History of the Parsis*, vol. 1 (New Delhi: Cosmo, 1999), 182–3.
19 Choksy (1989), 91.
20 Firby (1988), 66.
21 R. Ehrlich, "The Celebration and Gifts of the Persian New Year (Naw Ruz) According to an Arabic Source," *J.J. Modi Memorial Volume*, Bombay (1930), 95–101.
22 See www.bbc.co.uk/cbeebies/letscelebrate/watch/norouzclips/

23 Simmons, *Entertaining the Persian Way*, 36.

24 Ibid., 40.

25 Some of the information about the celebration of Mihragan in Yazd came from a paper presented by Dr. Bahman Moradian on "The Day of *Mihr*, Month of *Mihr*, and the ceremony of *Mihrized* in Yazd" at the Aram Society for Syro-Mesopotamian Studies conference, July 7, 2010.

26 Langer (2008), 144f, 288.

27 See M. Stausberg, "Monday Nights at the Banaji, Fridays at the Aslaji: Ritual Efficacy and Transformation in Bombay City," in M. Stausberg, ed., *Zoroastrian Rituals in Context* (Leiden, Boston: Brill, 2004), 653–718.

28 *Parsiana* (January 21, 2009), 34–6; 35.

29 M. M. J. Fischer, *Zoroastrian Iran Between Myth and Praxis*, unpublished Ph.D. dissertation, University of Chicago, 1975, 107.

30 Ibid., 75.

31 www.tatamotors.com

32 Firby (1988), 60.

33 R. Foltz, "Is Zoroastrianism an Ecological Religion?" *JSRNC 1.4* (2007): 413–30.

34 *Histories* 2.25; cited in De Jong (1997), 234.

35 Ibid., 52.

36 Foltz, "Is Zoroastrianism an Ecological Religion?", 427.

EPILOGUE

1 Adapted from D. J. Irani, trans. *The Gathas: The Hymns of Zarathushtra* (Newton, MA: Center for Ancient Iranian Studies, 1998), 33–5.

BIBLIOGRAPHY

SELECT BIBLIOGRAPHY

J. K. Choksy, *Purity and Pollution*, Austin, TX: University of Texas Press, 1989.

V. Curtis and S. Stewart (eds.), *Birth of the Persian Empire*, London: I.B. Tauris, 2005.

N. K. Firby, *European Travellers and Their Perceptions of Zoroastrians in the 17th and 18th Centuries*, Berlin: Dietrich Reimer Verlag, 1988.

J. R. Hinnells and A. V. Williams (eds.), *Parsis in India and the Diaspora*, London: Routledge, 2007.

A. de Jong, *Traditions of the Magi: Zoroastrianism in Greek and Latin Literature (Religions in the Graeco-Roman World 133)*, Leiden: Brill, 1997.

P. Kreyenbroek and S. N. Munshi, *Living Zoroastrianism: Urban Parsis Speak about Their Religion*, Richmond: Curzon, 2001.

R. Langer, *Pīrān und Zeyāratgāh: Schreine und Wallfahrtstätten der Zarathustrier im neuzeitlichen Iran*, Leuven, Paris, and Walpole, MA: Peeters, 2008.

F. Mehr, *The Zoroastrian Tradition: An Introduction to the Ancient Wisdom of Zarathushtra*, second ed., Costa Mesa, CA: Mazda, 2003.

K. P. Mistree and F. S. Shahzadi, *The Zarathushti Religion: A Basic Text*, Hinsdale, IL: FEZANA, 1998.

J. S. Palsetia, *The Parsis of India: Preservation of Identity in Bombay City*, Leiden: E.J. Brill, 2001.

R. Rivetna, ed., *The Legacy of Zarathushtra: An Introduction to the Religion, History and Culture of Zarathushtis (Zoroastrians)*, Hinsdale, IL: FEZANA, 2002.

J. Rose, *The Image of Zoroaster: The Persian Mage Through European Eyes*, New York: Bibliotheca Persica Press, 2000.

M. Stausberg, *Faszination Zarathushtra: Zoroaster und die Europäische Religionsgeschichte der Frühen Neuzeit (Religionsgeschichtliche Versuche und Vorarbeiten 42)*, 2 vols., Berlin and New York: Walter de Gruyter, 1998.

M. Stausberg, *Die Religion Zarathushtras. Geschichte-Gegenwart-Rituale*, Vols. 1 and 2, Stuttgart: Kohlhammer, 2002; Vol. 3. Stuttgart: Kohlhammer, 2004.

P. Vasunia, *Zarathushtra and the Religion of Ancient Iran: The Greek and Latin Sources in Translation*, Mumbai: KRCOI, 2007.

R. G. Williams and J. W. Boyd, *Ritual Art and Knowledge: Aesthetic Theory and Zoroastrian Ritual*, Columbia, SC: University of South Carolina, 1993.

SUPPLEMENTARY READING

M. Boyce, *A Persian Stronghold of Zoroastrianism*, Lanham, MD: University Press of America, 1989.

M. Boyce, *Textual Sources for the Study of Zoroastrianism*, Chicago, IL: University Of Chicago Press, 1990.

J. K. Choksy, *Conflict and Cooperation: Zoroastrian subalterns and Muslim elites in Medieval Iranian society*, New York: Columbia University Press, 1997.

V. Curtis and S. Stewart (eds.), *The Age of the Parthians*, London: I.B.Tauris, 2007.

V. Curtis and S. Stewart (eds.), *The Sasanian Era*, London: I.B. Tauris, 2008.

B. N. Dhabhar, The *Persian Rivayats of Hormazyar Framarz and Others*, Bombay: K.R. Cama Oriental Institute, reprint 1999.

M. M. J. Fischer, *Mute Dreams, Blind Owls and Dispersed Knowledges: Persian Poesis in the Transnational Circuitry*, Durham, NC, and London: Duke University Press, 2004.

P. J. Godrej and F. P. Mistree (eds.), *A Zoroastrian Tapestry: Art, Religion, Culture*, Ahmadebad: Mapin, 2002.

J. R. Hinnells, *The Zoroastrian Diaspora*, Oxford: Oxford University Press, 2005.

R.G. Hovanissian and G. Sabagh, (eds.), *The Persian Presence in the Islamic World*, Cambridge: Cambridge University Press, 1998.

F. M. Kotwal, and J. W. Boyd, *A Guide to the Zoroastrian Religion*, Chico, CA: Scholars Press, 1982.

J. Rose, *Zoroastrianism: An Introduction*, London and New York: I.B. Tauris, 2011.

J. R. Russell, *Zoroastrianism in Armenia*, Cambridge, MA: Harvard University Press, 1987.

S. Shaked, *Dualism in Transformation*, London: SOAS, 1994.

S. Shaked, *From Zoroastrian Iran to Islam*, Aldershot: Variorum, 1995.

M. Stausberg, ed., *Zoroastrian Rituals in Context*, Leiden: E.J. Brill, 2004.

M. L. West, *The Hymns of Zoroaster: A New Translation of the Most Ancient Sacred Texts of Iran*, London: I.B. Tauris, 2010.

(PARSI) FICTION IN ENGLISH

Perin Barucha   *The Fire Worshippers*, Bombay: Strand Book Club, 1968.
Boman Desai   *The Memory of Elephants*, London: Deutsch, 1988.
Firdaus Kanga   *Trying to Grow*, New Delhi: Penguin India, reprint 2008.
B. K. Karanjia   *More of an Indian*, New Delhi: Penguin India, 1970.
Ashok Mathur   *A Little Distillery in Nowgong*, Vancouver: Arsenal Pulp Press, 2009.
Dina Mehta   *And Some Take a Lover*, Kolkata: Rupa & Co., 1992.
Rohinton Mistry   *A Fine Balance*, New York: Vintage, reprint 2001.
                   Such a Long Journey, New York: Vintage, reprint 1992.

BIBLIOGRAPHY

	Tales from Firozsha Baag, New York: Penguin, reprint 1998.
	Family Matters, New York: Vintage, 2003.
Bapsi Sidhwa	*The Crow Eaters*, Minneapolis: Milkweed, reprint 2006.
	Cracking India, Minneapolis: Milkweed, reprint 2006.
	An American Brat, Minneapolis: Milkweed, reprint 2006.
Thrity Umrigar	*Bombay Time*, New York: Picador, 2002.
	The Space Between Us, New York and London: Harper Perennial, 2007.

FILMS

Earth (1998)
Little Zizou (2008)
Sixth Happiness (1997): film version of *Trying to Grow*
Such a Long Journey (1998)
See also *fiveparsifilms.blogspot.com* for five short films on Parsi themes, directed by Kaevan Umrigar.

INDEX